TIMELESS TRUTHS OF THE SECRET DOCTRINE

A COMPILATION

FIONA C. ODGREN

Order this book online at www.trafford.com
or email orders@trafford.com

Most Trafford titles are also available at major online book retailers.

Print information available on the last page.

ISBN: 978-1-4907-8226-3 (sc)
ISBN: 978-1-4907-8228-7 (hc)
ISBN: 978-1-4907-8227-0 (e)

Library of Congress Control Number: 2017906963

Trafford rev. 06/14/2017

Trafford PUBLISHING® www.trafford.com
North America & international
toll-free: 1 888 232 4444 (USA & Canada)
fax: 812 355 4082

This book is dedicated in loving memory of my late husband and spiritual mentor, Klas-Goran Odgren (George), who introduced me to the inspirational writings of Helena Petrovna Blavatsky and her Teachers, the Masters Morya and Koot Hoomi.

The proceeds of this book will be donated to the Theosophical Order of Service in Canada which funds three major projects: *The Tibetan Delek Hospital* in Dharamsala Northern India, the educational sponsorship of children from pre-school to collegiate levels and the support of special projects at *The Golden Link College* in the Philippines, and the funding of animal welfare initiatives at *The Besant Animal Welfare Dispensary* at Adyar, Chennai, India.

ACKNOWLEDGMENTS

This compilation would not have become a reality without the expertise, help, and encouragement of a number of people. I am in debt and deep gratitude to all of them.

First of all, profound thanks to Denise McDermott-King, author and editor, who again offered both her technological and literary skills. Then to Sandra and W. Robert Earle gratitude for their professional assistance with the pictures, as well as to my exceptionally helpful neighbour, Ken Garvin, who was always available to steer me through computer problems.

Further acknowledgements go to certain professionals who offered assistance, especially Will Thackara of the Theosophical University Press, California for permission to use some photos from the Pasadena Archives. Gratitude also to Alexandra Cousins of the McMichael Canadian Art Collection, Ontario, for arranging permission for use of the exceptional painting by Lawren Harris, *Lake and Mountains* (1927), oil on paperboard (30.3 x 38cm), a gift of the Founders, Robert and Signe McMichael (1972), for the cover of the book.

Finally but not least my greatest appreciation is offered to three individuals responsible for *The Secret Doctrine*: the intrepid enigmatic Russian Helena Petrovna Blavatsky, and her inspiring Mentors, the Masters Koot Hoomi and Morya.

FOREWORD

In October 1888 a unique philosophical work was published in London, England, the like of which had never before seen the light of day in European civilization. It carried a mysterious title: *The Secret Doctrine*. In January 1889 a second volume appeared. The impressive content of these two substantial tomes, the first dedicated to Cosmogenesis, the unfoldment of the Cosmos, and the second to Anthropogenesis, the development of humankind, bore a compelling sub-heading: *The Synthesis of Science, Religion and Philosophy*. At the outset, the books were deemed a success with at least a thousand copies being sold within days of being available to the public.

The author was none other than the enigmatic, well-traveled Russian noblewoman, Helena Petrovna Blavatsky, founder of the "modern" theosophical movement which was officially established in New York City by her and two other individuals: distinguished American government official, military man, and journalist, Colonel Henry Steel Olcott, and a young Anglo-Irish lawyer, Willam Quan Judge in November, 1875.

H.P.B., as she was called by her friends, initiated preliminary work on *The Secret Doctrine* during her six year stay (1879-1885) and theosophical endeavours in the spiritual Motherland of the world - India. However, it was not destined to be completed until three years before her untimely passing at the relatively young age of 59 in 1891 in London, England.

Prior to this extraordinary work, H.P.B. had produced in New York in 1877 another mammoth book in two volumes called *Isis Unveiled*. In this case, the first part was dedicated to Science and the second to Theology with the title page declaring the entire work to be "A Master Key to the Mysteries of Ancient and Modern Science and Theology." A thoroughly ambitious project indeed, but one which could not have been written without Blavatsky's profound link and connection with two Himalayan sages known as the Masters Koot Hoomi and Morya. The latter, a six foot eight Rajput prince, was her specific spiritual teacher who had appeared to her in visions since her childhood. Eventually, at age 20, she met him personally "in the flesh" so to speak, when he was part of an entourage of Indian Maharajahs visiting Queen Victoria.

Initially, *The Secret Doctrine* was planned and envisaged in the early 1880s as a further expansion of *Isis Unveiled* to help clarify many unanswered questions that book posed for serious spiritual seekers. The idea was to present monthly sections in the already thriving magazine, *The Theosophist*. However, that was not to materialize due to various reasons including multiple delays concerning H.P.B.'s health and the eventual necessity for her to leave India because of medical issues.

At first, H.P.B. went to stay in Germany, and it was there that she undertook seriously the work on *The*

Secret Doctrine. However, what she started was an entirely new project, not a new version of *Isis Unveiled.* Interestingly, she also intimated in letters to friend and British theosophist, A.P. Sinnett, that her spiritual Teacher, Morya, had agreed to help in the work. She further commented that both Mahatmas Morya and Koot Hoomi were often in her presence for the purposes of helping with this extraordinary endeavour.

Let it be noted that most of *The Secret Doctrine* was written during a time of great trial and distractions for H.P.B. when she was the butt and ridicule of considerable slander as a result of the infamous Coulomb affair, the scurrilous Hodgson Report with its biased and inaccurate observations, and the unfair criticism of previous friends who had become traitors to the theosophical cause. In addition, she was undergoing many challenges to her health, such as Bright's Disease, high blood pressure, and severe arthritis. Indeed, we are fortunate that even two volumes of this erudite and profound work were completed before her passing.

H.P.B.'s life was saved on two separate occasions by Morya while she was in the midst of this effort. The first rescue occurred in January 1885 when she was preparing to leave India. She was in a coma and not expected to live, but her Teacher, the Master Morya came and gave her the choice of either passing on in peace and ending her martyrdom, or living on for a few years to complete Volume two of *The Secret Doctrine.* The visit of Morya was in fact witnessed by a number of H.P.B.'s closest co-workers at the Theosophical headquarters in Adyar, Madras: the English Cooper-Oakley sisters, Isabel and Laura, the ardent Hindu ascetic Damodar K. Mavalankar, the East Indian chela, Banajii Nath, and the President of the German Theosophical Society, Dr. Franz Hartman. The second occurred some years later in Ostende, prior to HPB moving permanently to London.

Soon after the seemingly first "divine intervention and rescue," H.P.B. re-settled in Wurzburg, Central Germany. There she planned to be as reclusive as possible for she was consumed with the overwhelming desire to complete *The Secret Doctrine*. Apparently, if she had not been so maligned and ostracized by detractors and traitors, which also contributed greatly to her poor health, a further two volumes were planned. One of them was to be an account of the lives of those "Great Ones" and advanced souls who are called in the East and in the Ageless Wisdom, Adepts, Rishis, Sages, and Mahatmas or Masters; they are also considered to be part of the Spiritual Hierarchy overseeing the evolvement of humanity.

Many papers were discovered subsequent to H.P.B.'s passing which some surmised to be parts of intended third and fourth volumes. There is no definitive evidence to prove, though, these were part of planned future volumes. However, Annie Besant, the subsequent leader of the International Theosophical Society, did publish these papers collectively in book form in 1897 and it was named *The Secret Doctrine - Volume III*.

During this intense period in Wurzburg, H.P.B. had eventually a personal companion and very dear friend who not only helped with editing the manuscripts but also supervised the running of the apartment and tending domestic needs so she (H.P.B.) could concentrate fully on her writing and the mammoth task on hand. The Countess Wachtmeister acted in many ways as her personal secretary and proved to be a pillar of strength during this very critical time. The Countess was Anglo-French by birth and her late husband had been stationed at the Court of St. James in London, England as a highly respected Swedish ambassador.

Interestingly, the Countess wrote a book about her personal experiences of her stay with H.P.B. in Wurzburg which was entitled *Reminiscences of H.P. Blavatsky and the Secret Doctrine* (published in 1893). It provides us today with fascinating insights into the circumstances under which this remarkable work was produced. Some truly astounding events took place which those unfamiliar with the esoteric world would describe as being "miraculous." The Countess describes in her memoirs the circumstances with regard to the writing of *The Secret Doctrine* as follows:

"The circumstance which ... excited my wonder when I began to help Madame Blavatsky ... was the poverty of her traveling library. Her manuscripts were full to overflowing with references, quotations, allusions from a mass of rare and recondite works on subjects of the most varied kinds...."

"Shortly after my arrival in Wurzburg she took occasion to ask me if I knew anyone who could go for her to the Bodleian library (at Oxford). It happened that I did know someone I could ask, so my friend verified a passage that H.P.B. had seen in the astral light, with the title of the book, the chapter, page and figures all correctly noted."

"Once a very difficult task was assigned to me, namely to verify a passage taken from a manuscript in the Vatican. Having made the acquaintance of a gentleman who had a relative in the Vatican, I with some difficulty succeeded in verifying the passage. Two words were wrong, but all the remainder correct, and strangely enough, I was told that these words, being considerably blurred, were difficult to decipher."

Both Masters Morya, and Koot Hoomi were purported to supervise closely the work by various means, including dictation and the facilitation of Blavatsky's access to knowledge via astral sight. Interestingly, H.P.B. explained to the Countess the process of accessing this material as follows:

"Well, you see, what I do is this. I make what I can only describe as a sort of vacuum in the air before me, and fix my sight and my will upon it, and scene after scene passes before me like the successive pictures of a diorama, or, if I need a reference of information from some book, I fix my mind intently, and the astral counterpart of the book appears, and from it I take what I need. The more perfectly my mind is freed from distractions and mortification, the more energy and intentness it possesses, the more easily I can do this ...."

It needs to be clarified that H.P.B. never claimed to be the sole author of *The Secret Doctrine*. She was, in fact, a conduit chosen by advanced souls, in particular the Masters Morya and Koot Hoomi, to help revive and bring into the public arena the teachings of the Ancient, Ageless Wisdom to prepare humanity for the coming transformative new era and dispensation ahead.

Letters received by theosophist and eminent German scholar, Dr. Hubbe-Schleiden, from both the Masters Morya and Koot Hoomi in January 1886, verify categorically three individuals were responsible for the content of The Secret Doctrine: Koot Hoomi, Morya, and Upasika - in other words their "chela" or disciple, H.P.B., by means of her "luminous Higher Self." Dr. Hubbe-Schleiden was the first President of the German Theosophical Society, a close friend of H.P.B. and he considered *The Secret Doctrine* a work of utmost importance. Copies of the original letters he received from the Masters exist today and are in the Archives of The Theosophical Society in Pasadena.

The text was completed in long hand in early 1888 and comprised a mammoth manuscript over three feet high. Blavatsky then turned the writings over to two brothers, Archibald and Bertram Keightley, who were part of her inner group of close associates in London. They offered to type up the entire work and help with the final editing. Being very literary gentlemen who had attained degrees at Cambridge they were well qualified for this daunting project.

By the fall, the work was at long last ready for publication, the first volume being published in October of the same year, and the second in January of 1889, in the nation's capital. Later, copies were made available across the Atlantic Ocean in New York, with the unstinting help of co-founder, W.Q. Judge. Eventually, too, this extraordinary philosophical work was made available at the International Headquarters of the Theosophical Society in Adyar, Madras, India.

In the Preface to the first volume of *The Secret Doctrine* H.P.B. provides us with some significant statements regarding the goal of the work and the cosmic truths presented. She writes:

"These truths are in no sense put forward as a revelation; nor does the author claim the position of a revealer of mystic lore, now made public for the first time in the world's history. For what is contained in this work is to be found scattered throughout thousands of volumes embodying the scriptures of the great Asiatic and early European religions, hidden under glyph and symbol, and hitherto left unnoticed because of this veil. What is now attempted is to gather the oldest tenets together and to make them one harmonious, unbroken whole. The sole advantage which the writer has over her predecessors is that she need not resort to personal speculations and theories. For this work is a partial statement of what she herself has been taught by more advanced students, supplemented, in a few details, only by the results of her own study and observation...."

H.P.B. continues: "It is perhaps desirable to state unequivocally that the teachings, however fragmentary and incomplete, contained in these volumes, belong neither to the Hindu, the Zoroastrian, the Chaldean, nor the Egyptian religion, neither to Buddhism, Islam, Judaism nor Christianity exclusively. *The Secret Doctrine* is the essence of all these. Sprung from it in their origins, the various religious schemes are now made to merge back into their original element, out of which every mystery and dogma has grown, developed, and become materialised."

One may well ask what were the reasons for H.P.B. along with her Masters to make these truths available for the public at that particular time? It is suggested that the Adepts and Sages watching over the evolution of man were concerned about certain increasing trends in that period of the Victorian era: the growth of materialistic thinking due to the development of science, the increase of crystallized thought in orthodox religion, plus the growing obsession with spiritualistic seances. The world was becoming mired in too much materiality of various kinds, and was in need of a spiritual revival based on ancient truths. In fact, it is suggested that "the soul was becoming with every generation more atrophied and paralyzed." A deeper understanding of religions and nature based on underlying core realities was needed to offset those disturbing trends.

So what further can be said with regard to the specific content in these two remarkable volumes? A very comprehensive Introductory opens the first volume and sets the stage for what is to follow. States H.P.B. by way of preparation that *"The Secret Doctrine* is the universally diffused religion and wisdom of the ancient, pre-historic world." And she goes on to say: "The Wisdom Religion is the inheritance of all the nations, the world over" and also "it reconciles all religions, strips every one of its outward human garments, and shows the root of each to be identical with that of every other religion."

Furthermore: "It proves the necessity of an absolute Divine Principle in nature, and denies Deity no more than it does the Sun." It is also clarified that the outline of a few fundamental truths from the Secret Doctrine of the Archaic Ages was now permanently permitted to see the light of day, after long millenniums of the most profound silence and secrecy. And the truths to be found in *The Secret Doctrine* which are also referred to as "esoteric science," "is not the fancy of one or several isolated individuals but the uninterrupted record covering thousands of generations of Seers whose respective experiences were made to test and verify the traditions passed orally by one early race to another of exalted beings who watch over Humanity. The flashing gaze of these Seers have penetrated into the very kernel of matter and recorded the soul of things there, where an ordinary profane, however learned man would have perceived but the external work of form."

In India this esoteric science and Ancient Wisdom is referred to as Atma Vidya (Atma meaning Spirit, and Vidya, Knowledge) and as comprising "the formulation in human language of the nature, structure, destiny and operation of the Cosmos and the multitude of beings, which infill it." But what H.P.B. also emphasizes is "that which remains unsaid could not be contained in a hundred such volumes." So only a part of the veil has been lifted but the little that is given is surely better than complete silence on these vital truths.

The extensive Introductory is followed by the Proem which provides us with "Three Fundamental Propositions" which are the most significant tenets and pillars of the entire work. They can be summarized briefly as follows:

1. There is as the Source of all life - One Absolute Reality - about which speculation is impossible since it transcends human thought.

2. There is a law of periodicity which governs all life.

3. All souls are one with the Universal Oversoul, which is an aspect of the Absolute.

After the Proem, the main content of Volume I presents seven major Stanzas outlining certain stages in the unfoldment of the Cosmos and each comprise a varied number of verses. Mysteriously, these Stanzas and verses are known as the *Book of Dzyan* and are deemed to have been the work of divinely inspired Seers many thousands of years ago, even preceding the ancient Vedas of India. There is no clear explanation as to who or what Dzyan is, but one may note an interesting connection between the Sanskrit word for meditation (*Dhyana*) and Dzyan, and also with the later term referring to a type of Buddhism and meditation coined as "Zen."

These Stanzas and their verses contain very sacred, erudite, and cryptic descriptions with regard to the emergence of the Cosmos which were originally in the ancient language of Senzar; later they were translated into Sanskrit, then Tibetan, and lastly English by H.P.B. with the guidance of her spiritual Masters. However, as illumined British author and spiritual teacher, Sri Krishna Prem, commented with regard to these Stanzas, the important thing is to recognize that the Universe is a great mystery, and that these Stanzas are "but a pointer to its existence." H.P.B.'s Commentary is an attempt "to colour the same pointer in other and more familiar hues but neither Stanzas or Commentary make pretence of being a logically unimpeachable whole."

Interestingly, according to Blavatsky, these unique and compelling stanzas and verses are purported to have existed in an esoteric and secret Tibetan manuscript known as *The Book of Kiu-te*. H.P.B., who spent altogether at least five years in Tibet under the tutelage of spiritual Masters in both monasteries and remote Ashrams, refers to subterranean crypts and cave libraries cut in the rock, where monasteries are situated in the mountains, existing in Tibet and on the borders of China.

She writes in the Introductory to Volume I that along the ridge of the Altyne-Toga there exists a hamlet with a poor-looking temple. Beneath it, pilgrims have reported, is a collection of books more extensive than the British Museum. In that collection she affirms there exists *The Very Old Book* from which the Volumes of *Kiu-te* and the *Stanzas of Dzyan* were compiled. Tradition states this parent volume was taken down in Senzar from the words of Divine Beings who dictated it to the "Sons of Light" (i.e., sages) in Central Asia at the beginning of the fifth stage of development for humanity, which is known as the Fifth Root Race in the Ageless Wisdom. This book apparently describes Cosmic Evolution and explains the origin of everything on Earth including physical man. It stops short at the death of Krishna and the beginning of the cycle known as the Kali Yuga (approximately 5,000 years ago).

Researchers have tried to track down the so-called *Book of Kiu-te* in Tibet - if not its parent volume, *The Very Old Book*. The American Tibetan scholar, theosophist, and Buddhist author, David Reigle undertook exhaustive research and travels in Tibet which included assistance from His Holiness, the Dalai Lama. He attempted to track down this purported source of the Stanzas in *The Secret Doctrine* and subsequently wrote a book on his finds entitled *The Secret Books of Madame Blavatsky*. In this he presents the fascinating hypothesis that *The Book of Kiu-te* is related to a lost esoteric manuscript of the Kalachakra teachings of Mahayana Buddhism.

The English translation of the Stanzas is very poetic, strangely beautiful, and visually quite graphic, but also extremely obscure at times. H.P.B., with the help of her Masters, elaborates on the meanings of these verses and in these commentaries much is found to ignite the soul.

Part II of Volume I is a fascinating elucidation of fundamental symbols contained in the great religions of the world. It includes a broad spectrum including the cross, the circle, the lotus, the tree of life, the serpent, the dragon, and various geometric shapes such as the sphere, interlaced triangles, the square, the cube and so forth. This section provides enriching concepts and ideas which provide us with much on which to reflect.

In Part III, Blavatsky and her Masters outline the contrasting views of Science and the Wisdom of the Ancients and meets scientific objections by anticipation. Interestingly, it touches on some heart-stopping and uncanny prophecies regarding the nature of the atom, and the concept of radiant matter, with its subsequent discovery of x-rays and its positive application to medical science.

It is interesting to note that in Sylvia Cranston's biography of Blavatsky, the author speaks of the growing interest shown in the 20th century in the study of *The Secret Doctrine* by people of the scientific communities in certain large universities in the USA. It has been indicated that the true appreciation of this work will not fully come into fruition until the 21st century and in that light it is encouraging to read of increasing numbers of groups gathering together today to gain greater understanding of this erudite, challenging work.

Volume II presents further Stanzas and verses from the same divine source but now the emphasis is on human evolution from spiritual, mental, psychic and physical viewpoints. It traces a strange and compelling saga of man from millions of years ago as an ethereal spiritual entity, gradually descending into matter and developing through many changes and various stages on our Earth, described as Root Races. Panoramic accounts are also provided of antediluvian civilizations and continents. The origin of the lower Kingdoms of nature are also presented and discussed in conjunction with human evolution.

Part II of Volume II also provides further fascinating material on ancient symbolism with special emphasis on the seven-fold constitution of man including the divine and immortal aspects and the contrasting mortal and temporary aspects, which constitute the personality. In the final and third section, the Science of the day again is the focus with Anthropology especially being considered in the light of the Ageless Wisdom.

The Secret Doctrine is not a work to be studied with the analytical, concrete mind, as if it were an academic treatise, but instead the far-reaching ideas are to be contemplated with the more intuitive side of our nature. One is not going to be able to comprehend all the knowledge provided, even after many readings, for one must allow space and time to meditate on the wisdom offered, allowing the themes to sink in and percolate. Magically, then, insights and new understandings will surface, and, as Blavatsky once commented with regard to the effects of studying the work, "new pathways will be carved in the brain."

It has been the experience of this compiler, over several decades, that making the effort to study *The Secret Doctrine* is a thoroughly worthwhile endeavour that reaps untold spiritual dividends. And collating the knowledge offered in these two books according to major themes has greatly enriched and enhanced the experience.

Many abridgements and edited versions of the two volumes have appeared over the years. Yet, as far as this writer is aware, no comprehensive collation, devoted to a wide spectrum of major themes in this unique work, has ever taken place. Let it be noted, this particular compilation is based on a facsimile of the original edition of 1888 produced by the Theosophical University Press, Pasadena, California, in 1977.

It is the earnest hope of this writer that this thematic presentation will not only ease the study of theosophical enthusiasts, but it will also motivate others to contemplate the hidden, esoteric treasures contained in these extraordinary tomes. In truth, this book opens up before us vistas of cosmic grandeur and in doing so not only stretches both our mental and spiritual capacities, but expands our consciousness to embrace increasingly broader horizons.

Fiona C. Odgren

CONTENTS

Illustrations

Centerfold

Master Morya

Master Koot Hoomi

THE ABSOLUTE
ONE ETERNAL BE-NESS

1. An Omnipresent, Eternal, Boundless, and Immutable PRINCIPLE on which all speculation is impossible, since it transcends the power of human conception and could only be dwarfed by any human expression or similitude. It is beyond the range and reach of thought - in the words of Mandukya, "unthinkable and unspeakable."

To render these ideas clearer to the general reader, let him set out with the postulate that there is one absolute Reality which antecedes all manifested, conditioned, being. This Infinite and Eternal Cause - dimly formulated in the "Unconscious" and "Unknowable" of current European philosophy - is the rootless root of "all that was, is, or ever shall be." It is of course devoid of all attributes and is essentially without any relation to manifested finite Being. It is "Be-ness" rather than Being (in Sanskrit, *Sat*), and is beyond all thought or speculation. *SD 1, p. 14*

2. The idea of Eternal Non-Being, which is the One Being, will appear a paradox to anyone who does not remember that we limit our ideas of being to our present consciousness of existence; making it a specific instead of a generic term. An unborn infant, could it think in our acceptation of that term, would necessarily limit its conception of being in a similar manner, to the intra-uterine life which alone it knows; and were it to

1

endeavour to express to its consciousness the idea of life after birth (death to it), it would, in the absence of data to go upon, and of faculties to comprehend such data, probably express that life as "Non-Being which is Real Being."

In our case the One Being is the noumenon of all the noumena which we know must underlie phenomena, and give them whatever shadow of reality they possess, but which we have not the senses or the intellect to cognize at present. The impalpable atoms of gold scattered through the substance of a ton of auriferous quartz may be imperceptible to the naked eye of the miner, yet he knows that they are not only present there but that they alone give his quartz any appreciable value; and this relation of the gold to the quartz may faintly shadow forth that of the noumenon to the phenomenon. But the miner knows what the gold will look like when extracted from the quartz, whereas the common mortal can form no conception of the reality of things separated from the Maya which veils them, and in which they are hidden. Alone the Initiate, rich with the lore acquired by numberless generations of his predecessors, directs the "Eye of Dangma" (the spiritual seership of a purified Soul - Ed.) toward the essence of things on which no Maya can have any influence. *SD 1, p. 45*

3. The "Absolute Consciousness," they tell us, "behind" phenomena, which is only termed unconsciousnes in the absence of any element of personality, transcends human conception. Man, unable to form one concept except in terms of empirical phenomena, is powerless from the very constitution of his being to raise the veil that shrouds the mystery of the Absolute. Only the liberated Spirit is able to faintly realise the nature of the source whence it sprung and whither it must eventually return....

As the highest Dhyan Chohans (Archangels - Ed.), however, can but bow in ignorance before the awful mystery of Absolute Being; and since, even in that culmination of conscious existence - "the merging of the individual in the universal consciousness" - to use a phrase of Fichte's - the Finite cannot conceive the Infinite, nor can it apply to its own standard of mental experiences, how can it be said that the "Unconscious" and the Absolute can have even an instinctive impulse or hope of attaining clear self-consciousness? A Vedantin would never admit this Heglian idea; and the Occultist would say that it applies perfectly to the awakened MAHAT, the Universal Mind already projected into the phenomenal world as the first aspect of the changeless ABSOLUTE but never to the latter. "Spirit and Matter, or Purusha and Prakriti are but the two primeval aspects of the One and Secondless" we are taught. *SD 1, p. 51*

4. Paranishpanna, remember, is the *summum bonum*, the Absolute, hence the same as Paranirvana. Besides being the final state it is that condition of subjectivity which has no relation to anything but the one absolute truth (Para-marthasatya) on its plane. It is that state which leads one to appreciate correctly the full meaning of Non-Being, which, as explained, is *absolute*

Being. Sooner or later, all that now seemingly exists, will be in reality and actually in the state of Paranishpanna. But there is a great difference between *conscious* and *unconscious* "being."

The condition of Paranishpanna, without Paramartha, the Self-analysing consciousness ... is no bliss, but simply extinction (for Seven Eternities). Thus, an iron ball placed under the scorching rays of the sun will get heated through, but will not feel or appreciate the warmth, while a man will. It is only "with a mind clear and undarkened by personality, and an assimilation of the merit of manifold existences devoted to being in its collectivity (the whole living and sentient Universe), that one gets rid of personal existence, merging into becoming one with the Absolute, and continuing in full possession of Paramartha." *SD 1, pp. 53- 54*

5. Hence *Non-being* is "Absolute Being," in esoteric philosophy. In the tenets of the latter even Adi-Buddha (first or primeval wisdom) is, while manifested, in one sense an illusion, Maya, since all the gods, including Brahma, have to die at the end of the "Age of Brahma" (the Creator God - Ed.); the abstraction called Parabrahm alone - whether we call it Ensoph or Herbert Spencer's Unknowable - being "the One Absolute" Reality. The One secondless Existence is ADWAITA, "Without a Second," and all the rest is Maya, teaches the Adwaita philosophy. *SD 1, p. 54 (foot-note)*

6. The fundamental Law - the central point from which all emerged, around and toward which all gravitates, and upon which is hung the philosophy of the rest, is the One homogeneous divine SUBSTANCE-Principle," for it becomes "substance" on the plane of the manifested Universe, an illusion, while it remains a "principle" in the beginingless and endless abstract, visible and invisible SPACE. It is the omnipresent Reality: impersonal, because it contains all and everything. *Its impersonality is the fundamental conception* of the System. It is latent in every atom in the Universe, and is the Universe itself. The Universe is the periodical manifestation of this unknown Absolute-Essence.

To call it "essence" however, is to sin against the very spirit of the philosophy. For though the noun may be derived in this case from the verb esse, "to be," yet IT cannot be identified with a being of any kind, that can be conceived by human intellect. It is best described as neither Spirit nor matter, but both. "Parabrahmam and Mulaprakriti" are One, in reality, yet two in the Universal conception of the manifested, even in the conception of the One Logos, the first manifestation, to which, as the able lecturer in the "Notes on the Bhagavadgita" shows, IT appears from the objective standpoint of the One Logos as Mulaprakriti and not as Parabrahman; as its veil and not the one REALITY hidden behind, which is unconditioned and absolute. *SD 1, pp. 273-274*

7. "The latter (the one Reality - the Absolute) must never be mentioned in words or speech lest it should take away some of our spiritual energies that aspire towards Its state, gravitating ever onward unto IT spiritually, as the whole physical universe gravitates towards ITS manifested centre - cosmically." **SD 1, p. 290** (*Extracts from a Private Commentary hitherto kept secret.*)

8. The expression "All is One Number, issued from No Number" relates again to that universal and philosophical tenet just explained .... That which is absolute is of course No Number; but in its later significance it has an application in Space as in Time. It means that not only every increment of time is part of a larger increment, up to the most indefinitely prolonged duration conceivable by the human intellect, but also that no manifested thing can be thought of except as part of a larger whole: the total aggregate being the One manifested Universe that issues from the unmanifested or Absolute - called Non-Being or "No-Number," to distinguish it from BEING or "the One Number." **SD 1, pp. 87-88**

9. Moreover, Esoteric philosophy reconciles all religion, strips every one of its outward, human garments, and shows the root of each to be identical with that of every other great religion. It proves the necessity of an absolute Divine Principle in nature. It denies Deity no more than it does the Sun. Esoteric philosophy has never rejected God in nature, nor Deity as the absolute and abstract Ens. It only refuses to accept any of the gods of the so-called monotheistic religions, gods created by man in his own image and likeness, a blasphemous and sorry caricature of the Ever Unknowlable. **SD 1, Introduction p. xx**

10. "The knowledge of the absolute Spirit, like the effulgence of the sun, or like heat in fire, is naught else than the absolute Essence itself," says Sankaracharya. IT - is the "Spirit of the Fire," not fire itself; therefore, "the attributes of the latter, heat or flame, are not the attributes of the Spirit, but of that of which the Spirit is the unconscious cause." Is not the above sentence the true key-note of the later Rosicrucian philosophy? Parabrahm is, in short, the collective aggregate of Kosmos in its infinity and eternity, the "THAT" and "THIS" to which distributive aggregates cannot be applied. "In the beginning THIS was the Self, one only" (*Aitareya Upanishad*); the great Sankaracharya explains that "THIS" referred to the Universe (Jagat); the sense of the words, "In the beginning," meaning before the reproduction of the phenomenal Universe. *SD 1, p. 6 - 7*

11. The Secret Doctrine ... postulates a "One Form of Existence" as the basis and source of all things. But perhaps the phrase, the "One Form of Existence," is not altogether correct. The Sanskrit word is Prabhavapyaya, "the place, or rather plane, whence emerges the origination, and into which is the resolution of all things," says a commentator....

The Puranic Commentators explain it by Karana - "Cause" - but the Esoteric philosophy, by the *ideal spirit of that cause*. It is, in its secondary stage, the Svabhavat of the Buddhist philosopher, the eternal cause and effect, omnipresent yet abstract, the self-existent plastic Essence and the root of all things, viewed in the same dual light as the Vedantin views his Parabrahm and Mulaprakriti, the one under two aspects. *SD 1, p. 46*

ANGELS - MESSENGERS
OF THE DIVINE

1. The whole Kosmos is guided, controlled, and animated by almost endless series of Hierarchies of sentient Beings, each having a mission to perform, and who - whether we give to them one name or another, and call them Dhyan-Chohans or Angels - are "messengers" in the sense only that they are the agents of Karmic and Cosmic Laws. They vary infinitely in their respective degrees of consciousness and intelligence; and to call them all pure Spirits without any of the earthly alloy "which time is wont to prey upon" is only to indulge in poetical fancy. For each of these Beings either was, or prepares to become, a man, if not in the present then in a past or a coming cycle (Manvantara).

They are *perfected*, when not *incipient*, men; and differ morally from the terrestrial human beings on their higher (less material) spheres, only in that they are devoid of the feeling of personality and of the human emotional nature - two purely earthly characteristics. The former, or the "perfected," have become free from those feelings, because (a) they have no longer fleshly bodies - an ever-numbing weight on the Soul; and (b) the pure spiritual element being left untrammelled and more free, they are less influenced by maya than man can ever be, unless he is an adept who keeps his two personalities - the spiritual and the physical - entirely separated. *SD 1, pp. 274 - 275*

8

2. .... None of these Beings, high or low, have either individuality in the sense in which a man says, "*I am myself* and no-one else;" in other words, they are conscious of no such distinct separateness as men ... have on earth. Individuality is the characteristic of their respective hierarchies, not of their units; and these characteristics vary only with the degree of the plane to which those hierarchies belong; the nearer to the region of Homogeneity and the One Divine, the purer and the less accentuated that individuality in the Hierarchy.

They are finite, in all respects, with the exception of their higher principles - the immortal sparks reflecting the universal divine flame - individualized and separated only on the spheres of Illusion by a differentiation as illusive as the rest. They are "Living Ones," because they are the streams projected on the Kosmic screen of illusion from the ABSOLUTE LIFE; beings in whom life cannot become extinct, before the fire of ignorance is extinct in those who sense these "Lives." Having sprung into being under the quickening influence of the uncreated beams, the reflection of the great Central Sun that radiates on the shores of the river of Life, it is the inner principle in them which belongs to the waters of immortality, while its differentiated clothing is as perishable as man's body.

Therefore, Young was right in saying that "Angels are men of a superior kind" and no more. There are neither "ministering" nor "protecting" angels; nor are they "Harbingers of the Most High" still less the "Messengers of wrath" of any God such as man's fancy has created.

To appeal to their protection is as foolish as to believe that their sympathy may be secured by any kind of propitiation; for they are, as much, as man himself is, the slaves and creatures of immutable Karmic and Kosmic Law. The reason for it is evident. Having no element of personality in their essence they can have no personal qualities, such as attributed by men, in their exoteric religions, to their anthropomorphic God....

"Man can neither propitiate nor command the Devas," it is said. But, by paralyzing his lower personality, and arriving thereby at the full knowledge of the non-separateness of his higher SELF from the One absolute SELF, man can even during his terrestrial life, become as "One of Us." Thus it is, by eating of the fruit of knowledge which dispels ignorance, that man becomes like one of the Elohim or the Dhyanis; and once on their plane the Spirit of Solidarity and perfect Harmony, which reigns in every hierarchy, must extend over him and protect him in every particular. *SD 1, pp. 275 - 276*

3. In sober truth, as just shown, every "Spirit" so-called is either a *disembodied or a future man.* As from the highest Archangel (Dhyan Chohan) down to the last conscious "Builder" (the inferior class of Spiritual Entities), all such are men, having lived aeons ago, in other Manvantaras, or on this or other Spheres; so the interior, semi-intelligent and non-intelligent Elementals - are all future men. That fact alone - that a spirit is endowed with intelligence - is a proof to the Occultist that that Being must have been a man, and acquired

10

his knowledge and intelligence throughout the human cycle. *SD 1, p. 277*

4. The AH-HI (Dhyan-Chohans) are the collective hosts of spiritual beings - the Angelic Hosts of Christianity, the Elohim and "Messengers" of the Jews - who are the vehicle for the manifestation of the divine or universal thought and will. They are the Intelligent Forces that give to and enact in Nature her "laws," while themselves acting according to laws imposed upon them in a similar manner by still higher Powers; but they are not "the personifications" of the powers of Nature, as erroneously thought.

This hierarchy of spiritual Beings through which the Universal Mind comes into action is like an army - a 'Host,' truly - by means of which the fighting power of a nation manifests itself, and which is composed of army corps, divisions, brigades, regiments, and so forth, each with its separate individuality or life, and its limited freedom of action and limited responsibilities, each contained in a larger individuality, to which its own interests are subservient, and each containing lesser individualities in itself. *SD 1, p. 38*

5. The "Army" ... is the Host of angelic Beings (Dhyan-Chohans) appointed to guide and watch over each respective region from the beginning to the end of Manvantara. They are the "Mystic Watchers" of the Christian Kabalists and Alchemists, and relate, symbolically as well as cosmologically, to the numerical system of the Universe. The numbers with which these celestial Beings are connected are extremely difficult to explain, as each number refers to several groups of distinct ideas, according to the particular group of "Angels" which it is intended to represent. *SD 1, p. 119*

6. To the highest (worlds - Ed), we are taught, belong the seven orders of the purely divine Spirits; to the six lower ones belong hierarchies that can occasionally be seen and heard by men, and who do communicate with their progeny of the Earth; which progeny is indissolubly linked with them, each principle in man having its direct source in the nature of those great beings, who furnish us with the respective invisible elements in us. *SD 1, p. 133*

7. ... as the doctrine teaches, there are no such privileged beings in the universe, whether in our or in other systems, in the outer or the inner worlds, as the angels of the Western Religion and the Judean. A Dhyan Chohan has to become one; he cannot be born or appear suddenly on the plane of life as a full-blown angel. The Celestial Hierarchy of the present Manvantara will find itself transferred in the next cycle of life into higher, superior worlds, and will make room for a new hierarchy, composed of the elect ones of our mankind.

Being is an endless cycle within the one absolute eternity, wherein move numberless inner cycles finite and conditioned. Gods, created as such, would evince no personal merit in being gods. Such a class of beings, perfect only by virtue of the special immaculate nature inherent in them, in the face of suffering and struggling humanity, and even of the lower creation, would be the symbol of an eternal injustice quite Satanic in character, an ever present crime. It is an anomaly and impossibility in Nature.

.... How is it possible to conceive that those "gods," or angels, can be at the same time their own emanations and their personal selves? Is it in the same sense in the material world, where the son is (in one way) his father, being his blood, the bone of his bone and the flesh of his flesh? To this the teachers answers "Verily it is so." But one has to go deep into the mystery of BEING before one can fully comprehend this truth. *SD 1, pp. 221 - 222*

8. The Devas, Pitris, Rishis; the Suras and the Asuras; the Daityas and Adityas; the Dunavas and Gandharvas, etc., etc., have all their synonyms in our Secret Doctrine, as well as in the Kabala and the Hebrew Angelology; but it is useless to give their ancient names, as it would only create confusion. Many of these may be also known, in the Christian hierarchy of divine and celestial powers. All those Thrones and Dominions, Virtues and Principalities, Cherubs, Seraphs and demons, the various denizens of the Sidereal World, are the modern copies of archaic prototypes. The very symbolism in their names, when transliterated and arranged in Greek and Latin, are sufficient to show it, as will be proved in several cases further on. *SD 1, p. 92*

9. The Doctrine teaches that, in order to become a divine, fully conscious god, - aye, even the highest - the Spiritual primeval INTELLIGENCES (angels - Ed.) must pass through the human stage. And when we

13

say human, this does not apply merely to terrestrial humanity, but to the mortals that inhabit any world, i.e., to those Intelligences that have reached the appropriate equilibrium between matter and spirit, as we have now, since the middle point of the Fourth Root Race of the Fourth Round was passed. .... The Mind-born Sons, the Rishis, the Builders (Angels), etc., were all men - of whatever forms and shapes - in other worlds and the preceding Manvantaras. *SD 1, pp. 106 - 107*

10. There are three chief groups of Builders and as many of the Planetary Spirits and the Lipika (the Recording Angels - Ed.), each group being again divided into Seven sub-groups. It is impossible, even in such a large work as this, to enter into a minute examination of even the three principal groups, as it would demand an extra volume. The "Builders" are the representatives of the first "Mind-born" Entities, therefore of the primeval Rishi-Prajapati; also of the Seven great Gods of Egypt, of which Osiris is the chief; of the Seven Amshaspends of the Zoroastrians, with Ormazd at their head; or the "Seven Spirits of the Face"; the Seven Sephiroth (of the Kabala) separated from the first Triad etc. etc.

They build or rather rebuild every "System" after the "Night." The second group of the builders is the Architect of our planetary chain exclusively; and the third, the progenitor of our Humanity - the Macrocosmic prototype of the microcosm.

The Planetary Spirits are the informing spirits of the Stars in general and of the Planets especially. They rule the destinies of men who are all born under one or other of their constellations; the second and third groups pertaining to other systems have the same function and all rule various departments of Nature. In the Hindu exoteric Pantheon they are the guardian deities who preside over the eight points of the compass - the four cardinal and four intermediate points - and are called *Loka-Palas*, "Supporters or guardians of the World" (in our visible Kosmos), of which Indra (East), Yama (South), Varuna (West), and Kuvera (North) are the chief; their elephants and their spouses pertaining of course to fancy and afterthought, though all of them have an occult significance. *SD 1, pp. 127 - 128*

11. "Four winged wheels at each corner ... for the four holy ones and their armies (hosts)" .... These are the "four Maharajahs" or great Kings of the Dhyan Chohans, the Devas who preside, each over one of the four cardinal points. They are the Regents or Angels who rule over the Cosmical Forces of North, South, East and West, Forces having each a distinct occult property. These BEINGS are also connected with Karma, as the latter needs physical and material agents, to carry out her decrees, such as the four kinds of winds, for instance, professedly admitted by Science to have their respective evil and beneficent influences upon the health of Mankind and every living thing.

There is occult philosophy in that Roman Catholic doctrine which traces the various public calamities, such as epidemics of disease, and wars and so on, to the invisible "Messengers" from North and West. "The glory of God comes from the way of the East" says Ezekiel, while Jeremiah, Isaiah, and the psalmist assure their readers that all the evil under the Sun come from the North and the West - which proposition, when applied to the Jewish nation sounds like an undeniable prophecy for themselves. And this accounts also for St. Ambrose (On Amos, ch. iv.) declaring that it is precisely for that reason "we curse the North-Wind, and that during the ceremony of baptism we begin by turning towards the West (Sidereal), to renounce the better, him who inhabits it; after which we turn to the East.*" SD 1, pp. 122 - 123*

12. Belief in the "Four Maharajahs" - the Regents of the Four cardinal points - was universal and is now that of Christians, who call them, after St. Augustine, "Angelic Virtues," and "Spirits" when enumerated by themselves, and "Devils" when named by the Pagans. But where is the difference between the Pagans and the Christians in this cause? Following Plato, Aristotle explained that the term was understood only as meaning the incorporeal principles placed at each of the four great divisions of our Cosmical world to supervise them. Thus, no more than the Christians did, do they *adore* and *worship* the Elements and the cardinal (imaginary) points, but the "gods" that ruled these respectively.

For the Church there are two kinds of Sidereal beings, the Angels and the Devils. For the Kabalist and Occultist there is but one; and neither of them makes any difference between "the Rectors of Light" and the Cosmocratores (the Builders - Ed.) .... It is not the

"Rector" or "Maharajah" who punishes or rewards, with or without "God's" permission or order, but man himself - his deeds or Karma, attracting individually and collectively (as in the case of whole nations sometimes), every kind of evil and calamity. *SD 1, pp. 123 - 124*

13. In the Egyptian temples, according to Clemens Alexandrinus, an immense curtain separated the tabernacle from the place for the congregation. The Jews had the same. In both, the curtain was drawn over five pillars (the pentacle) symbolizing the five senses and five Root races esoterically, while the four colours of the curtain represented the four cardinal points and the four terrestrial elements. The whole was an allegorical symbol. It is through the four high Rulers over the four points and Elements that our five senses may become cognisant of the hidden truths of Nature....

For what was the meaning of the square tabernacle raised by Moses in the wilderness, if it had not the same cosmical significance? "Thou shalt make an hanging .... of blue, purple, and scarlet" and "five pillars of shittim wood for the hanging ... four brazen rings in the four corners thereof ... boards of fine wood for the four sides, North, South, West and East ... of the Tabernacle ... with Cherubims of cunning work." (Exodus, ch. xxvi, xxxvii.)

The Tabernacle and the square courtyard, Cherubim and all, were precisely the same as those in the Egyptian temples. The square form of the Tabernacle meant just the same thing as it still means to this day, in the exoteric worship of the Chinese and Tibetans - the four cardinal points signifying that which the four sides of the pyramids, obelisks, and other such square erections mean. Josephus (the Jewish historian - Ed.) takes care to explain the whole thing. He declares that the Tabernacle pillars are the same as those raised at Tyre to the four Elements which were placed on pedestals whose four angles faced the four cardinal points: adding that "the angles of the pedestals had equally the four figures of the Zodiac" on them, which represented the same orientation. (*Antiquities I, VIII, ch. xxii.*) *SD 1, pp. 125 - 126*

14. If the student would know more of them (the Regents of the four cardinal points - Ed.), he has but to compare the Vision of Ezekiel (ch. i.) with what is known of Chinese Buddhism (even in its exoteric teachings); and examine the outward shape of these "Great Kings." In the opinion of the Rev. Joseph Edkins, they are "the Devas who preside each over one of the four continents into which the Hindus divide the world."

Each leads an army of spiritual beings to protect mankind and Buddhism. With the exception of favouritism towards Buddhism, the four celestial beings are precisely this. They are the protectors of mankind and also the Agents of Karma on Earth, whereas the Lipika (the Recording Angels - Ed.) are concerned with Humanity's hereafter. At the same time they are the four living creatures "who have the likeness of a man" of Ezekiel's vision, called by the translators of the Bible, "Cherubim," "Seraphim," etc.; and by the Occultists, "the winged Globes," the "Fiery Wheels," and in the Hindu Pantheon by a number of different names. All these "Gandharvas, the "Sweet Songsters," the Asuras, Kinnaras, and Nagas, are the allegorical descriptions of the "four Maharajahs."

.... But Ezekiel plainly describes the four Cosmic Angels: "I looked, and behold, a whirl-wind, a cloud and fire unfolding it ... also out of the midst thereof came the likeness of a man. And every one had four faces and four wings ... the face of a man, and the face of a lion, the face of an ox, and the face of an eagle ..." ... "Now as I beheld the living creatures behold one wheel upon the Earth with his four faces ... as it were a wheel in the middle of a wheel ... for the support of the living creature was in the wheel ... their appearance was like coals of fire...." etc. (Ezekiel, ch. i.) *SD 1, pp. 126 - 127*

ATLANTIS AND ATLANTEANS

1. Plato is the first sage among the classics who speaks at length of the divine Dynasties, and locates them on a vast continent which he calls Atlantis. Bailly was not the first nor last to believe the same, and he had been preceded and anticipated in this theory by Father Kircher. This learned Jesuit writes in "Oedipus Aegyptiacus" (Vol. 1., p. 70) : -

"I confess, for a long time I had regarded all this (dynasties and the Atlantis) as pure fables ... to the day when, better instructed in oriental languages, I judged that all those legends must be, after all, only the development of a great truth...."

As de Rougemont shows, Theopompus, in his Meropis, made the priests of Phrygia and Asia Minor speak exactly as the priests of Sais did when they revealed to Solon the history and fate of Atlantis. According to Theopompus, it was a unique continent of an indefinite size, and containing two countries inhabited by *two races* - a fighting warrior race, and a pious, meditative race, which Theopompus symbolizes by two cities. (These were the early Aryans i.e., fifth Root race - and the bulk of the Fourth Root Races - the former pious and meditative ..., the latter - a fighting race of sorcerers, who were rapidly degenerating owing to their uncontrolled passions.) *(footnote SD 2, p. 371)*

The pious "city" was *continually visited by the gods*; the belligerent "city" was inhabited by various beings *invulnerable* to iron, liable to *be mortally wounded only by stone and wood.*

.... It is certain that, whether "chimera" or reality, the priests of the whole world had it from one and the same source: the universal tradition about the third great continent which perished some 850,000 years ago. A continent inhabited by two distinct races; distinct physically and especially morally; both deeply versed in primeval wisdom and the secrets of nature; mutually antagonistic in their struggle, during the course and progress of their double evolution. Whence even the Chinese teachings upon the subject, if it is but a *fiction*? Have they not recorded the existence once upon a time of a *holy* island ... and beyond which were the lands of the *immortal men*? Do they not still believe that the remnants of those *immortal* men - who survived when the holy island had become black with sin and perished - have found refuge in the great desert of Gobi, where they still reside invisible to all, and defended from approach by hosts of Spirits? *SD 2, pp. 370 - 372*

2. That not only the last island of Atlantis, spoken of by Plato, but a large continent, first divided, and then broken later on into seven peninsulas and islands (called *dwipas*), preceded Europe, is sure. It covered the whole of the North and South Atlantic regions, as well as portions of the North and South Pacific, and had islands even in the Indian Ocean (relics of Lemuria). The claim is corroborated by Indian Puranas, Greek writers, and Asiatic, Persian, and Mahommedan traditions. Wilford, who confuses sorely the Hindu and the Mussalman legends, shows this, however clearly. (*See Vol. VIII., X. and XI. of Asiatic Researches*.) And his facts and quotations from the *Puranas* give direct and conclusive evidence that the Aryan Hindus and other ancient nations were earlier navigators than the Phoenicians, who are all credited with having been the first seamen that appeared in the post-diluvian times. This is what is given in the *Journal of the Asiatic, III, pp. 325, et. seq.*: -

"In their distress the few nations who survived (in the war between Devatas and Daityas) raised their hands to Bhagavan, 'Let him who can deliver us, be our King;' using the word I'T (a *magic* term not understood by Wilford, evidently) which echoed through the whole country."

Then comes a violent storm, the waters of the *Kali* are strangely agitated, "when there appeared from the waves .. a man, afterwards called I'T, at the head of a numerous army, saying abhayan, no fear" ... and scattered the enemy. "The King I'T," explains Wilford," is a subordinate incarnation of M'rira (*Mrida*, a form of Rudra, probably?) who "re-established peace and prosperity throughout all Sankha-dwipa through *Barbaradesa*, Hissat'han and Awasthan or Arabia ...." etc., etc.

Surely if the Hindu Puranas give a description of wars on continents and islands beyond Western Africa in the Atlantic Ocean; if their writers speak of *Barbaras* and other people such as Arabs - they who were never known to navigate or cross the *Kala pani* (the black waters of the Ocean) in the days of Phoenician navigation - then their *Puranas* must be older than those Phoenicians (placed at from 2,000 to 3,000 years B.C.). At any rate those traditions must have been older; as - "In the above accounts" writes an adept, "the Hindus speak of this island as *existing* and in great power; it must, therefore, have been more than eleven thousand years ago." *SD 2, pp. 405 - 406*

3. Asburj (or Azburj), whether the peak of Tenriffe or not, was a volcano, when the sinking of the "western Atala" (or hell) began, and those who were saved told the tale to their children. Plato's Atlantis perished between the water below and fire above; the great mount vomiting flames all the while. "The 'fire-vomiting Monster' survived alone, out of the ruins of the unfortunate island."

Do the Greeks, accused of borrowing a Hindu fiction (Atala), and inventing from it another (Atlantis), stand also accused of getting their geographical notions and the number seven from them?

"The famous Atlantis exists no longer, but we can hardly doubt that it did once," says Proclus, "for Marcellus who wrote a history of Ethiopian affairs, and says that such, and so great an island once existed and this is evidenced by those who composed histories relative to the external sea. *For they relate that in this time there were seven* islands in the Atlantic Sea sacred to Persephone.... And, besides this, the inhabitants of the last island (Poseidonus) *preserved the memory of the prodigious magnitude* of the Atlantic Island as related by their ancestors, and of it governing for many periods all the islands in the Atlantic sea. From this isle one may pass to other large islands beyond, which are not far from the firm land, near which is the true sea."

"These seven dwipas (inaccurately rendered islands) constitute according to Marcellus, the body of the famous Atlantis" writes Wilford himself ...." This evidently shows *that Atlantis is the old continent....* The Atlantis was destroyed after a violent storm; this is well known to the Puranics (writers of the Hindu *Puranas* - Ed.), some of whom assert that in consequence of this dreadful convulsion of nature, six of the dwipas disappeared."

Enough proofs have now been given to satisfy the greatest sceptic. Nevertheless, direct proofs based on exact science are also added. Volumes might be written, however, to no purpose for those who will neither see nor hear, except through the eyes and ears of their respective authorities. *SD 2, pp. 408 - 409*

4. No more striking confirmation of our position could be given, than the fact that the ELEVATED RIDGE in the Atlantic basin, 9,000 feet in height, which runs for some two or three thousand miles southwards from a point near the British Islands, first slopes towards South America, then *shifts almost at right angles* to proceed in a SOUTH-EASTERLY *line toward the African coast*, whence it runs on southward to Tristan d'Acunha. This ridge is a remnant of an Atlantic continent, and, could

24

it be traced further, would establish the reality of a submarine horse-shoe junction with a former continent in the Indian Ocean. *SD 2, p. 333*

5. Several times the writer has put to herself the question: "Is the story of Exodus - in its details at least - as narrated in the Old Testament, original? Or is it, like the story of Moses himself and many others, simply another version of the legends told of the Atlanteans?" For who, upon hearing the story told of the latter, will fail to perceive the great similarity of the fundamental features? The anger of "God" at the obduracy of Pharoah, his command to the "chosen" ones, to spoil the Egyptians, before departing, of their "jewels of silver and jewels of gold" (Exod. xi.); and finally the Egyptians and their Pharoah drowned in the Red Sea. For here is a fragment of the earlier story from the Commentary (in the Archives of the Himalayan Brotherhood - Ed.) : -

"And the 'great King of the dazzling Face,' the chief of all the Yellow-faced, was sad seeing the sins of the Black-faced.

"He sent his air-vehicles (Viwan) to all his brother chiefs (chiefs of other nations and tribes) with pious men within saying: 'Prepare. Arise ye men of the good law, and cross the land while (yet) dry.'

'The Lords of the storm are approaching. Their chariots are nearing the land. One night and two days only shall the Lords of the Dark Face (the Sorcerers) live on this patient land. She is doomed and they have to descend with her. The nether Lords of the Fires (the Gnomes and fire Elementals) are preparing their magic Agneyastra (fire-weapons worked by magic). But the Lords of the Dark Eye ("Evil Eye") are stronger than they (the Elementals) and they are the slaves of the mighty ones. They are versed in Ashtar (Vidya, the highest magical knowledge). Come and use yours (i.e., your magic powers in order to counteract those of the Sorcerers). Let every Lord of the Dazzling Face (an adept of the White Magic) cause the Viwan of every lord of the Dark Face to come into his hands (or possession), lest any (of the Sorcerers) should by its means escape from the waters, avoid the rod of the Four (Karmic Deities) and save his wicked' (followers, or people).

'May every yellow face send sleep from himself (mesmerize?) to every black face. May even they (the Sorcerers) avoid pain and suffering. May every man true to the Solar Gods bind (paralyze) every man under the lunar gods, lest he should suffer or escape his destiny.

'And may every yellow face offer of his life-water (Blood) to the speaking animal of a black face, lest he awakens his master .... (Some wonderful, artificially-made beast, similar in some way to Frankenstein's creation, which spoke and warned his master of every approaching danger. The master was a 'black magician," the mechanical animal was informed by a *djin*, an Elemental, according to the accounts. The blood of a pure man alone could destroy him.) *(footnote SD 2, p. 427)*

'Let their destiny be accomplished. We are the servants of the great Four (the Four Karmic gods, called the Four Maharajahs in the SD). May the Kings of light return.'"

"The great King fell upon his dazzling Face and wept .... When the Kings assembled the waters had already moved .... But the nations had now crossed the dry lands. They were beyond the water mark. Their Kings reached them in their Viwans, and led them on to the lands of Fire and Metal (East and North)." *SD 2, pp. 426 - 428*

6. Still in another passage (in the Commentary of the Himalayan Brotherhood's Archives - Ed.) it is said: -

".... Stars (meteors) showered on the lands of the black Faces; but they slept. The speaking beasts (the magic watchers) kept quiet. The nether lords waited for order, but they came not, for their masters slept. The waters arose, and covered the valleys from one end of the earth to the other. High lands remained, the bottom of the Earth (the lands of the antipodes) remained dry. There dwelt those who escaped; the men of the yellow-faces and of the straight eye (the frank and sincere people).

"When the Lords of the Dark Faces awoke and bethought themselves of their Viwans (flying machines - Ed.) in order to escape from the rising waters, they found them gone."

Then a passage shows some of the more powerful magicians of the "Dark Face" - who awoke earlier than the others - pursuing those who had "spoilt them" and who were in the rear-guard, for "the nations that were led away, were as thick as the stars of the milky way," says a more modern Commentary, written in Sanskrit only.

"Like as a dragon-snake uncoils slowly its body, so the Sons of men, led on by the Sons of Wisdom, opened their folds, and spreading out, expanded like a running stream of sweet waters.... Many of the faint-hearted among them perished on their way. But most were saved."

Yet the pursuers, "whose heads and chest soared high above the waters," chased them "for three lunar terms" until finally reached by the rising waves, they perished to the last man, the soil sinking under their feet and the earth engulfing those who had desecrated her. *SD 2, pp. 427 - 428*

7. This sounds a good deal like the original material upon which the similar story in *Exodus* was built many hundred thousands of years later. The biography of Moses, the story of his birth, childhood and rescue from the Nile by Pharoah's daughter, is now shown to have been adapted from the Chaldean narrative about Sargon. And if so, the Assyrian tile in the British Museum being a good proof of it, why not that of the Jews robbing the Egyptians of their jewels, the death of Pharaoh and his army, and so on? The gigantic magicians of Rutta and Daitya, the "lords of the Dark Face," may have become in the later narrative the

Egyptian Magi, and the yellow-faced nations of the Fifth Race, the virtuous sons of Jacob, the "chosen people,"

.... It would be impossible, in view of the limited space at our disposal, to go any further into the description of the Atlanteans, in whom the whole East believes as much as we believe in the ancient Egyptians, but whose existence the majority of the Western scientists deny, as they have denied, before this, many a truth, from the existence of Homer down to that of the carrier pigeon. The civilization of the Atlanteans was greater even than that of the Egyptians. It is their degenerate descendants, the nation of Plato's Atlantis, which built the first Pyramids in the country, and that certainly before the advent of the "Eastern Aetheopians," as Herodotus calls the Egyptians. This may be well inferred from the statement made by Ammianus Marcellinus, who says of the Pyramids that "there are subterranean passages and winding retreats, which it is said, men skilful in the ancient mysteries, by means of which they divined the coming of a flood, constructed in different places lest the memory of all their sacred ceremonies should be lost."

These men who "divined the coming of floods" were not Egyptians, who never had any, except the periodical rising of the Nile. Who were they? The last remnants of the Atlanteans, we maintain. Those races which are dimly suspected by Science, and thinking of which Mr. Ch. Gould, the well-known geologist, says: "Can we suppose that we have at all exhausted the great museum of nature? Have we, in fact, penetrated yet beyond its antechambers? Does the written history of man, comprising a few thousand years, embrace the whole course of his intelligent existence? Or have we in the long mythical eras, extending over hundreds of thousands of years, and recorded in the chronologies of Chaldea and of China, shadowy mementos of pre-historic man, handed down by tradition, and perhaps transported by a few survivors to existing lands from others, which, like fabled (?) Atlantis of Plato, may have been submerged, or the scene of some great catastrophe which destroyed them with all their civilization." *SD 2, pp. 428 – 429*

BUDDHA, BUDDHAS, AND BUDDHISM

1. The Hindu Reformer limited his public teachings to the purely moral and physiological aspect of the Wisdom-Religion, to Ethics and MAN alone. Things "unseen and incorporeal," the mystery of Being outside our terrestrial sphere, the great Teacher left entirely untouched in his public lectures, reserving the hidden Truths for a select circle of his Arhats. The latter received their Initiation at the famous Saptaparna cave (the Sattapanni of Mahavansa) near Mount Baibhar (the Webhara of the Pali MSS.). This cave was in Rajagriha, the ancient capital of Magadha, and was the Cheta cave of Fa-hian, as rightly suspected by some archaeologists.

Time and human imagination made short work of the purity and philosophy of these teachings, once that they were transplanted from the secret and sacred circle of the Arhats, during the course of their work of proselytism, into a soil less prepared for metaphysical conceptions than India; i.e., once they were transferred into China, Japan, Siam, and Burma. How the pristine purity of these grand revelations was dealt with may be seen in studying some of the so-called "esoteric" Buddhist schools of antiquity in their modern garb, not only in China and other Buddhist countries in general, but even in not a few schools in Tibet, left to the care of uninitiated Lamas and Mongolian innovators. *SD 1, pp. xx - xxi*

2. Thus the reader is asked to bear in mind the very important difference between *orthodox* Buddhism - i.e., the public teachings of Gautama the Buddha, and his esoteric *Budhism* (Budhism with one d refers to wisdom - Ed.). His Secret Doctrine, however, differed in no wise from that of the initiated Brahmins of his day. The Buddha was a child of the Aryan soil, a born Hindu, a Kshatriya and a disciple of the "twice born" (the initiated Brahmins) or Dwijas. His teachings, therefore, could not be different from their doctrines, for the whole Buddhist reform merely consisted in giving out a portion of that which had been kept secret from every man outside of the "enchanted" circle of Temple-Initiates and ascetics.

Unable to teach all that had been imparted to him - owing to his pledges - though he taught a philosophy built upon the ground work of the true esoteric knowledge, the Buddha gave to the world only its outward material body and kept its soul for his Elect. Many Chinese scholars among Orientalists have heard of the "Soul Doctrine." None seem to have understood its real meaning and importance. *SD 1, p. xxi*

3. Considering the sacredness for the Buddhists of every line written upon Buddha or his "Good Law," the loss of nearly 76,000 *tracts* does seem miraculous. Had it been *vice versa*, every one acquainted with the natural course of events would subscribe to the statement that of these 76,000, five or six thousand treatises *might have* been destroyed during the persecutions in, and emigration from, India. But as it is well ascertained that

Buddhist Arhats began their religious exodus, for the purpose of propagating the new faith beyond Kashmir and the Himalayas, as early as the year 300 before our era, and reached China in the year 61 A.D. when Kashyapa, at the invitation of the Emperor Ming-ti, went there to acquaint the "Son of Heaven" with the tenets of Buddhism, it does seem strange to hear the Orientalists speaking of such a loss as though it were really possible.

They do not seem to allow for one moment the possibility that the texts may be lost only for the West and *for themselves*; or, that the Asiatic people should have the unparalleled boldness to keep their most sacred records out of the reach of foreigners, thus refusing to deliver them to the profanation and misuse of races even so "vastly superior" to themselves. *SD 1, pp. xxvii-xxviii*

4. It is wrong and unjust to regard the Buddhists and Advaitee Occultists as atheists. If not all of them philosophers, they are, at any rate, all logicians, their objections and arguments being based on strict reasoning. Indeed if the Parabrahman of the Hindus may be taken as a representative of the hidden and nameless deities of other nations, this absolute Principle will be found to be the prototype from which all the others were copied. *SD 1, p. 6*

5. The true Buddhist, recognising no "personal god," nor any "Father" and "Creator of Heaven and earth," still believes in an absolute consciousness, "Adi-Buddhi"; and the Buddhist philosopher knows that there

33

are Planetary Spirits, the "Dhyan Chohans." But though he admits of "spiritual lives," yet, as they are temporary in eternity, even they, according to his philosophy, are "the maya of the day," the illusion of a "day of Brahma," a short manvantara of 4,320,000,000 years. *SD 1, p. 635*

6. In its turn, rationalistic science greets the Buddhists and the Svabhavikas as the "positivists" of the archaic ages. If we take a considered view of the philosophy of the latter, our materialists may be right in their own way. The Buddhists maintained that there is no creator, but an infinitude of Creative powers, which collectively form the one eternal substance, the essence of which is inscrutable - hence not a subject for speculation for any true philosopher. Socrates invariably refused to argue upon the mystery of universal being, yet no-one would ever have thought of charging him with atheism, except those who were bent upon his destruction. *SD 1, p. 4*

7. In the Northern Buddhist system, or the popular exoteric religion, it is taught that every Buddha, while preaching the good law on earth, manifests himself simultaneously in three worlds: in the formless, as Dhyani Buddha, in the World of forms, as a Bodhisattva, and in the world of desire, the lowest (or our world) as a man.

Esoterically the teaching differs: the divine purely Adi-Buddha monad manifests as the universal Buddhi (the *Maha-buddhi* or Mahat in Hindu philosophies) the spiritual, omniscient and omnipotent root of divine intelligence, the highest *anima mundi* or the Logos.

This descends "like a flame spreading from the eternal Fire, immoveable, without increase or decrease, ever the same to the end" of the cycle of existence, and becomes universal life on the Mundane Plane. From this Plane of conscious Life shoot out, like seven fiery tongues, the Sons of Light (the *logoi* of Life); then the Dhyani-Buddhas of contemplation: the concrete forms of their formless Fathers - the Seven Sons of Light, still themselves, to whom may be applied the Brahmanical mystic phrase: "Thou art 'THAT' - *Brahm*." It is from these Dhyani-Buddhas that emanate their *chhayas* (Shadows) the Bodhisattvas, and of the terrestrial Buddhas, and finally of men. The "Seven Sons of Light" are also called "Stars." *SD 1, p. 572*

8. Unwise are those who, in their blind and, in our age, untimely hatred of Buddhism, and by re-action, of "Budhism," (wisdom - Ed.) deny its esoteric teachings (which are those also of the Brahmins), simply because the name suggests what to them, as Monotheists, are noxious doctrines. *SD 1, p. xix*

9. There is a curious piece of information in the Buddhist exoteric traditions. The exoteric or *allegorical* biography of Gautama Buddha show this great Sage dying of an indigestion of *pork* and *rice*, a very prosaic end, indeed, having little of the solemn element in it.

This is explained as an allegorical reference to his having been born in the "Boar," or Varaha-Kalpa when Brahma assumed the form of that animal to raise the Earth out of the "Waters of Space." And as the Brahmins descend direct from Brahma and are, so to speak, identified with him; and as they are at the same time the mortal enemies of Buddha and Buddhism, we have the curious allegorical hint and combination. Brahminism (of the Boar, or Varaha Kalpa) has slaughtered the religion of Buddha in India, swept it away from its face; therefore Buddha, identified with his philosophy, is said to have died from the effects of eating of the flesh of a wild hog.

The idea alone of one who established the most rigorous vegetarianism and respect for animal life - even to refusing to eat eggs as *vehicles of a latent future life* - dying of a meat indigestion, is absurdly contradictory and has puzzled more than one Orientalist. But this explanation, unveiling the allegory, explains all the rest. The Varaha, however, is no simple boar, and seems to have meant at first some antediluvian lacustrine animal "delighting to sport in water." (*Vaya Puranna*.) *SD 1, pp. 368-369, foot-note*

10. The MS. from which these ... explanations are taken belongs to the group called *"Tongshaktichi Sangye Songa,"* or the Records of the "Thirty-five Buddhas of Confession," as they are exoterically called. These personages, however, though called in the Northern Buddhist religion "Buddhas," may just as well be called Rishis, or Avatars, etc., as they are "Buddhas who have preceded Sakyamuni" only for the Northern followers of the ethics preached by Gautama. These great Mahatmas, or Buddhas, are a universal and common property: they are *historical* sages - at any rate for all the Occultists who believe in such hierarchy of Sages,

36

the existence of which has been proved to them by the learned ones of the fraternity. They are chosen from among some ninety-seven Buddhas in one group and fifty three in another, mostly imaginary personages, who are really the personifications of the powers of the first-named (the Logos - Ed.).

These "baskets" of the oldest writings on "palm leaves" are kept very secret. Each MS. has appended to it a short synopsis of the history of the sub-race to which the particular "Buddha-La" belonged. The one special MS. from which the fragments ... are extracted and then rendered into a more comprehensible language, is said to have been copied from stone tablets which belonged to a Buddha of the earliest day of the Fifth Race, who had witnessed the Deluge and the submersion of the chief continents of the Atlantean race.

The day when much, if not all, of that which is given here from the archaic records, will be found correct, is not far distant. Then the modern symbologists will acquire the certitude that even Odin, or the god Woden, the highest god in the German and Scandinavian mythology, is one of these thirty-five Buddhas; one of the earliest, indeed, for the continent to which he and his race belonged, is one of the earliest. So early, in truth, that in the days when tropical nature was to be found, where now lie eternal unthawing snows, one could cross almost by dry land from Norway via Iceland and Greenland, to the lands that at present surround Hudson's Bay. *SD 2, p. 423*

CIVILIZATIONS OF THE PAST

1. ... no one will deny that between the great civilizations of antiquity, such as those of Egypt and India, there stretched the dark ages of crass ignorance and barbarism ever since the beginning of the Christian era up to our modern civilization; during which period all recollections of these traditions were lost.

As said in *Isis Unveiled*: "Why should we forget that, ages before the prow of the adventurous Genoese clove the Western waters, the Phoenician vessels had circumnavigated the globe, and spread civilization in regions now silent and deserted? What archeologists will dare assert that the same hand which planned the Pyramids of Egypt, Karnak, and the thousand ruins now crumbling to oblivion of the sandy banks of the Nile, did not erect the monumental Nagkon-Wat of Cambodia? Or trace the hieroglyphics on the obelisks and doors of the deserted Indian village, newly discovered in British Columbia by Lord Dufferin?"

"Do not the relics we treasure in our museums - last momentos of the long 'lost arts' - speak loudly in favour of ancient civilization? And do they not prove, over and over again, that nations and continents that have passed away have buried along with them arts and sciences, which neither the first crucible ever heated in a mediaeval cloister, nor the last cracked by a modern chemist, have revived, nor will - at least in the present century?"

And the same question may be put now that was put then; it may be once more asked: "How does it happen that the most advanced standpoint that has been reached in our times, only enables us to see in the dim distance up the Alpine path of knowledge the monumental proofs that earlier explorers have left to mark the plateaux they had reached and occupied?"

"If modern masters are so much in advance of the old ones, why do they not restore to us, the lost arts of our postdiluvian forefathers? Why do they not give us the unfading colours of Luxor - the Tyrian purple; the bright vermillion and dazzling blue which decorate the walls of this place, and are as bright as on the first day of their application? The indestructible cement of the pyramids and of ancient aqueducts; the Damascus blade, which can be turned like a corkscrew in its scabbard without breaking; the gorgeous unparalleled tints of the stained glass that is found amid the dust of old ruins and beams in the windows of ancient cathedrals?"

"And if chemistry is so little able to rival even the early medieval ages in some arts, why boast of achievements which, according to strong probability, were perfectly known thousands of years ago. The more archeology and philology advance, the more humiliating to our pride are the discoveries which are daily made, the more glorious testimony do they bear on behalf of those who, perhaps on account of the distance of their remote antiquity, have been until now considered ignorant flounderers in the deepest mire of superstition."

Among other arts and sciences, the ancients - ay, as an heirloom from the Atlanteans - had those of astronomy and symbolism, which included the knowledge of the Zodiac. *SD 2, pp. 430 -431*

2. It is with the advent of the divine Dynasties that the first civilizations were started (the later Lemurians - Ed.). And while some regions of the Earth, a portion of mankind preferred leading a nomadic and patriarchal life, and in others savage man was hardly learning to build a fire and to protect himself against the Elements, his brothers - more favoured than he by their Karma, and helped by the divine intelligence which informed them - built cities, and cultivated arts and sciences. Nevertheless, and civilization notwithstanding, while their pastoral brethren enjoyed wondrous powers as their birthright, they, the builders, could now obtain theirs only gradually; even these being generally used for power over physical nature and selfish and unholy purposes.

Civilization has ever developed the physical and intellectual at the cost of the psychic and spiritual. The command and the guidance over his own psychic nature, which foolish men now associate with the supernatural, were with early Humanity innate and congenital, and came to man as naturally as walking and thinking. "There is no such thing as magic" philosophises "SHE," the author (Rider Haggard - Ed.) forgetting that "magic" in her early day still meant the great SCIENCE of WISDOM, and that Ayesha could not possibly know anything of the modern perversion of thought - "though there is such a thing as knowledge of the Secrets of Nature." But they have become Secrets only in our race, and were public property with the Third (Root Race - Ed.). *SD 2, pp. 318 - 319*

CONSCIOUSNESS

1. In the occult teachings the Unknown and the Unknowlable MOVER, or the Self-Existing, is the absolute divine Essence. And thus being *Absolute* Consciousness, and *Absolute* Motion - to the limited senses of those who describe this indescribable - it is unconsciousness and immoveableness. Concrete consciousness cannot be predicated of abstract Consciousness, any more than the quality wet can be predicated of water - wetness being its own attribute and the cause of the wet quality in other things.

Consciousness implies limitations and qualifications; something to be conscious of, and someone to be conscious of it. But Absolute Consciousness contains the cognizer, the thing cognized, and the cognition, all three in itself and all three one. No man is conscious of more than the portion of his knowledge that happens to have been recalled to his mind at any particular time, yet such is the poverty of language that we have no term to distinguish the knowledge we are unable to recall to memory. To forget is synonymous with not to remember. How much greater must be the difficulty of finding terms to describe, and to distinguish between, abstract metaphysical facts or differences. It must not be forgotten, also, that we give names to things according to the appearances they assume for ourselves.

We call absolute consciousness "unconsciousness," because it seems to us that it must be necessarily so, just as we call the Absolute, "Darkness," because to our finite understanding it appears quite impenetrable, yet we recognize fully that our perception of such things does not do them justice. We involuntarily distinguish in our minds, for instance, between absolute consciousness, and unconsciousness, by secretly endowing the former with some indefinite quality that corresponds, on a higher plane than our thoughts can reach, with what we know as consciousness in ourselves. But this is not any kind of consciousness that we can manage to distinguish from what appears to us as unconsciousness. *SD 1, p. 56*

2. Everything in the Universe, throughout all its kingdoms, is CONSCIOUS: i.e., endowed with a consciousness of its own kind and on its own plane of perception. We men must remember that because we do not perceive any signs - which we can recognise - of consciousness, say, in stones, we have no right to say that no consciousness exists there. There is no such thing as either "dead" or "blind: matter, as there is no "Blind" or "Unconscious" Law. These find no place among the conceptions of Occult philosophy. The latter never stops at surface appearances, and for it the noumenal essences have more reality than their objective counterparts; it resembles therein the medieval Nominalists, for whom it was the Universals that were the realities and the particulars which existed only in name and human factor. *SD 1, p. 274*

3. Esoteric philosophy teaches that everything lives and is conscious, but not all life and consciousness are similar to those of human or even animal beings. Life we look upon as "the one form of existence," manifesting in what is called matter; or, as in man, what, incorrectly separating them, we name Spirit, Soul and Matter. Matter is the vehicle for the manifestation of soul on this plane of existence, and soul is the vehicle on a higher plane for the manifestation of spirit, and these three are a trinity synthesized by Life, which pervades them all. The idea of universal life is one of those ancient conceptions of its liberation from anthropomorphic theology.

Science, it is true, contents itself with tracing or postulating the signs of universal life, and has not yet been bold enough even to whisper "Anima Mundi!" The idea of "crystalline life," now familiar to science, would have been scouted half a century ago (written 1888 - Ed.). Botanists are now searching for the nerves of plants; not that they suppose that plants can feel or think as animals do, but because they believe that some structure, bearing the same relation functionally to plant life that nerves bear to animal life, is necessary to explain vegetable growth and nutrition. It hardly seems possible that science can disguise from itself much longer, by the mere use of terms such as "force" and "energy," the fact that things that have life are living things, whether they be atoms or plants. ***SD 1, p. 49***

4. According to Hegel (German philosopher - Ed.), the "Unconscious" would never have undertaken the vast and laborious task of evolving the Universe, except in the hope of attaining clear Self-Consciousness. In this connection it is to be borne in mind that in designating Spirit, which the European Pantheists use as equivalent to Parabrahm (the Absolute - Ed.), as unconscious, they do not attach to that expression of "Spirit" - one employed in the absence of a better to symbolise a profound mystery - the connotation it usually bears. *SD 1, p. 51*

5. Dreamless sleep is one of the seven states of consciousness known in Oriental esotericism. In each of these states a different portion of the mind comes into action; or as a Vedantin would express it, the individual is conscious in a different plane of his being. The term "dreamless sleep," in this case is applied allegorically to the Universe to express a condition somewhat analogous to that state of consciousness in man, which, not being remembered in a waking state, seems a blank, just as the sleep of the mesmerised subject seems to him an unconscious blank when he returns to his normal condition, although he has been talking and acting as a conscious individual would. *SD 1, p. 47*

THE CONTINENTS OF
THE ROOT-RACES

1. It may be useful to agree upon the names to be given to the Continents on which the four great Races (Root Races - Ed.) preceded our Adamic Race, were born, lived, and died. Their archaic and esoteric names were many and varied with the language of the nationality which mentioned them in its annals and scriptures. That which in the Vendidad (sacred text of Zoroastrianism), for instance, is referred to as Airyanem Vaego wherein was born the original Zoroaster, is called in the Puranic literature "Sveta-Dwipa," "Mount Meru," the abode of Vishnu, etc. etc.; and in the Secret Doctrine is simply named the land of the "Gods" under their chiefs the "Spirits of this Planet."

Therefore, in view of the possible, and even very probable confusion that may arise, it is considered more convenient to adopt, for each of the four Continents constantly referred to, a name more familiar to the cultured reader. It is proposed, then, to call the first continent, or rather the first *terra firma* on which the first Race was evolved by the divine progenitors:-

I."The Imperishable Sacred Land"

The reason for this same as explained as follows: This "Sacred Land" ... is stated never to have shared the fate of the other continents; because it is only one whose destiny it is to last from the beginning to the end of the Manvantara throughout each Round. It is the cradle of the first man and the dwelling of the last divine mortal, chosen as a *Sishta* for the future seed of humanity. Of this mysterious and sacred land very little can be said, except, perhaps, according to a poetical expression in the Commentaries (of the Himalayan Brotherhood - Ed.) that the "pole-star has its watchful eye upon it, from the dawn to the close of the twilight of 'a day' of the GREAT BREATH."

II. The "Hyperborean" will be the name chosen for the Second Continent, the land which stretched out its promontories southward and westward from the North Pole to receive the Second Race, and comprised the whole of what is now known as Northern Asia. Such was the name given by the oldest Greeks to the far-off and mysterious region, whither their tradition made Apollo the "Hypoborean" travel every year. Astronomically, Apollo is of course the Sun, who abandoning his Hellenic sanctuaries, loved to visit annually his far-away country, where the Sun was said never to set for one half of the year.

But historically, or better, perhaps, ethnologically and geologically, the meaning is different. The land of the Hypoboreans, the country that extended beyond Boreas, the frozen-hearted god of snows and hurricanes, was neither an ideal country, as surmised by the mythologists, nor yet a land in the neighbourhood of Scythia and the Danube. It was a real Continent, a *bona-fide* land which knew no winter in those early days, nor have its sorry remains more than one night and day during the year, even now. The nocturnal shadows never fall upon it, said the Greeks; for it is the *land of the Gods*, the favourite abode of Apollo, the god of light, and its inhabitants are his beloved priests and servants. This may be regarded as poetical fiction now; but it was poetised *truth* then.

III. The third Continent, we propose to call "Lemuria." The name is an invention, or an idea, of Mr. P. L. Sclater, who asserted, between 1850 and 1860, on zoological grounds the actual existence, in prehistoric times, of a Continent which he showed to have extended from Madagascar to Ceylon and Sumatra. It included some portions of what is now Africa; but otherwise this gigantic Continent, which stretched from the Indian ocean to Australia, has now wholly disappeared beneath the waters of the Pacific, leaving here and there only some of its highland tops which are now islands. Mr. A. R. Wallace, the naturalist, "extends the Australia of tertiary periods to new Guinea and the Solomon Islands, and perhaps to Fiji;" and from its Marsupial types he infers "a connection with the Northern Continent during the Secondary period," writes Mr. C. Gould in *"Mythical Monsters."*

IV. "Atlantis" is the Fourth Continent. It would be the first historical land, were the tradition of the ancients to receive more attention than they have hitherto. The famous island of Plato of that name was but a fragment of this great Continent.

V. The Fifth Continent was America; but as it is situated at the Antipodes, it is Europe and Asia Minor, almost coeval with it, which are generally referred to by the Indo-Aryan Occultists as the fifth. If their teaching followed the appearance of the Continents in their geological and geographical order, then this classification would have to be altered. But as the sequence of the Continents is made to follow the order of evolution of the Races, from the first to the fifth, our Aryan Root-race, Europe must be called the fifth great Continent.

The Secret Doctrine takes no account of islands and peninsulas, nor does it follow the modern geographical distribution of land and sea. Since the day of its earliest teachings and the destruction of the great Atlantis, the face of the earth has changed more than once. There was a time when the delta of Egypt and Northern Africa belonged to Europe, before the formation of the Straits of Gibraltar, and a further upheaval of the continent, changed entirely the face of the map of Europe. The last serious change occurred some 12,000 years ago, and was followed by the submersion of Plato's little Atlantic island, which he calls Atlantis after its parent continent. Geography was part of the mysteries, in days of old. Says the Zohar: "These secrets of land and sea were divulged *to the men of sacred science,* but not to the geographers. *SD 2, pp. 6 - 9*

2. But the main point for us lies not in the agreement or disagreement of the Naturalists as to the duration of geological periods, but rather in their perfect accord on one point, for a wonder, and this a very important one. They all agree that during "The Miocene Age" - whether one or ten million years ago - Greenland and even Spitzbergen, the remnant of our Second or Hypoborean Continent, "had almost a tropical climate." Now the pre-Homeric Greeks had preserved a vivid tradition of this "Land of the Eternal Sun," whither their Apollo journeyed yearly. "During the Miocene Age, Greenland (in N. lat. 70 degrees) developed an abundance of trees, such as the Yew, the Redwood, the Sequoia, allied to the Californian species, Beeches, Planes, Willows, Oaks, Poplars, and Walnuts, as well as a Magnolia and a Zamia," says Science; in short Greenland had Southern plants unknown to Northern regions. *SD 2, p. 11*

3. And now the natural question rises. If the Greeks knew in the days of Homer, of a Hypoborean land, i.e., a blessed land beyond the reach of Boreas, the god of winter and of the hurricane, an ideal region which the later Greeks and their classes have vainly tried to locate by searching for it beyond Scythia, a country where nights were short and days long, and beyond that land a country where the sun never set and the palm grew freely - and if they knew all this, who then told them of it? In their day and for ages previously, Greenland must certainly have been covered with perpetual snows with never-thawing ice, just as it is now.

Everything tends to show that the land of the short nights and the long days was Norway or Scandanavia, beyond which was the blessed land of eternal light and summer; and to know of this, their tradition must have descended to the Greeks from some people more ancient than themselves, who were acquainted with those climatic details of which the Greeks themselves could know nothing.

.... The archaic teachings, and likewise the Puranas (ancient Indian myths - Ed.) - for one who understands the allegories of the latter - contain the same statements. Suffice, then, to us the strong probability that a people, now unknown to history, lived during the Miocene period (250,000,000 years ago) of modern science, at a time when Greenland was an almost tropical island. *SD 2, pp. 11 - 12*

CREATION - THE RE-AWAKENING
OF COSMOS

1. Behold, Oh Lanoo! The Radiant Child of the two, the unparalleled refulgent glory, bright Space, son of dark Space, who emerges from the depths of the great dark waters! It is Oeaohoo, the Younger.... He shines forth as the Sun. He is the Blazing Divine Dragon of Wisdom. *SD 1, Stanza III v. 7*

"Bright Space, son of dark Space," corresponds to the Ray dropped at the first thrill of the new "Dawn" into the great Cosmic depths, from which it re-emerges differentiated as Oeaohoo the younger, (the "new Life"), to become, to the end of the life-cycle, the germ of all things. He is "the Incorporeal man (the Heavenly Man, the Logos - Ed.) who contains in himself the divine Idea," - the generator of Light and Life, to use an expression of Philo Judaeus. He is called the Blazing Dragon of Wisdom," because, firstly, he is that which the Greek philosophers called the Logos, the Verbum of the Thought Divine; and secondly, because in Esoteric philosophy the first manifestation, being the synthesis or the aggregate of Universal Wisdom, Oeaohoo, "the Son of the Son," contains in himself the Seven Creative Hosts (The Sephiroth), and is thus the essence of manifested Wisdom. "He who bathes in the light of Oeaohoo (the Logos and new Life - Ed.) will never be deceived by the veil of Maya." **SD 1, pp. 71 - 72**

2. AN Archaic Manuscript - a collection of palm leaves made impermeable to water, fire, and air, by some specific unknown process - is before the writer's eye. On the first page is an immaculate white disk within a dull background.

On the following page, the same disk, but with a central point. The first, the student knows to represent Kosmos in Eternity, before the re-awakening of still slumbering Energy, the emanation of the Word in later systems. The point in the hitherto immaculate disk, Space and Eternity in Pralaya, denotes the dawn of differentiation. It is the Point in the Mundane Egg, the germ within the latter which will become the Universe, the ALL, the boundless, periodical Kosmos, this germ being latent and active, periodically and by turns.

The one circle is divine Unity, from which all proceeds, whither all returns. Its circumference - a forcibly limited symbol, in view of the limitation of the human mind - indicates the abstract, ever incognisable PRESENCE, and its plane, the Universal Soul, although the two are one. Only the face of the Disk being white and the ground all around black, shows clearly that its plane is the only knowledge, dim and hazy though it still is, that is attainable by man. It is on this plane that the Manvantaric manifestations (re-awakenings of Cosmos - Ed.) begin for it is in this SOUL that slumbers, during the Pralaya, the Divine Thought, wherein lies concealed the plan of every future Cosmogony and Theogony. *SD 1, p. 1*

3. From the beginning of man's inheritance, from the first appearance of the architects of the globes he lives in, the unrevealed Deity was recognised and considered under its only philosophical aspect - universal motion, the thrill of the creative Breath in Nature. Occultism sums up the "One Existence" thus: "Deity is a arcane, living (or moving) FIRE, and the eternal witnesses to this unseen Presence are Light, Heat, Moisture," - this trinity including, and being the cause of every phenomenon in Nature. As an eternal abstraction it is the EVER-PRESENT; as a manifestation, it is finite, both in the coming direction and the opposite, the two being the alpha and the omega of successive reconstructions.

Kosmos - the NOUMENON - has naught to do with the causal relations of the phenomenal World. It is only with reference to the Intra-cosmic soul, the ideal Kosmos in the immutable Divine Thought, that we may say: "It never had a beginning nor will it have an end." With regard to its body or Cosmic organization, though it cannot be said that it had a first, or will ever have a last construction, yet at each new Manvantara, its organizations may be regarded as the first and the last of its kind, as it evolutes, every time on a higher plane...." *SD 1, pp. 2 - 3*

4. Upon inaugurating an active period, says the Secret Doctrine, an expansion of this Divine essence from without inwardly and from within outwardly, occurs an obedience to eternal and immutable law, and the phenomenal or visible universe is the ultimate result of the long chain of cosmical forces thus progressively set in motion. In like manner, when the passive condition is resumed, a contraction of the Divine essence takes place, and the previous work of creation is gradually and progressively undone. The visible universe becomes disintegrated, its material dispersed; and 'darkness' solitary and alone, broods once more over the face of the 'deep.' To use a Metaphor from the Secret Books, which will convey the idea still more clearly, an out-breathing of the 'unknown essence' produces the world; and an inhalation causes it to disappear. This process has been going on from all eternity, and our present universe is but one of an infinite series, which had no beginning and will have no end. *SD 1, p. 4*

5. ... when the so-called "Creation," or formation of a planet, is accomplished by that force which is designated by the Occultists LIFE and by Science "energy," then the process takes place from within outwardly, every atom being said to contain in itself creative energy of the divine breath. Hence, whereas after an absolute pralaya, or when the pre-existing material consists but of ONE Element, and BREATH "is everywhere," the latter acts from without inwardly: after a minor pralaya, everything having remained in *status quo* - in a refrigerated state, so to say, like the moon - at the first flutter of manvantara, the planet or planets begin their resurrection to life from within outwardly. *SD 1, pp. 11 - 12 (foot-note)*

6.. ... nature runs down and disappears from the objective plane, only to re-emerge after a time of rest out of the subjective and to re-ascend once more. Our Kosmos and nature will run down only to reappear on a more perfect plane after every PRALAYA. *SD 1, p. 149*

7. ... just as the fecundation of an egg takes place before it is dropped; so the non-eternal periodical germ which becomes later in symbolism the mundane egg, contains in itself, when it emerges from the said symbol "the promise and potency" of all the Universe. Though the idea *per se* is, of course, an abstraction, a symbolical mode of expression, it is a symbol truly, as it suggests the idea of infinity as an endless circle. It brings before the mind's eye the picture of Kosmos emerging from and in Boundless space, a Universe as shoreless in magnitude if not as endless in its objective manifestation.

The simile of an egg also expresses the fact taught in Occultism that the primordial form of everything manifested, from atom to globe, from man to angel, is spheroidal, the sphere having been with all nations the emblem of eternity and infinity - a serpent swallowing its tail. To realize the meaning, however, the sphere must be thought of as seen from its centre. The field of vision or of thought is like a sphere whose radii proceed from one's self in every direction, and extends out into Space, opening up vistas all around. It is the symbolical circle of Pascal and the Kabalists, "whose centre is everywhere and circumference is nowhere," a conception which enters into the compound idea of this emblem. *SD 1, pp. 64 - 65*

8. The reader has to bear in mind that the Stanzas given treat only of the Cosmogony of our own planetary system and what is visible around it, after a Solar Pralaya (rest period for our Solar System - Ed.). The secret teachings with regard to the Evolution of the Universal Kosmos cannot be given, since they could not be understood by the highest minds in this age, and there seem to be very few initiates, even among the greatest, who are allowed to speculate upon the subject. Moreover the Teachers say openly that not even the highest Dhyani-Chohans (i.e., Archangels - Ed.) have ever penetrated the mysteries beyond those boundaries that separate the milliards of Solar Systems from the "Central Sun," as it is called. Therefore, that which is given, relates only to our visible Kosmos (solar system - Ed.), after a "Night of Brahma." *SD 1, p. 13*

9. This teaching, however, although it would not be "entirely rejected" by Science, is sure to be repudiated as an integral whole. For it avers that there are only seven Self-born primordial "gods" emanated from the trinitarian ONE. In other words, it means that all the worlds or sidereal bodies (always on strict analogy) are formed one from the other, after the primordial manifestation at the beginning of the "Great Age" is accomplished.

The birth of the celestial bodies in Space is compared to a crowd or multitude of "pilgrims" at the festival of the "Fires." Seven ascetics appear on the threshold of the temple with seven lighted sticks. At the light of these the first row of pilgrims light their incense sticks. After which every ascetic begins whirling his stick around his head in space and furnishes the rest with fire. Thus with the heavenly bodies. A laya-centre (a nucleus of rest and "negativeness," also called a "zero point" - Ed.) is lighted and awakened into life by the fires of another "pilgrim," after which the new "centre" rushes into space and becomes a comet. It is only after losing its velocity, and hence its fiery tail, that the "Fiery Dragon" settles down into quiet and steady life as a regular respectable citizen of the sidereal family.

Born in the unfathomable depths of Space, out of the homogenous Element called the World Soul, every nucleus of Cosmic matter, suddenly launched into being, begins life under the most hostile circumstances. Through a series of countless ages, it has to conquer for itself a place in the infinitude. It circles round and round between denser and already fixed bodies, moving by jerks, and pulling towards some given point or centre that attracts it, trying to avoid like a ship drawn into a channel dotted with reefs and sunken rocks, other bodies that draw and repel it in turn; many perish, their mass disintegrating through stronger masses, and when born within the insatiable stomachs of various suns. Those which move slower and are propelled into an elliptic course are doomed to annihilation sooner or later. Others moving in parabolic curves generally escape destruction owing to their velocity. *SD 1, pp. 203 - 204*

THE CROSS AND CIRCLE SYMBOLS

1. Something of the divine and the mysterious has ever been ascribed, in the minds of the ancient philosophers, to the shape of the circle. The old world, consistent in its symbolism with its pantheistic intuition, uniting the visible and the invisible Infinitudes into one, represented Deity and its outward VEIL alike - by a circle. This merging of the two into a unity and the name theos given indifferently to both, is explained and becomes thereby still more scientific and philosophical.

Plato's etymological definition of the word theos has been shown elsewhere. He derives it from the verb ... "to move," as suggested by the motion of the heavenly bodies which he connects with deity. According to the Esoteric philosophy, this Deity is during its "nights" and its "days" (i.e., cycles of rest or activity) "the *eternal perpetual motion*," "the EVER-BECOMING, as well as the ever universally present and the ever Existing." The latter is the root-abstraction, the former - the only possible conception in human mind, if it disconnects this deity from any shape or form. It is a perpetual, never-ceasing evolution circling back to its incessant progress through aeons of duration into its original status - ABSOLUTE UNITY. *SD 2, p. 545*

2. The Cross, say the Kabalists, repeating the lesson of the Occultists, is one of the *most* ancient - nay, perhaps, the most ancient of symbols. This is demonstrated at the very beginning of the *Proem* (Vol. 1.). The Eastern Initiates show it coeval with the circle of Deific infinitude and the first differentiation of the Essence, the union of spirit and matter. SD 2, p. 541

3. The Spirit of Life and Immortality was everywhere symbolized by a circle; hence the serpent biting its tail, representing the circle of Wisdom in infinity; as does the astronomical cross - the cross within a circle, and the globe with two wings added to it, which then became the sacred *Scarabaeus* (beetle - Ed.) of the Egyptians, its very name being suggestive of the secret idea attached to it. For the Scarabaeus is called in Egypt (in the *papyri*) *Khopirron* and *Khopri* from the verb Khopron "to become," and has thus been made a symbol and an emblem of human life and of the successive *becomings* of man, through the various peregrinations and metempsychoses (reincarnations) of the liberated Soul. This mystical symbol shows plainly that the Egyptians believed in reincarnation and the successive lives and existences of the Immortal entity. Being, however, an esoteric doctrine, revealed only during the mysteries by the priest-hierophants and the Kings-Initiates to the candidates, it was kept secret.

The incorporeal intelligences (the Planetary Spirits, or Creative Powers) were always represented under the form of circles. In the primitive philosophy of the Hierophants these *invisible* circles were the prototypic causes and builders of all the heavenly orbs, which were their *visible* bodies or coverings, and of which they were the souls. It was certainly a universal teaching in antiquity. (See Ezekiel, ch. 1)

"Before the mathematical numbers," says *Proclus* (in Quinto Libro, EUCLID), there are the *Self-moving* numbers; before the figures apparent - the vital figures, and before producing the material worlds which move in a Circle, the Creative Power produced the *invisible* Circles." ***SD 2 p. 552***

4. The vision of the prophet Ezekiel reminds one forcibly of this mysticism of the circle, when he beheld a *whirl-wind* from which came out "one wheel upon the earth" whose work *"was* as it were a wheel in the middle of a wheel (ch. i. vv. 4 - 16) ..."for the Spirit of the living creature was in the wheels" (v. 20).

"*Spirit* whirleth about continually and returneth again according to his circuits" - says Solomon (Eccles. i. 6), who is made in the English translation to speak of the "Wind," and in the *original text* to refer both to the Spirit and the Sun. But the Zohar ... in explanation of this verse, which is, perhaps, rather hazy and difficult to comprehend, says that "it seems to say that the sun moves in circuits, whereas it refers to the Spirit under the Sun, called the holy Spirit, that moves circularly, toward both sides, that they (It and the Sun) *should be united in the same Essence.*" ***SD 2, pp. 552 - 553***

5. The Brahmanical "Golden Egg," from within which emerges Brahma, the creative deity, is the "circle with the Central Point" of Pythagoras, and its fitting symbol. In the Secret Doctrine the concealed UNITY - whether representing *PARABRAHMAN*, or the "GREAT EXTREME" of Confucius, or the Deity concealed by PHTA, the Eternal Light, or again the Jewish EN-SOPH, is always found to be symbolized by a circle or the "nought" (absolute No-Thing and Nothing, because it is infinite and the ALL); while the god-manifested (by its works) is referred to as the *diameter of that circle*. **SD 2, p. 553**

6. Alone, among the Apostles of the Western religion, Paul seems to have fathomed - if not actually revealed - the archaic mystery of the Cross. As for the rest of those, who, by unifying and individualizing the Universal Presence, have thus synthesized it into one symbol - the central Point in the Crucifix - they have shown thereby that that they have never seized the true Spirit of the teaching of Christ, and by their interpretations they have degraded it in more than one way. They have forgotten the Spirit of that universal symbol and have selfishly monopolized it - as though the Boundless and the Infinite can ever be limited and conditioned to one manifestation individualized in one man, or even in one nation! **SD 2, p. 556**

7.The four arms of the "X," the decussated cross, and of the "Hermetic," pointing to the four cardinal points - were well understood by the mystical minds of the Hindus, Brahmins and Buddhists, thousands of years before it was heard of in Europe, and that symbol was and is found all over the world. They bent the ends of that cross and made of it their Swastica now the Wan of the Buddhist Mongolian. It implies that the "Central point" is not limited to one individual, however perfect. That the Principle (God) is in Humanity, and Humanity, as all the rest, is in it, like drops of water are in the ocean, the four ends being toward the four cardinal points, hence losing themselves in infinity. *SD 2, p. 556*

8. The "Ankhe-tie" (the Egyptian cross - Ed.) does not belong to Egypt alone. It exists under the name of pasa, a cord which Siva holds in the hand of his right back arm (Siva having four arms). .... The pasa is held in the hand in such a way that is the first finger and the hand near the thumb which make the cross or loop and crossing.... Hence the cruciform (pasa) in his hand, when he is represented as an ascetic, the *Mayayogin*, has no phallic signification, and it, indeed requires a strong imagination bent in this direction to find such even in an astronomical symbol. As an emblem of "door, gate, mouth, the place of outlet" it signifies the "strait gate" that leads to the kingdom of heaven....

It is *a Cross in a Circle and Crux Ansata*, truly; but it is a Cross on which all the human passions have to be crucified before the Yogi passes the "strait gate," the narrow circle that widens into an infinite one, as soon as the *inner* man has passed the threshold. *SD 2, pp. 548 - 549*

9. Isarim, an Initiate, is said to have found at Hebron, on the dead body of Hermes, the well-known *Smaragdine* tablet, which is said, contained the essence of Hermetic wisdom.... "Separate the earth from the fire, the subtile from the gross .... Ascend from the earth to heaven and then descend again to earth," was traced on it." The *riddle* of the cross is contained in these words, and its double mystery is solved to the Occultist. ***SD 2, p. 556***

10. Enough was said in the text about the *Swastica* and the *Tau*. Verily may the Cross be traced back into the very depths of the unfathomable Archaic Ages! Its Mystery deepens rather than clears, as we find it on the statues of Easter Island - in old Egypt, in Central Asia engraved on rocks as Tau and Swastica, in pre-Christian Scandinavia, everywhere! The author of the "Hebrew Egyptian Mystery" stands perplexed before the endless shadow it throws back into antiquity, and is unable to trace it to any particular nation or man. ***SD 2, pp. 557 - 558***

11. So it is, but the spirit of it (the cross) has ever been misunderstood. "To crucify before (not against) the sun" is a phrase used of initiation. It comes from Egypt and primarily from India. The enigma can be unriddled only by searching for its key in the Mysteries of Initiation. ***SD 2, p. 558***

CYCLES OF BEING

1. The second assertion of the Secret Doctrine is the absolute universality of that law of periodicity, of flux and reflux, ebb and flow, which physical science has observed and recorded in all departments of nature. An alternation such as that of Day and Night, Life and Death, Sleeping and Waking, is a fact so common, so perfectly universal and without exception, that it is easy to comprehend that in it we see one of the absolutely fundamental laws of the universe. *SD 1, p. 17*

2. The Days and Nights of Brahma: This is the name given to the Periods called MANVANTARA (Manu-antara, or between the Manus) and PRALAYA (Dissolution); one referring to the active periods of the Universe, the other to its times of relative and complete *rest* - according to whether they occur at the end of a "Day," or an "Age" (a life) of Brahma. These periods, which follow each other in regular succession, are also called *Kalpas*, small and great, the minor and the Maha Kalpa; though properly speaking, the Maha-Kalpa is never a "day," but a whole life or age of Brahma, for it is said in the Brahma Vaivarta: "Chronologers compute a Kalpa by the Life of Brahma; minor Kalpas, as Smavarta and the rest, are numerous." In sober truth they are infinite; as they have never had a commencement, i.e., there never was a first Kalpa, nor will there ever be a last one, in Eternity.

One *Parardha* - in the ordinary acceptation of this measure of time - or half of the existence of Brahma (in the present Maha Kalpa) has already expired; the last Kalpa was the Padma, or that of the Golden Lotus; the present one being Varaha (the "boar" incarnation, or Avatar). *SD 1, p. 368*

3. There are many kinds of *Pralaya*, but three chief ones specially mentioned in old Hindi books; and of these, as Wilson shows: - The first is called NAIMITTIKA occasional or incidental, caused by the intervals of "Brahma's Days;" it is the destruction of creatures of all that lives and has a form, but not of the substance which remains in status quo till the new DAWN in that "Night." The other is called PRAKRITIKA - and occurs at the end of the Age or Life of Brahma, when everything that exists is resolved into the primal element, to be remodelled at the end of that longer night.

But the third, *Atyantika*, does not concern the Worlds of the Universe, but only the individualities of some people; it is thus individual pralaya or NIRVANA; after having reached which, there is no more future existence possible, no rebirth till after the *Maha Pralaya*. The latter night lasting as it does 311,040,000,000,000 years, and having the possibility of being almost doubled in case the lucky Jivanmukti reaches Nirvana at an early period of a Manvantara, is long enough to be regarded as *eternal*, if not endless. The *Bhagavata* (XII, iv, 35) speaks of a fourth kind of Pralaya the *Nitya* or constant dissolution, and explains it as the change which takes place imperceptibly in everything in this Universe from the globe down to the atom - without cessation. It is growth and decay (life and death). *SD 1, pp. 370 - 371*

4. These exoteric figures accepted throughout India (i.e., the Brahmanical chronology, see *pp. 68-70, SD 1 - Ed.*) ... dovetail pretty nearly with those of the secret works. The latter, moreover, amplify them by a division into a number of esoteric cycles never mentioned in Brahmanical poular writings - one of which, the division of the Yugas into racial cycles, is given elsewhere as an instance. The rest, in their details, have of course never been made public. They are, nevertheless, known to every *"Twice-born"* (Dwija, or Initiated) Brahmin, and the Puranas contain references to some of them in veiled terms, which no matter-of-fact Orinetalist has yet endeavoured to make out, nor could he if he would.

These sacred astronomical cycles are of immense antiquity, and most of them pertain ... to the calculations of Narada and Asuramaya. The latter has the reputation of a giant and a sorcerer. But the antediluvian giants (the Gibborim of the Bible) were not all bad or Sorcerers, as Christian Theology, which sees in every Occultist a servant of the Evil one, would have it; nor were they worse than many of "the faithful sons of the Church."

A Torquemada and a Catherine de Medicis certainly did more harm in their day and in the name of their master than any Atlantean giant or demigod of antiquity ever did; whether his name was Cyclops or Medusa, or yet the Orphic Titan, the *anguipedal* monster known

67

as Ephialtes. There were *good* "giants" in days of old just as there are *bad* "pigmies" now; and the Rakshasas and Yakshas of Lanka are no worse than our modern dynamiters and certain Christian and civilised generals during modern wars. Nor are they myths.

As the Brahmanical figures given (*SD 2, pp. 68-70 - Ed.*) ... are approximately the basic calculations of our esoteric system, the reader is requested to take them carefully in mind. *SD 2, p. 70*

5. ... a few more facts may be added to the information ... known to every Orientalist (i.e., the exoteric chronological, Brahmanical figures such as the period of a complete Manvantara or "One Day" of Brahma and the cycles of the Yugas). The sacredness of the cycle of 4320 with additional cyphers, lies in the fact that the figures which comprise it taken separately or joined in various combinations, are each and all symbolical of the greatest mysteries in nature. Indeed, whether one takes the 4 separately, or the 3 by itself, or the two together making 7, or again the three added together and yielding 9, all these numbers have their application in the most sacred and occult things, and record the workings of nature in her eternally periodical phenomena. They are never erring, perpetually recurring numbers, unveiling, to him who studies the secrets of nature, a truly divine System, an intelligent plan in Cosmogony, which results in natural cosmic divisions of times, seasons, invisible influences, astronomical phenomena with their action and reaction on terrestrial and even moral nature; on birth, death, and growth, on health and disease. All these natural events are based and depend upon cyclical processes in the Kosmos itself, producing periodic agencies which, acting from without, affect the Earth and all that lives and breathes on it, from one end to the other of any Manvantara. *SD 2, pp. 73 - 74*

6. In *Isis Unveiled* we wrote that which we now repeat: - "*We are at the bottom of a cycle evidently in a transitory state.* Plato divides the intellectual progress of the universe during every cycle into fertile and barren periods. In the sublunary regions, the spheres of the various elements remain eternally in perfect harmony with the divine nature; 'but their parts,' owing to a too close proximity to earth and their comingling with the *earthy* ... are sometimes according, and sometimes contrary to divine nature.' When those circulations - which Eliphas Levi calls 'currents of the astral light' - in the universal ether which contains in itself every element, take place in harmony with the divine spirit, our earth and everything pertaining to it enjoys a fertile period. The occult power of plants, animals, and minerals magically sympathize with the 'superior natures,' and the divine soul of man is in perfect intelligence with these 'inferior' ones.

But during the barren periods, the latter lose their magic sympathy, and the spiritual sight of the majority of mankind is so blinded as to lose every notion of the superior powers of its own divine spirit. We are in a barren period: the eighteenth century, during which the malignant fever of scepticism broke out so irrepressibly,

has entailed unbelief as a hereditary disease upon the nineteenth. The divine intellect is veiled in man; his animal brain alone *philosophises.*" And philosophizing alone, how can it understand the "SOUL DOCTRINE"?
SD 2, p. 74

DELUGES AND NOAH

1. We have said ... that the great Flood had several meanings, and that it referred, as also does the FALL, to both spiritual and physical, cosmic and terrestrial events; as above, so it is below. The ship or ark - navis - in short, being the symbol of the female generative principle, is typified in the heavens by the Moon, and on Earth by the Womb: both being the vessels and bearers of the seeds of life and being, which the sun or Vishnu, the male principle, vivifies and fructifies.

The first Cosmic Flood refers to primordial creation, or the formation of heaven and the Earths; in which case Chaos and the great Deep stand for the "Flood," and the Moon for the "mother" from whom proceed all the life-germs. But the terrestrial Deluge and its story has also its dual application. In one case it has reference to that mystery when mankind was saved from utter destruction ... at the end of the Third Race, and in the other to the real and historic Atlantean submersion. In both cases the "Host" - or the Manu which saved the seed - is called Vaivasvata Manu. *SD 2, p. 139*

2. The "Deluge" is undeniably a *universal tradition.* "Glacial periods" were numerous and so were the "Deluges," for various reasons. Stockwell and Croil enumerate some half dozen Glacial periods and subsequent Deluges - the earliest of all being dated by them 850,000, and the last about 100,000 years ago. But which was *our* Deluge? Assuredly the former, the one which to this date remains recorded in the traditions of all the peoples, from the remotest antiquity the one that finally swept away the last peninsulas of Atlantis, beginning with Ruta and Daitya and ending with the (comparatively) small island mentioned by Plato (Poseidon - Ed.). This is shown by the agreement of certain details in all the legends. It was the last of its gigantic character.

The little deluge, the traces of which Baron Bunsen found in central Asia, and which he places at about 100,000 years B.C., had nothing to do with either the semi-universal Deluge, or Noah's flood - the latter being a purely mythical rendering of old traditions - nor even with the submersion of the last Atlantean island; at least only a moral connection.

Our Fifth (Root) Race (the non-initiated portions) hearing of many deluges, confused them, and now know of but one. This one altered the whole aspect of the globe in its interchange and shifting of land and sea. *SD 2, p. 141*

3. ... like all other legends, that of the Deluge had more than one meaning. It refers in Theogony, to *pre-cosmic transformations*, to *spiritual correlations* - however absurd the term may sound to a scientific ear - and also to subsequent Cosmogony; to the great FLOOD of WATERS (matter) in CHAOS, awakened and fructified by those Spirit-Rays which were swamped by, and *perished* in, the mysterious differentiation - a

pre-cosmic mystery, the Prologue to the drama of Being.

All this goes to show that the semi-universal deluge known to geology (first glacial period) must have occurred just at the time allotted to it by the Secret Doctrine: namely, 200,000 years (in round numbers) after the commencement of the FIFTH (Root) RACE, or about the time assigned by Messrs, Croil and Stockwell for the first glacial period; i.e., about 850,000 years ago. Thus, as the latter disturbance is attributed by geologists and astronomers to "an extreme eccentricity of the Earth's orbit," and as the Secret Doctrine attributes it to the same source, but with the addition of another factor, the shifting of the Earth's axis - a proof of which may be found in the *Book of Enoch*, if the veiled language of the *Puranas* is not understood - all this should tend to show that the ancients knew something of the "modern discoveries" of Science. Enoch, when speaking of "the great inclination of the Earth," which "is in travail," is quite significant and clear. ***SD 2, pp. 144 - 145***

4. Is not this evident? Nuah as Noah, *floating* on the waters in his ark; the latter being the emblem of the Argha, or Moon, the feminine principle; Noah is the "spirit: falling into matter. We find him as soon as he descends upon the Earth, planting a vineyard, drinking of the wine, and getting drunk on it, *i.e.*, the pure spirit becomes intoxicated as soon as it is finally imprisoned in matter. The seventh chapter of *Genesis* is only another version of the First. Thus, while the latter reads:

"and darkness was upon the face of the deep. And the spirit of God moved upon the face of the waters," in ch. 7 it is said "... and the waters prevailed ... and the ark went (with Noah, the spirit) upon the face of the waters." Thus Noah, if identical with the Chaldean Nuah, is the spirit *vivifying* matter, which latter is Chaos, represented by the DEEP, or the Waters of the Flood. In the Babylonian legend (the pre-cosmical blended with the terrestrial event) it is Istar (Astaroth or Venus the lunar goddess) who is shut up in the ark and sends out "a dove in search of dry land." **SD 2, p. 145**

5. As all such Cataclysms are periodical and cyclical, and as Manu Vaivasvata figures as a *generic* character under various circumstances and events, there seems to be serious objections to the supposition that the first "great flood" had any allegorical, as well as a cosmic meaning, and that it happened at the end of the Satya Yuga, the "age of Truth," when the *Second Root* race, "the Manu with bones," made its primeval appearance as "the Sweat-Born." **SD 2, p. 146**

6. The Second Flood - the so-called "universal" - which affected the Fourth Root Race (now conveniently regarded by theology as "the accursed race of giants," the Cainites, and "the sons of Ham") is that flood which was first perceived by geology. If one carefully compares the accounts in the various legends of the Chaldees and other exoteric works of the nations, it will be found that all of them agree with the orthodox narratives given in the Brahmanical books. And it may be perceived that while, in the first account, "there is no God or mortal yet on Earth," when Manu Vaivasvata lands on the Himavan; in the second, the Seven Rishis are allowed to keep him company; this showing that whereas some accounts refer to the sidereal and cosmic FLOOD before the so-called creation, the others treat, one of the Great Flood of Matter on Earth, and the other of a real watery deluge.

In the *Satapatha Brahmana*, Manu finds that "the Flood had swept away all living creatures and he alone was left" - *i.e., the seed of life* alone remained from the previous dissolution of the *Universe*, or *Mahapralaya*, after a "Day of Brahma"; and the *Mahabharata* refers simply to the geological cataclysm which swept away nearly all the Fourth Race to make room for the Fifth. Therefore is Vaivasvata Manu shown under three distinct attributes in our esoteric Cosmogony; as the "Root-Manu" on Globe A in the Fifth Round; (b) as the seed of life" on Globe D in the Fourth Round; and (c) as the "Seed of Man" at the beginning of every Root-Race - in our Fifth Race especially. ***SD 2, pp. 146 - 147***

7. The story as told in the "Mahabharata" strikes the key-note, and yet it needs to be explained by the secret sense contained in the Bhagavad Gita. It is the *prologue to the drama* of our (Fifth) Humanity. While Vaivasvata was engaged in devotion on the river bank, a fish craves his protection from a bigger fish. He saves and places it in a jar, where, growing larger and larger, it communicates to him the news of the forthcoming deluge. It is the well-known "Matsya Avatar," the first Avatar of Vishnu, the *Dagon* (the man-fish - Ed.) of the

Chaldean Xisuthrus, and many other things besides. The story is too well-known to need repetition. Vishnu orders a ship to be built, in which Manu is said to be saved along with the seven Rishis, the latter, however, being absent from other texts. Here the seven Rishis stand for the *seven Races*, the seven principles, and various other things; for there is a again a double mystery involved in this manifold allegory. *SD 2, p. 139*

DEVOTION

1. When moved by the law of Evolution, the Lords of Wisdom infused into him (man - Ed.) the spark of consciousness, the first feeling it awoke to life and activity was a sense of solidarity, of one-ness with his spiritual creators. As the child's first feeling is for its mother and nurse, so the first aspirations of the awakening consciousness in primitive man were for those whose element he felt within himself, and who yet were outside, and independent of him. DEVOTION arose out of that feeling, and became the first and foremost motor in his nature; for it is the only one which is natural in our heart, which is innate in us, and which we find alike in human babe and the young of the animal.

This feeling of irrepressible, instinctive aspiration in primitive man is beautifully, and one may say intuitionally, described by Carlyle. "The great antique heart," he exclaims, "how like a child's in its simplicity, like a man's in its earnest solemnity and depth! Heaven lies over him wheresoever he goes or stands on the earth; making all the earth a mystic temple to him, the earth's business all a kind of worship. Glimpses of bright creatures flash in the common sunlight; angels yet hover, doing God's messages among men.... Wonder, miracle, encompasses the man; he lives in an element of miracle.... A great law of duty, high as these two infinitudes (heaven and hell) dwarfing all else, annihilating all else - it was a reality, and it is one: the garment only of it is dead; the essence of it lives through all times and all eternity!"

It lives undeniably, and has settled in all its ineradicable strength and power in the Asiatic Aryan heart from the Third Race direct through its first "mind-born" sons, - the fruits of *Kriyashakti*. As time rolled on the holy caste of Initiates produced but rarely, and from age to age, such perfect creatures: beings apart, inwardly, though the same as those who produced them outwardly. *SD 1, pp. 210 - 211*

2. There is no nation in the world in which the feeling of devotion or of religious mysticism is more developed and prominent than in the Hindu people. See also what Max Muller says of this idiosyncracy and national feature in his works. This is direct inheritance from the primitive conscious men of the Third Race. *SD 1, pp. 210 - 211*

DIVINE KINGS AND INSTRUCTORS

1. Since traditions and even Chronicles of such dynasties of divine Kings - of gods reigning over men followed by dynasties of Heroes or Giants - exist in the annals of every nation, it is difficult to understand how all peoples under the sun, some of whom are separated by vast oceans and belong to different hemispheres, such as the ancient Peruvians and Mexicans, as well as Chaldeans, could have worked out the same "fairy tales" in the same order of events. However, as the Secret Doctrine teaches history - we are as entitled to our beliefs as anyone else, whether religionist or skeptic. And that Doctrine says that the Dhyani-Buddhas of the two higher groups, namely, the "Watchers" or the "Architects," furnished the many and various races with divine kings and leaders. It is the latter who taught humanity their arts and sciences, and the former who revealed to the incarnated Monads that had just shaken off their vehicles of the lower Kingdoms - and who had, therefore, lost every recollection of their divine origin - the great spiritual truths of the transcendental worlds. *SD 1, pp. 266 - 267*

2. From Manu, Thot-Hermes, Oannes-Dagon, and Edris-Enoch, down to Plato and Panadores, all tell us of seven divine dynasties, of seven Lemurians, and seven Atlantean divisions of the Earth; of the seven primitive and dual gods who descend from their celestial abode and reign on Earth, teaching mankind Astronomy,

Architecture, and all the other sciences that have come down to us. These Beings appear first as "Gods" and Creators; then they merge in nascent man, to finally emerge as "divine-Kings and Rulers." But this fact has been gradually forgotten. As Bosuage adds, the Egyptians themselves confessed that science flourished in their country, only since Isis-Osiris, whom they continue to adore as gods, "though they had become Princes in human form." And he adds of Osiris-Isis (the divine androgyne): "It is said that this (Isis-Osiris) built cities in Egypt, stopped the over-flowing of the Nile, invented agriculture, the use of the vine, music, astronomy, and geometry." *SD 2, p. 366*

3. The chronology of the divine Kings and Dynasties, like that of the age of humanity, has ever been in the hands of the priests and was kept secret from the profane multitudes.

When was it? History is silent on the subject. Fortunately we have the Dendera Zodiac, the planisphere on the ceiling of one of the oldest Egyptian temples, which records the fact. This Zodiac with its mysterious three *Virgos* between the *Lion* and *Libra*, has found its Oedipus, who understood the riddle of these signs, and justified the truthfulness of those priests who told Herodotus that : - (a) The poles of the Earth and the Ecliptic had formerly coincided; and (b) That ever since their first Zodiacal records were commenced, the Poles have been three times within the plane of the Ecliptic, as the Initiates taught. *SD 2, p. 368*

4. Bailly had not sufficient words at his command to express his surprise at the *sameness* of all such traditions about the *divine* races."What are finally," he exclaims, "all those reigns of Indian *Devas* and Persian *Peris?* .... Or, those reigns and dynasties of the Chinese legends; those *Tien-hoang* or the *Kings of Heaven* quite distinct from the *Ti-hoang,* the Kings on Earth, ... a distinction which is in perfect accord with that other one made by the Greeks and the Egyptians, in enumerating *their dynasties of Gods, of demi-*gods, and of mortals."

"Now," says Panadoras, "it is before that time (Menes) that the *reign of the seven gods who rule the world took place.* It was during that period that those benefactors of humanity *descended* on Earth and taught men to calculate the course of the sun and moon by the twelve signs of the Ecliptic." ***SD 2, pp. 368 - 369***

5. ... Herodotus was shown by the priests of Egypt the statues of their human Kings and Pontiffs-piromis (the archi-prophets or Maha-Chohans of the temples) *born from the other* (without the intervention of woman) who had reigned before Menes, their first *human* King. These statues, he says, were enormous colossi in wood, three hundred and forty-five in number, *each of which had his name, his history and his annals.* And they assured Herodotus (unless the most truthful of historians, the "Father of History," is now accused of fibbing, just in this instance) that no historian could ever understand or write an account of these superhuman Kings, unless he had studied and learned the history of *the three Dynasties* that preceded the human, namely, the DYNASTIES OF THE GODS, that of demi-gods, and of the Heroes, or giants. These "three dynasties" are the three (Root) Races (the Third, Fourth, and Fifth Root Races - Ed.).

Translated into the language of the Esoteric doctrine, these three dynasties would also be those of the Devas, of Kimpurushas, and of Danavas and Daityas - otherwise gods, celestial spirits, and giants or Titans. "Happy are those who are born, even from the condition of gods, as men, in Bharata-Varsha!" exclaim the incarnated gods themselves, during the Third Root-Race. Bharata is India, but in this case it symbolized the chosen land in those days, and was considered the best ... as it was the land of active (spiritual) works *par excellence*; the land of initiation and of divine knowledge. ***SD 2, p. 369***

EGYPT AND INITIATION

1. Broadly calculated, it is believed by the Egyptologists that the great Pyramid was built 3,350 B.C. ... and that Menes and his Dynasty existed 750 years before the Fourth Dynasty (supposed to have built the Pyramids) had appeared.... Thus 4,000 years B.C. is the age assigned to Menes. Now Sir J. Gardener Wilkinson's declaration that *"all the facts lead to the conclusion* that the Egyptians had already made very great progress in the arts of civilization *before the age of Menes,* and perhaps before they immigrated into the valley of the Nile"... is very suggestive as destroying the hypothesis.

The Schesoo-Hor (*"the servants of Horus"*) were the people who had settled in Egypt; and as M.G. Maserpo affirms, it is to this prehistoric race "that belongs the honour ... of having founded the principal cities of Egypt and established the most important sanctuaries." This was *before* the great Pyramid epoch, and when Egypt had hardly arisen from the waters. Yet "they possessed the hieroglyphic form of writing special to the Egyptians, and must have been already considerably advanced in civilization." It was, says Lenormant, "the country of the great pre-historic sanctuaries, seats of the sacerdotal dominion, which played the most important part in the origin of civilization."

What is the date assigned to the people? We hear of 4,000, at the utmost of 5,000 years B.C. (Maspero).

Now it is claimed that it is by means of the cycle of 25,868 years (the Sidereal Year) that the approximate year of the erection of the Great Pyramid can be ascertained. "Assuming that the long narrow downward passage was directed towards the pole star of the pyramid builders, astronomers have shown that .... Alpha Draconis, the then pole-star, was in the required position about 3,350 B.C., as well as in 2,170 B.C." (Proctor, quoted by Staniland Wake.) But we are also told that "this relative position of Alpha Draconis and Alcyone being an extraordinary one ... it could not occur again for a whole sidereal year." This demonstrated that, since the Dendera Zodiac (on the ceiling of one of the oldest Egyptian temples - Ed.) shows the passage of three sidereal years, the great Pyramid must have been built 78,000 years ago, or in any case that this possibility deserves to be accepted at least as readily as the later date of 3,350 B.C. *SD 2, pp. 431- 432*

2. "Every time I hear people talking of the religion of Egypt" writes M. Gaston Maspero, the great French Egyptologist ..., "I am tempted to ask which of the Egyptian religions they are talking about? Is it of the Egyptian religion of the 4th Dynasty, or of the Egyptian religions of the Ptolemaic period? Is it of the religion of the rabble, or that of the leaned men? Of that which was taught in the schools of Heliopolis, or of that other which was in the minds and conceptions of the Theban sacerdotal class? For between the first tomb of Memphis, which bears the cartouche of a king of the third dynasty, and the last stones at Esneh under

Caesar-Philippus, the Arabian, there is an interval of at least five thousand years.

.... Egypt has passed during those five thousand years through many vicissitudes of life, moral and intellectual. Chapter XVII of the *Book of the Dead* which seems to contain the exposition of the system of the world as it was understood at Heliopolis during the time of the first dynasties, is known to us only by a few copies of the eleventh and twelfth dynasties. Each of the verses composing it was already at the time interpreted in three or four different ways.... Fifteen centuries later, the number of readings had increased considerably. Time had, in its course, modified the ideas about the universe and the forces that ruled it. During the hardly 18 centuries that Christianity exists, it has worked, developed, and transformed most of its dogmas; how many times, then might not the Egyptian clergy have altered its dogmas during those fifty centuries that separate Theodosius from the King Builders of the Pyramids?"

Here we believe the eminent Egyptologist is going too far. The exoteric dogmas may often have been altered, the esoteric, never. He does not take into account the sacred immutability of the primitive truths, revealed only during the mysteries of initiation. The Egyptian priests have forgotten much, they altered nothing. The loss of a good deal of the primitive teaching was due to the sudden deaths of the great Hierophants, who passed away before they had time to reveal all to their successors; mostly, to the absence of worthy heirs to the knowledge. Yet they have preserved in their rituals and dogmas the principal teachings of the secret doctrine.

.... All this is now shown to have been the source and origin of Christian dogmas. That which the Jews had from Egypt, through Moses and other initiates, was confused and distorted enough in later days; and that which the Church got from both, is still more misinterpreted. *SD 1, pp. 311 - 312*

3. It is on this "knowledge" (the astronomical knowledge of the builders of the Pyramid - Ed.) that the programme of the MYSTERIES and of the series of Initiation was based: thence, the construction of the Pyramids, the everlasting record and the indestructible symbols of these Mysteries and Initiations on Earth, as the courses of the stars are in heaven.

The cycle of Initiation was a reproduction in miniature of that great series of Cosmic changes to which astronomers have given the name of tropical or sidereal year. Just as, at the close of the cycle of the sidereal year (25,868 years), the heavenly bodies return to the same relative positions as they occupied at its outset, so at the close of the cycle of Initiation the inner man has regained the pristine state of divine purity and knowledge from which he set out on his cycle of terrestrial incarnation.

Moses, an Initiate into the Egyptian Mystagogy, based the religious mysteries of the new nation which he created, upon the same abstract formula derived from

86

this sidereal cycle, which he symbolized under the form and measurements of the tabernacle, that he is supposed to have constructed in the wilderness. .... On these data, the later Jewish High priests constructed the allegory of Solomon's Temple.... Thus if the measurements of this allegorical temple, the symbol of the cycle of Initiation coincide with those of the great Pyramid, it is due to the fact that the former were derived from the latter through the Tabernacle of Moses. *SD 1, pp. 314 - 315*

4. The "King's Chamber" in Cheops' Pyramid is thus an Egyptian "Holy of Holies." On the days of the Mysteries of Initiation, the candidate, representing the solar god, had to descend into the Sarcophagus, and represent the energizing ray, entering into the fecund womb of nature. Emerging from it on the following morning, he typified the resurrection of life after the change called Death.

In the great MYSTERIES his figurative death lasted two days, when with the Sun, he rose on the third morning, after a last night of the most cruel trials. While the postulant represented the Sun - the all-vivifying Orb that "resurrects" every morning but to impart life to all - the Sarcophagus was symbolic of the female principle. Thus, in Egypt; its form and shape changed with every country, provided it remained a vessel, a symbolic navis or boat-shaped vehicle, and a container, symbolically, of germs or the germ of life. In India, it is the "golden" Cow through which the candidate for Brahmanism has to pass if he desires to be a Brahmin, and to become DWIJA ("reborn a second time"). *SD p. 461*

5. "To crucify before (not against) the sun" is a phrase used for initiation. It comes from Egypt, and primarily from India. The enigma can be unriddled only by searching for its key in the Mysteries of Initiation. The initiated adept, who had successfully passed through all the trials, was *attached*, not *nailed*, but simply tied on a couch in the form of a tau ... thus plunged in a deep sleep (the *"Sleep of Siloam"* it is called to this day among the Initiates in Asia Minor, in Syria, and even higher Egypt). He was allowed to remain in this state for three days and three nights, during which time his Spiritual Ego was said to confabulate with the "gods," descend into Hades, Amenti, or Patala (according to the country), and do works of charity to the invisible beings, whether souls of men or Elemental Spirits; his body remains all the time in a temple crypt or subterranean cave. In Egypt, it was placed in the Sarcophagus in the King's Chamber of the Pyramid of Cheops, and carried during the night of the approaching third day to the entrance of a gallery, where at a certain hour the beams of the rising Sun struck full on the face of the entranced candidate, who awoke to be initiated by Osiris and Thoth, the God of Wisdom. *SD 2, p. 558*

THE ELEMENTS

1. Metaphysically and esoterically there is but one ELEMENT in nature, and at the root of it is the Deity; and the so-called seven elements of which five have already manifested and asserted their existence, are the garment, *the veil, of that deity*; direct from the essence whereof comes MAN, whether physically, psychically, mentally or spiritually considered. Four elements only are generally spoken of in later antiquity, five admitted only in philosophy. For the body of ether is not fully manifested yet, and its noumenon is still "the Omnipotent Father - Aether, the synthesis of the rest."

But what are these "ELEMENTS" whose compound bodies have now been discovered by Chemistry and Physics to contain numberless sub-elements, even the sixty or seventy of which no longer embrace the whole number suspected. Let us follow their evolution from the *historical* beginnings, at any rate.

The four Elements were fully characterized by Plato when he said that they were that "which composes and decomposes the *compound bodies*. Hence Cosmolatry was never, even in its worst aspect, the fetishes which adore or worship the passive external form and matter of any object, but looked ever to the noumenon therein. Fire, Air, Water, Earth, were but the visible garb, the symbols of the informing, invisible Souls or Spirits - the Cosmic Gods to whom worship was offered by the ignorant, and simple, respectful recognition by the wiser. In their turn the phenomenal subdivisions of the noumenal Elements were informed by the Elementals, so called, the "Nature Spirits" of lower grades. *SD 1, pp. 460 - 461*

2. For clearer understanding on the part of the general reader, it must be stated that Occult Science recognises Seven Cosmical Elements - four entirely physical, and the fifth (Ether) semi-material, as it will become visible in the air towards the end of our Fourth Round, to reign supreme over the others during the whole of the Fifth. The remaining two are as yet absolutely beyond the range of human perception. These latter will, however, appear as presentiments during the 6th and 7th (Root) Races of this Round, and will become known in the 6th and 7th Rounds respectively.

These seven elements with their numberless Sub-Elements far more numerous than those known to Science are simply conditional modifications and aspects of the one and only Element. This latter is not *Ether*, not even *Akasha* but the *Source* of these. The Fifth Element now advocated quite freely by Science, is not the Ether hypothesised by Sir Isaac Newton - although he calls it by that name, having associated it in his mind probably with the Aether, "Father-Mother" of Antiquity. As Newton intuitionally says, "Nature is a perpetual circulatory worker, generating fluids out of solids, fixed things out of volatile, and volatile out of fixed, subtile out of gross, and gross out of subtile. ....

Thus, perhaps may all things be originated from Ether," (Hypoth, 1675). *SD 1, p. 12 - 13*

3. Now speaking of Elements, it is made the standing reproach of the Ancients, that they "supposed their Elements simple and undecomposable." Once more this is an unwarrantable statement; as, at any rate, their initiated philosophers can hardly come under such an imputation, since it is they who have invented allegories and religious myths from the beginning. Had they been ignorant of the heterogeneity of their Elements they would have had no personifications of Fire, Air, Water, Earth, and Aether; their Cosmic gods and goddesses would never have been blessed with such posterity, with so many sons and daughters, elements born *from* and *within each respective Element.*

Alchemy and occult phenomena would have been a delusion and a snare, even to theory, had the Ancients been ignorant of the potentialities and correlative functions and attributes of every element that enters into the composition of Air, Water, Earth, and even *Fire* - the latter a terra icognito to this day to modern Science, which is obliged to call it Motion, evolution of light and heat, state of ignition, - defining it by its outward aspects, in short, and remaining ignorant of its nature. *SD 1, pp. 140 - 141*

4. Of these (Seven Elements), four elements are now fully manifested, while the fifth - Ether - is only partially so, as we are hardly in the second half of the Fourth Round, and consequently, the fifth Element will manifest fully only in the Fifth Round. The Worlds, including our own, were of course, as germs, primarily evolved from the ONE Element in its second stage ("Father-Mother," the differentiated World's Soul, not what is termed the "Over-Soul" by Emerson), whether we call it, with modern Science, Cosmic dust and Fire Mist, or with Occultism - Akasa, Jivatma, divine Astral Light, or the "Soul of the World." But this first stage of Evolution was in due course of time followed by the next. No world, as no heavenly body, could be constructed on the objective plane, had not the Elements been sufficiently differentiated already from their primeval *Ilus*, resting in *Laya*.

The latter term is a synonym of Nirvana. It is, in fact, the Nirvanic dissociation of all substances, merged after a life-cycle into the latency of their primary conditions. It is the luminous but bodiless shadow of the matter that was, the realm of negativeness - wherein lie latent during their period of rest the active Forces of the Universe. **SD 1, pp. 461**

5. ... not alone the elements of our planets, but even those of all its sisters in the Solar System, differ as widely from each other in their combinations, as from the Cosmic elements beyond our Solar limits. Therefore, they cannot be taken as a standard for comparison with the same in other worlds. Enshrined in their virgin, pristine state within the bosom of the Eternal Mother, every atom born beyond the threshold of her realm is doomed to incessant differentiations. **SD 1, p. 143**

EVOLUTION

1. The whole order of nature evinces a progressive march towards a *higher life*. There is design in the action of the seemingly blinded forces. The whole process of evolution with its endless adaptations is a proof of this. The immutable laws that weed out the weak and feeble species, to make room for the strong, and which ensure the "survival of the fittest," though so cruel in their immediate action - all are working toward the grand end. The very *fact* that adaptations *do* occur, that the fittest do survive in the struggle for existence, shows that what is called "unconscious Nature" is in reality an aggregate of forces manipulated by semi-intelligent beings (Elementals) guided by Higher Planetary Spirits (Dhyan Chohans), whose collective aggregate forms the manifested verbum of the unmanifested LOGOS, and constitutes at one and the same time the MIND of the Universe and its immutable LAW. *SD1, pp. 277-278*

2. The first lesson taught in Eastern Philosophy is, that the incognizable Cause does not put forth evolution, whether consciously or unconsciously, but only exhibits periodically *different aspects of itself* to the perception of finite Minds. *SD 2, p. 487*

3. It now becomes plain that there exists in Nature a triple evolutionary scheme, for the formation of the three *periodical Upadhis* (vehicles - Ed.); or rather three separate schemes of evolution, which in our system are inextricably interwoven and interblended at every point. These are the Monadic (or spiritual), the intellectual, and the physical evolution. These three are the finite aspects or the reflections on the field of Cosmic Illusion of ATMA, the seventh (and highest principle - Ed.), the ONE REALITY.

1. The Monadic is, as the name implies, concerned with the growth and development into still higher phases of activity of the Monad in conjunction with:-

2. The Intellectual, represented by the Manasa-Dhyanis (the Solar Devas, or the Agnishwatta Pitris) the "givers of intelligence and consciousness" to man and:-

3. The Physical, represented by the Chhayas of the Lunar Pitris, round which Nature has concreted the present physical body. This body served as the vehicle for the "growth" (to use a misleading word) and the transformations through Manas and - owing to the accumulation of experiences - of the finite into the INFINITE, of the transient into the Eternal and Absolute.

Each of these three systems has its own laws, and is ruled and guided by different sets of the highest Dhyanis or "Logoi." Each is represented in the constitution of man, the Microcosm of the great Macrocosm; and it is the union of these three streams in him which makes him the complex being he now is.

"Nature," the physical evolutionary Power, could never evolve intelligence unaided - she can only create "senseless forms," as will be seen in our "ANTHROPOGENESIS." The "Lunar Monads" cannot progress, for they have not yet had sufficient touch with the forms created by "Nature" to allow of their accumulating experiences through its means. It is the Manasa Dhyanis who fill up the gap, and they represent the evolutionary power of Intelligence and Mind, the link between "Spirit" and "Matter" - in this Round. **SD 1, pp. 181-182**

4. It would be interesting to obtain a glimpse of the mental representation of Evolution in the Scientific brain of a materialist. What is EVOLUTION? If asked to define the full and complete meaning of the term, neither Huxley nor Haeckel will be able to do it any better than Webster does: "the act of unfolding; the process of growth, development; as the evolution of a flower from a bud, or an animal from the egg."

Yet the bud must be traced through its parent-plant to the seed and the egg to the animal or bird that laid it; or, at any rate to the speck of protoplasm from which it expanded and grew. And both the *seed* and the *speck* must have the latent potentialities in them for the reproduction and gradual development, the unfolding of the thousand and one forms or phases of evolution, through which they must pass before the flower or the animal are fully developed? Hence, the future plan, if not a DESIGN, *must be there.* Moreover, that *seed has to be traced,* and its nature ascertained. Have the Darwinists been successful in this? Or will the Moneron be cast in our teeth? But this atom of the

Watery Abysses is *not* homogeneous matter; and there must be something or somebody that had moulded and cast it into being.

Here Science is once more silent. But since there is no self-consciousness as yet in either speck, seed, or germ, according to both Materialists and Psychologists of the modern school - Occultists agreeing in this for once with their natural enemies - what is it that guides the force or forces so unerringly in this process of evolution? *Blind* force? As well call *blind* the brain which evolved in Haeckel his "Pedigree of Man" and other lucabrations. We can easily conceive that the said brain lacks an important centre or two. For, whoever knows anything of the anatomy of the human, or even of any animal body, and is still an *atheist* and a *materialist*, must be "hopelessly insane," according to Lord Herbert, who rightly sees in the frame of man's body and the coherence of its parts, something so strange and paradoxical that he holds it "to be the greatest miracle of nature."

Blind forces, "and *no* design" in anything under the Sun; when no sane man of Science would hesitate to say that, even from the little he knows and has hitherto discovered of the forces at work in Kosmos, he sees very plainly that every part, every speck and atom are in harmony with their fellow atoms and these with the whole, each having its distinct mission throughout the life-cycle. But, fortunately the greatest, the most eminent thinkers and scientists of the day are now beginning to rise against this "Pedigree," and even

Darwin's *natural selection* theory, though its author had never, probably, contemplated such widely stretched conclusions.

The remarkable work of the Russian Scientist N.T. Danilevsky - "Darwinisim, a Critical Investigation of the Theory" - upsets it completely and without appeal, and so does de Quatrefages in his last work. Our readers are recommended to examine the learned paper by Dr. Bourges ... called *"Evolutionary Psychology; the Evolution of Spirit, etc."* in which he reconciles entirely the two teachings - namely: those of the physical and spiritual evolutions. He explains the origin of the variety of organic forms, made to fit their environments with such evident intelligent design, by the existence and the mutual help and *interaction* of two principles in (manifest) nature, the inner Conscious Principle adapting itself to physical nature and the innate potentialities in the latter. Thus the French Scientist has to return to our old friend - *Archaeus*, or the life-Principle - without naming it, as Dr. Richardson has done in England in his "Nerve-Force," etc. The same idea was recently developed in Germany by Baron Hellenbach, in his remarkable work, "Individuality in the light of Biology and modern Philosophy."

We find the same conclusion arrived at in still another excellent volume of another Russian deep thinker, N.N. Strachof - who says in his "Fundamental Conceptions of Psychology and Physiology": "The most clear, as the most familiar, type of development may be found in our own mental or physical evolution, which has served others as a model to follow.... If organisms are *entities* ... then it is only just to conclude and assert that the organic life strives to beget psychic life; but it would be still more correct and in accordance with the spirit of these two categories of evolution to say, that *the true cause of organic life is the tendency of spirit to manifest in substantial form which contains the complete explanation for the lowest, never the reverse."* This is admitting, as Bourges does in the Memoire above quoted, the identity of this mysterious, integrally acting and organizing Principle with the Self-Conscious and Inner Subject which we call the Ego and the world at large - the Soul. Thus, gradually, all the best Scientists and Thinkers are approaching the Occultists in their general conclusions. ***SD 2, pp. 653-654***

5. But it is still urged that the author of "Esoteric Buddhism" (A.P. Sinnett - Ed.) has "preached Darwinism" all along. Certain passages would undoubtedly seem to lend countenance to this inference. Besides which the occultists themselves are ready to concede partial correctness to the Darwinian hypothesis, in later details, bye-laws of Evolution, and after the midway point of the Fourth Race. Of that which has taken place, physical science can really know nothing, for such matters lie entirely outside of its sphere of investigation. But, what the Occultists have never admitted, nor will they ever admit, is that man was an ape in this or in any other Round; or that he ever could be one, however much he may have been "ape-like." This is vouched by the very authority from whom the author of "Esoteric Buddhism" got his information (the Master Koot Hoomi - Ed.). **SD 1, p. 187**

6. To calculate its (the Earth's) age, however, as the pupil is asked to do ... is rather difficult, since we are not given the figures of the great Kalpa, and are not allowed to publish those of our small Yugas, except to the approximate duration of these. **SD 1, p. 206**

7. Now the evolution of the *external* form or body round the astral is produced by the terrestrial forces, just as in the case of the lower kingdoms; but the evolution of the internal or real MAN is purely spiritual. It is now no more a passage of the impersonal Monad through many and various forms of matter - endowed at best with instinct and consciousness on quite a different plane - as in the case of external evolution, but a journey of the "pilgrim soul" through various *states of not only matter* but Self-consciousness and self-perception, or of *perception* from apperception. **SD 1, p. 175**

8. This tracing of "Spiral Lines" ("Fohat traces Spiral Lines to unite the Sixth to the Seventh ...." - See *Stanza V, v. 4* - Ed.) refers to the evolution of man's as well as Nature's principles; an evolution which takes place gradually (as will be seen in Book II, on "The origin of the Human Races"), as does everything else in nature. The Sixth principle in Man (Buddhi, the Divine Soul) though a mere breath, in our conception, is still something material when compared with divine "Spirit" (Atma) of which it is the carrier or vehicle. **SD 1, p. 119**

9. In short, Spirituality is on its ascending arc, and the animal or physical impedes it from steadily progressing on the path of its evolution only when the selfishness of the *personality* has so strongly infected the real *inner* man with its lethal virus, that the upward attraction has lost all its power on the thinking reasonable man. In sober truth, vice and wickedness are an *abnormal, unnatural* manifestation, at this period of our human evolution - at least they ought to be so. The fact that mankind was never more selfish and vicious than it is now, civilized nations having succeeded in making of the first an ethical characteristic, of the second an art, is an additional proof of the exceptional nature of the phenomenon. *SD 2, p. 110*

10. As regards that other question, of the priority of man to the animals in the order of evolution, the answer is as promptly given. If man is really the Microcosm of the macrocosm, then the teaching has nothing so very impossible in it, and is but logical. For, man becomes that macrocosm for the three lower kingdoms under him.

Arguing from a physical standpoint, all the lower kingdoms, save the mineral - which is light itself, crystallised and immetallised - from plants to the creatures which preceded the first mammalians, all have been consolidated in their physical structures by means of the "cast-off dust" of those minerals, and *the refuse of the human matter, whether from living or dead bodies, on which they fed and which gave them their outer bodies.* In his turn, man grew more physical, by re-absorbing into his system that which he had given out, and which became transformed in the living anima crucibles through which it had passed, owing to Nature's alchemical transmutations.

There were animals in those days of which our modern naturalists have never dreamed; and the stronger became physical man, the giants of those times, the more powerful were his emanations. Once that Androgyne "humanity" separated into sexes, transformed by Nature into child-bearing engines, it ceased to procreate its life through drops of vital energy oozing out of the body. But while man was still ignorant of his procreative powers on the human plane (before his Fall, as a believer in Adam would say,) all this vital energy, scattered far and wide from him, was used by nature for the production of the first mammal-animal forms.

Evolution is an *eternal cycle of becoming*, we are taught; and nature never leaves an atom unused. Moreover, from the beginning of the Round, all in Nature, tends to become Man. All the impulses of the dual, centripetal and centrifugal Force are directed towards one point - MAN. The progress in the succession of beings, says Agassiz, "consists in an increasing similarity of the living fauna, and, among the vertebrates, especially, in the increasing resemblance to man. Man is the end towards which all animal creation has tended from the first appearance of the first palaeozoic fishes."

Just so; but "the palaeozoic fishes" being at the lower curve of the arc of the evolution of *forms*, this Round began with astral man, the *reflection of the Dhyan Chohans, called the "Builders." Man is the alpha and the omega of objective creation.* As said in "Isis Unveiled," "all things had their origin in spirit - evolution having originally begun from above and proceeding downwards, instead of the reverse, as taught in the Darwinian theory." Therefore, the tendency spoken of by the eminent naturalist above quoted, is one inherent in every atom. Only, were one to apply it to both sides of the evolution, the observations made would greatly interfere with the modern theory, which has now almost become (Darwinian) law.

But in citing the passages from Agassiz' work with approval, it must not be understood that the occultists are making *any concession* to the theory, which derives man from the animal kingdom. The fact that in this Round he preceded the mammalia is obviously not impugned by the consideration that the latter (mammalia) follow in the wake of man. *SD 2, pp. 169 - 170*

11. Our teachings show that, while it is correct to say that nature had built, at one time, around the human astral form an *ape-like external shape*, yet it is as correct that this shape was no more that of the "missing link," than were the coverings of that astral form, during the course of its natural evolution through all the kingdoms of nature. Nor was it, as shown in the proper place, on this Fourth Round planet that such evolution took place, but only during the First, Second, and Third Rounds, when MAN was, in turn, "a stone, a plant, and an animal" until he became what he was in the First Root-Race of present humanity.

The real line of evolution differs from the Darwinian, and the two systems are irreconcilable, except when the latter is divorced from the dogma of "Natural Selection" and the like. ... for the "human" Monad, whether *immetalized* in the stone-atom, or *invegetalized* in the plant, or *inanimalized* in the animal, is still and ever a divine, hence also a HUMAN Monad. It ceases to be human only when it becomes *absolutely divine*. The terms "mineral," "vegetable" and "animal" *monad* are meant to create a superficial distinction; there is no such thing as a Monad (jiva), other than divine, and consequently having been, or having to become human. *SD 2, pp. 185 - 186*

12. Among many other objections to the doctrine of an endless evolution and re-involution (or re-absorption) of the Kosmos, a process which, according to the Brahminical and Esoteric Doctrine, is without a beginning or an end, the Occultist is told that it cannot be, since "by all the admissions of modern scientific philosophy it is a necessity of nature to run down." If the tendency of Nature "to run down" is to be considered so forcible an objection to occult Cosmogony, "How," we may ask, "do your Positivists and Free-thinkers and Scientists account for the phalanx around us of active stellar systems?" They had eternity to "run down" in; why, then, is not the Kosmos a huge inert mass?

Even the moon is only hypothetically believed to be a dead planet, "run down," and astronomy does not seem to be acquainted with many such dead planets. The query is unanswerable. But apart from this it must be noted that the idea of the amount of "transformable energy" in our little system coming to an end is based purely on the fallacious conception of a "white-hot, incandescent Sun" perpetually radiating away his heat without compensation into Space. To this we reply that nature runs down and disappears from the objective plane, only to re-emerge after a time of rest out of the subjective and to re-ascend once more. Our Kosmos and nature will run down only to reappear on a more perfect plane after every PRALAYA. *SD1, pp. 149 - 150*

FIRE - ITS ESOTERIC MEANING

1. There is a deep philosophy underlying the earliest worship in the world, that of the Sun and of Fire. Of all the Elements known to Science, Fire is the one that has ever eluded definite analysis.

What says the esoteric teaching with regard to fire? "Fire," it says, "is the most perfect and unadulterated reflection, in Heaven as on Earth, of the ONE FLAME. It is Life and Death, the origin and the end of every material thing. It is divine 'SUBSTANCE.'" Thus, not only the FIRE-WORSHIPPER, the Parsee, but even the wandering tribes of America, which proclaim themselves "born of fire," show more science in their creeds and truth in their superstitions, than all the speculation of modern physics and learning.

The Christian who says: "God is a living Fire," speaks of the Pentecostal "Tongues of Fire" and of the "burning bush" of Moses, is as much a fire-worshipper as any other "heathen." The Rosicrucians, among all the mystics and Kabalists, were those who defined Fire in the right and most correct way. Procure a ... lamp, keep it only supplied with oil, and you will be able to light at its flame, candles and fires of the whole globe without diminishing that flame. If the Deity, the radical One, is eternal and an infinite substance ("the Lord thy God is a consuming fire") and never consumed, then it does not seem reasonable that the Occult teaching should be held as unphilosophical when it says: "Thus were the Arupa and Rupa worlds formed: from ONE light, seven lights; from each of the seven, seven times seven," etc. etc. **SD 1, pp. 120 - 122**

2. The Spirit, beyond manifested nature, is the fiery BREATH in its absolute Unity. In the manifested Universe, it is the Central Spiritual Sun, the electric Fire of all Life. In our System it is the visible Sun, the Spirit of Nature, the terrestrial god. And in, on, and around the Earth, the fiery Spirit thereof - air, fluidic fire; water. liquid fire; *Earth*, solid fire. All is fire - *ignis*, in its ultimate constitution, or I, the root of which is O (*nought*) in our conceptions, the All in nature and its mind. *Pre-Mater* is divine fire. It is the Creator, the Destroyer, the Preserver.

The primitive names of the gods are all connected with fire, from AGNI, the Aryan, to the Jewish god, who "is a consuming fire." In India, God is called in various dialects, *Eashoor, Esur, Iswur,* and *Is'Vara,* in Sanskrit the Lord, from *Isa,* but this is primarily the name of Siva, the Destroyer; and the three Vedic chief gods are Agni (ignis), Vayu, and Surya - Fire, Air, and the Sun, three occult degrees of fire.

In the *Bhagavad Gita* we read, "Iswara resides in every mortal being and puts in motion, by his supernatural power, all things which mount on the Wheel of Time." It is the creator and the destroyer, truly. "The primitive fire was supposed to have an insatiable appetite for devouring. Maximus of Tyre relates that the ancient Persians threw into the fire combustible matter crying:

'Devour, oh Lord!' In the Irish language *Easam* or *Asam*, means 'to create,' and *Aesar* was the name of an ancient Irish god, meaning 'to light a fire,'" (Kenealy). **SD 2, p. 114**

3. It was not Zeno alone, the founder of the Stoics, who taught that the Universe evolves, when its primary substance is transformed from the state of fire into that of air, then into water, etc. Heracleitus of Ephesus maintained that the one principle that underlies all phenomena in Nature is fire. The intelligence that moves the Universe is fire, and fire is intelligence. And while Anaximenes said the same of air, and Thales of Miletus (600 years B.C.) of water, the Esoteric Doctrine reconciles all those philosophers by showing that though each was right the system of none was complete. **SD 1, p. 76 - 77**

4. In *Pistis Sophia* (a Gnostic text) the disciple says to Jesus: "Rabbi, reveal unto us the Mysteries of the Light (*i.e.,* the "*Fire of Knowledge or Enlightenment*") ... foreasmuch as we have heard thee saying that *there is another baptism of smoke*, and another baptism of the Spirit of Holy Light," i.e., the Spirit of FIRE. "I baptize you with water, but .... he shall baptize you with the Holy Ghost and with fire," says John of Jesus (Matt. iii. 2); meaning this esoterically.

The real significance of this statement is very profound. It means that he, John, a non-initiated ascetic, can impart to his disciples no greater wisdom than the mysteries connected with the plane of matter (water being a symbol of it). His gnosis was that of exoteric and ritualistic dogma of dead-letter orthodoxy; while the wisdom which Jesus, an Initiate of the higher mysteries, would reveal to them, was of a higher character, for it was the "Fire" Wisdom of the true gnosis or the *real spiritual* enlightenment. One was FIRE, the other the SMOKE. For Moses, the *fire* on Mount Sinai, and the spiritual wisdom imparted; for the multitudes of the "people" below, for the profane, Mount Sinai in (*through*) smoke, *i.e.*, the exoteric husks of orthodox or *sectarian ritualism.* **SD 2, p. 566**

5. All these - "Light," "Flame," "Hot," "Cold," "Fire," "Heat," "Water," and the "water of life" are all, on our plane, the progeny' or, as a modern physicist would say, the correlations of ELECTRICITY. Mighty word, and a still mightier symbol! Sacred generator of a no less sacred progeny; of fire - the creator, the preserver, and the destroyer; of light - the essence of our divine ancestors; of flame - the Soul of things. Electricity, the ONE life at the upper rung of Being, and Astral Fluid, the Athanor of the Alchemists, at its lowest .... **SD 1, p. 81**

6. *"One earth and man,"* says the Commentary (of the Himalayan Brotherhood - Ed.), *"being the products of the three Fires"* - whose three names answer, in Sanskrit, to *"the electric fire, the Solar fire, and the fire produced by friction,"* - these three fires, explained on the Cosmic and human planes, are Spirit, Soul, and Body, the three great Root groups, with their four additional divisions. These vary with the Schools, and become - according to their applications - the *upadhis* and the *vehicles*, or the *noumena* of these . .... In the metaphysical sense the "Fire by friction" means the Union between the *Buddhi*, the sixth, and *Manas*, the fifth principles, which thus are united or cemented together; the fifth merging partially into and becoming part of the monad; in the physical it relates to the *creative spark*, or germ, which fructifies and generates the human being. **SD 2, p, 247**

FOHAT - "COSMIC ELECTRICITY"

1. Fohat, being one of the most, if not the most important character in esoteric Cosmogony, should be minutely described. ... Fohat is one thing in the yet unmanifested Universe and another in the phenomenal and Cosmic World. In the latter, he is that Occult, electric, vital power, which, under the Will of the Creative Logos, unites and brings together all forms, giving them the first impulse which becomes in time law. But in the unmanifested Universe, Fohat is no more this, than Eros is the later brilliant winged Cupid or Love. Fohat has naught to do with Kosmos yet, since Kosmos is not born and the gods still sleep in the bosom of "Father-Mother," he is an abstract philosophical idea. He produces nothing yet by himself; he is simply the potential creative power in virtue of whose action the NOUMENON of all future phenomena divides, so to speak, but to reunite in a mystic supersensuous act, and emit the creative ray.

When the "Divine Son" breaks forth, then Fohat becomes the propelling force, the active Power which causes the ONE to become TWO and THREE - on the Cosmic plane of manifestation. The triple One differentiates into the many, and then Fohat is transformed into that force which brings together the elemental atoms and makes them aggregate and combine. *SD 1, p. 109*

2. Fohat is closely related to the "One Life." From the Unknown One, the Infinite TOTALITY, the manifested ONE, or the periodical, Manvantaric Deity, emanates; and this is the Universal Mind, which, separated from its Fountain-Source is the Demiurgos or the creative Logos of the Western Kabalists, and the four-faced Brahma of the Hindu religion.... By the action of the manifested Wisdom, or Mahat, represented by these innumerable centres of spiritual Energy in the Kosmos, the reflection of the Universal Mind, which is Cosmic Ideation and the intellectual Force accompanying such ideation, becomes objectively the Fohat of the Buddhist esoteric philosopher. Fohat, running along the seven principles of AKASHA, acts upon manifested substance or the One Element, as declared above, and by differentiating it into various centres of Energy, sets in motion the law of Cosmic Evolution, which, in obedience to the Ideation of the Universal Mind, brings into existence all the various states of being in the manifested Solar System. SD 1, p. 110

3. Fohat, then, is the personified electric vital power, the transcendental binding Unity of all Cosmic Energies, on the unseen as on the manifested planes, the action of which resembles - on an immense scale - that of a living Force created by WILL, in those phenomena where the seemingly subjective acts on the seemingly objective and propels it to action. Fohat is not only the living Symbol and Container of that Force, but is looked upon by the Occultists as an Entity - the forces he acts upon being cosmic, human and terrestrial, and exercising their influence on all those planes respectively.

On the Earthly plane his influence is felt in the magnetic and active force generated by the strong desire of the magnetizer. On the Cosmic, it is present in the constructive power that carries out, in the formation of things - from the planetary system down to the glow-worm and simple daisy - the plan in the mind of nature, or in the Divine Thought, with regard to the development and growth of that special thing. He is, metaphysically, the objectivised thought of the gods; the "Word made flesh," on a lower scale, and the messenger of Cosmic and human ideations; the active force in Universal Life. In his secondary aspect, Fohat is the Solar Energy, the electric vital fluid, and the preserving fourth principle, the animal Soul of Nature so to say, or - Electricity.

In India, Fohat is connected with Vishnu and Surya in the early character of the (first) God; for Vishnu is not a high god in the Rig Veda. The name Vishnu is from the root *vish*, "to pervade," and Fohat is called the "Pervader" and the Manufacturer, because he shapes the atoms from crude material. In the sacred texts of the Rig Veda, Vishnu also, is "a manifestation of the Solar Energy," and he is described as striding through the Seven regions of the Universe in three steps, the Vedic God having little in common with the Vishnu of later times. Therefore the two are identical in this particular feature, and one is the copy of the other. *SD 1, pp. 111 - 112*

4. This something, at present unknown to Western speculation, is called by the occultists Fohat. It is the "bridge" by which the "Ideas" existing in the "Divine Thought" are impressed on Cosmic substance as the "laws of Nature." Fohat is thus the dynamic energy of Cosmic Ideation; or regarded from the other side, it is the intelligent medium, the guiding power of all manifestation, the "Thought Divine" transmitted and made manifest through the Dhyan Chohans, the Architects of the visible world. .... Fohat in its various manifestations is the mysterious link between Mind and Matter, the animating principle electrifying every atom into life. *SD 1, p. 16*

5. He (Fohat) is the Steed, and Thought is the Rider (*i.e., he is under the influence of their guiding thought*) (the guiding thought of the Dhyan Chohans - Ed.). He passes like Lightening through the fiery clouds (cosmic mists); takes three and five, and seven strides through the seven regions above and the seven below (*the worlds to be*). He lifts his voice, and calls the innumerable sparks (*atoms*) and joins them together. *SD. 1, pp. 107 - 108, Stanza V, v. 2*

6. How does Fohat build them (the worlds - Ed.)? He collects the fiery dust. He makes balls of fire, runs through them, and round them, infusing life, there into, then sets them into motion; some one way, some the other way. They are cold, he makes them hot. They are dry, he makes them moist. They shine, he fans and cools them. Thus acts Fohat from one twilight to the other, during Seven Eternities. **SD 1, p. 144, Stanza VI, v. 4**

7. Fohat has several meanings. He is called the "Builder of the Builders," the Force that he personifies having formed our Septenary chain (our planetary chain). **SD 1, p. 139, foot-note**

8. He (Fohat) is One and Seven, and on the Cosmic plane is behind all such manifestations as light, heat, sound, adhesion, etc. etc., and is the "spirit" of ELECTRICITY, which is the LIFE of the Universe. As an abstraction, we call it the ONE LIFE; as an objective and evident Reality, we speak of a septenary scale of manifestation, which begins at the upper rung with the One Unknowable CAUSALITY, and ends as Omnipresent Mind and Life immanent in every atom of Matter. Thus, while science speaks of its evolution through brute matter, blind force, and senseless motion, the occultists point to intelligent LAW and sentient LIFE, and add that Fohat is the guiding Spirit of all this. Yet he is no personal god at all, but the emanation of those other Powers behind him whom the Christians call the "Messengers" of their God (who is in reality only the Elohim, or rather one of the Seven Creators called Elohim), and we, the "Messenger of the primordial Sons of Life and Light." **SD 1, p. 139, foot-note**

9. Fohat runs the Manus (or Dhyan Chohans) errands, and causes the ideal prototypes to expand from within without - viz., to cross gradually, on a descending scale, all the planes from the noumenon to the lowest phenomenon, to bloom finally on the last into full

objectivity - the acme of illusion, or the grossest matter.
SD 1, p. 63

10. The ancients represented it (Fohat) by a serpent,
for "Fohat hisses as he glides hither and thither (in
zigzags). The Kabala figures it with the Hebrew letter
Teth, whose symbol is the serpent which played such
a prominent part in the Mysteries. Its universal value
is nine, for it is the ninth letter of the alphabet and the
ninth door of the fifty portals or gateways that lead to
the concealed mysteries of being. It is the magical agent
par excellence, and designates in Hermetic philosophy
"Life infused into primordial matter," the essence that
composes all things, and the spirit that determines their
form. But there are two secret Hermetical operations,
one spiritual, the other material-correlative, and forever
united. Thou shalt separate the earth from the fire, the
subtile from the solid ... that which ascends from earth
to heaven and descends again from heaven to earth.
It (the subtile light), is the strong force of every force,
for it conquers every subtile thing and penetrates into
every solid. Thus was the world formed." (*Hermes*) **SD
1, p. 76**

11. Bear in mind that Fohat, the constructive Force
of Cosmic Electricity, is said metaphorically, to have
sprung like Rudra (Siva - Ed.) from Brahma "from the
brain of the Father and the bosom of the Mother"
and then to have metamorphosed himself into a male
and a female, *i.e.*, polarity, into positive and negative
electricity. He has *seven sons who are his brothers*; and
Fohat is forced to be born time after time whenever any

two of his son-brothers indulge *in too close contact* - whether an embrace or a fight. To avoid this, he binds together and unites those of unlike nature and separates those of similar temperament. This, of course, relates, as any one can see, to electricity generated by friction and to the law involving attraction between two objects of unlike, and repulsion between those of like polarity.

The Seven "Sons-brothers," however, represent and personify the seven forms of Cosmic magnetism called in *practical Occultism* the "Seven Radicals," whose co-operative and active progeny are, among other energies, Electricity, Magnetism, Sound, Light, Heat, Cohesion, etc. Occult Science defines all these as Super-sensuous effects in their hidden behaviour, and as objective phenomena in the world of senses; the former requiring abnormal faculties to perceive them - the latter, our ordinary physical senses. They all pertain to, and are, the emanations of, still more supersensuous spiritual qualities, not personated by, but belonging to, real and conscious CAUSES. To attempt a description of such ENTITIES would be worse than useless. The reader must bear in mind that, according to our teaching which regards this phenomenal Universe as a great *Illusion*, the nearer a body is to the UNKNOWN SUBSTANCE, the more it approaches *reality*, as being removed the farther from this world of MAYA. *SD 1, p. 145*

12. It is Fohat who guides the transfer of the principles from one planet to the other, from one star to another - child-star. When a planet dies, its informing principles are transferred to a laya or sleeping centre, with potential but latent energy in it, which is thus awakened into life and begins to form itself into a new sidereal body. *SD 1, p. 147*

GIANTS OF ANCIENT TIMES

1. To speak of a race nine *yatis*, or 27 feet high, in a work claiming a more scientific character than "Jack the Giant-Killer," is a somewhat unusual proceeding. "Where are your proofs? The writer will be asked. In History and tradition is the answer. Traditions about a race of giants in days of old are universal; they exist in oral and written lore. India had her Danavas and Daityas; Ceylon had her Rakshasas; Greece her Titans; Egypt, her colossal Heroes; Chaldea, her Izdubars (Nimrod); and the Jews their *Emims* of the land of Moab, with the famous giants, Anakim (*Numbers* xiii.33). Moses speaks of Og, a king who was nine cubits high (15 ft. 4 in.) and four wide (Deut. iii 11), and Goliath was "six cubits and a span in height (or 10ft. 7in)."

The only difference found between the "revealed Scripture" and the evidence furnished to us by Herodotus, Diodorus Sinclus, Homer, Plimy, Plutarch, Philostratus etc. etc., is this: While the pagans mention only *the skeletons of giants*, dead untold ages before, relics that some of *them had personally seen*, the Bible interpreters unblushingly demand that geology and archaeology should believe, that several countries were inhabited by such giants in the day of Moses; giants before whom the Jews were as grasshoppers, and who still existed in the days of Joshua and David. Unfortunately, their own chronology is in the way.

Either the latter or the giants have to be given up. *SD 2, p. 336*

2. It was the belief of entire antiquity, Pagan and Christian, that the earliest mankind was a race of giants. Certain excavations in America in mounds and in caves, have already yielded in isolated cases groups of skeletons of nine and twelve feet high. These belong to tribes of the early Fifth (Root) Race, now degenerated to an average size of between five and six feet. But we can easily believe that the Titans and Cyclopes of old really belonged to the Fourth (Atlantean) Race, and that all the subsequent legends and allegories found in the Hindu Puranas and the Greek Hesiod and Homer, were based on the hazy reminiscences of real Titans - men of a superhuman tremendous physical power, which enabled them to defend themselves, and hold at bay the gigantic monsters of the Mesozoic and early Cenozoic times - and of actual Cyclopes - three-eyed mortals.

It has been often remarked by observant writers, that the "origin of nearly every popular myth and legend could be traced invariably to a fact in nature."

In these fantastic creations of an exuberant subjectivism, there is always an element of the objective and real. The imagination of the masses, disorderly and ill-regulated as it may be, could never have conceived and fabricated ex nihilo so many monstrous figures, such a wealth of extraordinary tales, had it not had, to serve it as a central nucleus, those floating reminiscences, obscure and vague, which unite the broken links of the chain of time to form with them the mysterious, dream foundation of our collective consciousness. *SD 2, p. 293*

3. Of still standing witnesses to the submerged continents and the colossal men that inhabited them, there are still a few. Archeology claims several such on this globe, though beyond wondering "what these may be" - it never made any serious attempt to solve the mystery. Besides the Easter Island statues ..., to what epoch do the colossal statues, still erect and intact near Bamian, belong? (Sadly, they no longer exist due to their destruction by the Taliban - Ed.) Archeology assigns them to the first centuries of Christianity (as usual) and errs in this as it does in many other speculations. A few words of description will show the readers what are the statues of both Easter Isle and Bamian. We will first examine what is known of them to orthodox Science. In *"The Countries of the World,"* by Robert Brown, ... it is stated that -

"Teapi, Rapa-nui, or Easter Island, is an isolated spot almost 2,000 miles from the South American coast.... In length it is about twelve miles, in breadth four ... and there is an extinct crater 1,050 feet high in its centre. The island abounds in craters, which have been extinct for so long that no tradition of their activity remains....

"But who made the great stone images which are now the chief attraction of the island to visitors? *No one knows"* - says the reviewer. "It is more than likely that they were here when the present inhabitants (a handful of Polynesian savages) arrived .... Their workmanship *is of a high order* ... and it is believed that the race who formed them were the frequenters of the natives of Peru and other portions of South America.... Even at the date of Cook's visit, some of the statues measuring 27 feet in height and eight across the shoulders were lying over-thrown, while others still standing appeared much larger. One of the latter was so lofty that the shade was sufficient to shelter a party of thirty persons from the heat of the sun. The platforms on which these colossal images stood averaged from thirty to forty feet in length, twelve to sixteen broad ... all built of hewn stone in the Cyclopean style, very much like the walls of the Temple of Pachacamac, *or the ruins of Tia-Huanuco in Peru.*"

"There is no reason to believe that any of the statues have been built up, bit by bit, by scaffolding erected around them" - adds the journal very suggestively - without explaining how they could be built otherwise unless made by giants of the same size as the statues themselves. One of the best of these colossal images is now in the British Museum. The images of Ronororaka - the only one now found erect - are four in number, three deeply sunk in the soil, and one resting on the back of its head like the head of a man asleep. Their types, though all are long-headed, are different; and they are evidently meant for portraits, as the noses, the mouths and chins differ greatly in form, their head-dress, moreover - a kind of flat cap with a back piece attached to it to cover the back portion of the head - showing that the originals were no savages of the stone period. Verily, the question may be asked - "Who made them?" - but it is not archeology nor yet geology that is likely to answer, though the latter recognises in the island a portion of a submerged continent. *SD 2, pp. 336 - 337*

4. But who cut the Bamian, still more colossal statues, the tallest and most gigantic in the whole world for Bartholdi's "Statue of Liberty" is a dwarf when compared with the largest of the five images. Burnes, and several learned Jesuits who have visited this place, speak of a mountain "all honeycombed with gigantic cells," with two immense giants cut in the same rock.

For all those numberless gigantic ruins discovered one after the other in our day, all those immense avenues of colossal ruins that cross North America along and beyond the Rocky Mountains, are the work of the Cyclopes, the true and actual Giants of old. "Masses of enormous human bones" were found "in America, near Misorte," a celebrated modern traveller tells us, precisely on the spot which local tradition points out as the landing spot of those giants who overran America when it had hardly arisen from the waters. *SD 2, pp. 337 - 338*

5. Central Asian traditions say the same of the Bamian statues. What are they, and what is the place where they have stood for countless ages...? Bamian is a small, miserable, half-ruined town in Central Asia, half-way between Cabul and Balkh, at the foot of Kobhibaba, a huge mountain ... some 8,500 feet above the level of the sea. The whole valley is hemmed in by colossal rocks, which are full of perfectly natural and partially artificial caves and grottoes, once the dwellings of Buddhist monks who had established in them their viharas.... It is at the entrance of some of these that five enormous statues of what is regarded as Buddha have been discovered or rather *rediscovered* in our century (the 19th - Ed.), as the famous Chinese traveller, Hiouen-Thsang, speaks of, and saw them, when he visited Bamian in the VIIth century.

When it is maintained that no larger statues exist on the whole globe the fact is easily proven on the evidence of all the travellers who have examined them.... Thus the largest is 173 feet high, or seventy feet higher that the Statue of Liberty.... The second statue ... is only 120 feet (15 feet taller than the said "Liberty"). The third statue is only 60 feet high - the two others still smaller, the last being a little larger than the average tall man of our present race.

.... Hiouen Thsang, speaking of the colossal statue says that "the shining of the gold ornamentation that overlaid the statue" in his day "dazzled one's eyes," but of such gilding there remains not a vestige in modern times. The very drapery, in contrast to the figure itself, cut out in the standing rock, is made of plaster and modelled over the stone image. Talbot, who has made the most careful examination, found that this drapery belonged to a far later epoch. The statue itself has therefore to be assigned a far earlier period than Buddhism. Who does it represent in such case, it may be asked?

Once more tradition, corroborated by written records, answers the query and explains the mystery. The

Buddhist Arhats and Ascetics found the five statues, and many more, now crumbled down to dust, and as the three were found by them in colossal niches at the entrance of their future abode, they covered the figures with plaster, and over the old, modelled new statues made to represent Lord Tathagata (the Buddha - Ed.). The interior walls of the niches are covered to this day with bright paintings of human figures, and the sacred image of Buddha is repeated in every group. These frescoes and ornaments - which one of the Byzantine style of painting - are all due to the piety of the monk-ascetics, like some other minor figures and rock-cut ornamentations. But the five statues belong to the handiwork of the Initiates of the Fourth Race (the Atlantean - Ed.), who sought refuge, after the submersion of their continent, in the vastness and on the summits of the Central Asian mountain chains. Moreover, the five statues are an imperishable record of the esoteric teaching about the gradual evolution of the races.

The largest is made to represent the First (Root) race of mankind, its ethereal body being commemorated in hard, everlasting stone, for the instruction of future generations, as its remembrance would otherwise never have survived the Atlantean deluge. The second - 120 feet high - represents the sweat-born; and the third - measuring 60 feet - immortalizes the race that fell, and thereby inaugurated the first physical race, born of father and mother, the last descendants of which are represented in the Statues found on Easter Isle; but they were only from 20 to 25 feet in stature at the epoch when Lemuria was submerged after it had been nearly destroyed by volcanic fires. The Fourth Race was still smaller, though gigantic in comparison with our present Fifth Race, and the series culminated finally in the latter.

These are, then, the "Giants" of antiquity, the ante- and post-diluvian Gibborim of the Bible. They lived and flourished one million rather than between three and four thousand years ago. *SD 2, pp. 338 - 340*

6. ... (a) had there been no giants to move about such colossal rocks, there could never have been a Stonehenge, a Carnac (Brittany) and other such Cyclopean structures; and (b) were there no such thing as MAGIC, there could never have been so many witnesses to *oracular* and *speaking* stones. *SD 2, p. 341*

7. De Mirville - who seeks to justify the Bible - inquires very pertinently why the monstrous stones of Stonhenge were called in days of old *chior-gaur* (from *Cor,* "dance," whence *chorea,* and *gaurr,* a GIANT), or the dance of giants? And then he sends the reader to receive his reply from the Bishop of St. Gildas. But the authors of the *Voyage dans le Comte de Cornouailles, sur les traces des geants,* and of various learned works on the ruins of Stonehenge, Carnac and West Hoadley, give far better and more reliable information upon this particular subject. In those regions - true forests of rocks - immense monoliths are found, "some weighing over 5000,000 kilograms" (Cambry). These "hinging stones" of Salisbury Plain are believed to be the remains of a Druidical temple. But the Druids were historical men and not Cyclops nor giants. Who then, *if not giants, could ever raise such masses* (especially those at Carnac and West Hoadley), range them in such symmetrical order that they should represent the planisphere, and place them in such wonderful equipose that they seem to hardly touch the ground, are set in motion at the slightest touch of the finger, and would yet resist the efforts of twenty men who should attempt to displace them.

We say, that most of these stones are the relics of the last Atlanteans. We shall be answered that all the geologists claim them to be of a natural origin. That a rock when "weathering," i.e., losing flake after flake of its substance under influence of weather, assumes this form. That, the "tors" in West England exhibit curious forms, also produced by this cause....

But read what Geology has to say, and you will learn that often these gigantic masses do not even belong to the countries wherein they are now fixed; that their geological congeners often pertain to strata unknown in those regions and to be found only far beyond the seas.
SD 2, pp. 342 - 343

THE GREAT BREATH

1. The appearance and disappearance of the Universe are pictured as an outbreathing and inbreathing of "the Great Breath," which is eternal, and which, being Motion, is one of the three aspects of the Absolute - Abstract Space and Duration being the other two. When the "Great Breath" is projected, it is called the Divine Breath, and is regarded as the breathing of the Unknowable Deity - the One Existence - which breathes out a thought, as it were, which becomes the Kosmos. So also is it when the Divine breath is inspired again the Universe disappears into the bosom of "the Great Mother," who then sleeps "wrapped in her invisible robes." *SD 1, p. 43*

2. The Secret Doctrine points out, as a self-evident fact, that Mankind collectively and individually, is, with all manifested nature, the vehicle of the breath of One Universal Principle, in its primal differentiation; and of the countless "breaths" proceeding from that One BREATH in its secondary and further differentiations, as Nature with its many *mankinds* proceeds downwards toward the planes that are ever increasing in materiality. The primary breath informs the higher Hierarchies (of Angelic Hosts - Ed.); the secondary - the lower, on the constantly descending planes. *SD 2, p. 492*

3. The Secret Doctrine teaches us that everything in the universe, as well as the universe itself, is formed (created) during its periodical manifestations - by accelerated MOTION set into activity by the BREATH of the ever-to-be-unknown power (unknown to present mankind, at any rate) within the phenomenal world. *SD 2, pp. 551 - 552*

4. In the Anugita (part of the Asvamedha Parvan of *The Mahabharata*) a conversation is given between a Brahmana and his wife, on the origin of Speech and its occult properties. The wife asks how Speech came into existence, and which was prior to the other, Speech or Mind. The Brahmana tells her that the Apana (*inspirational breath*) becoming lord, charges that intelligence which does not understand Speech or Words, into the state of Apana, and thus opens the mind. Thereupon he tells her a story, a dialogue between Speech and Mind. ....

This allegory (the story the Brahmana tells his wife - Ed.) is at the root of the Occult law, which prescribes silence upon the knowledge of certain secret and invisible things perceptible only to the spiritual mind (the 6th sense - the buddhi - Ed.), and which cannot be expressed by "noisy" or uttered speech. This chapter of Anugita explains, says Arjuna Misra, Pranayama, or regulation of the breath in Yoga practices. This mode, however, without the previous acquisition of, or at least full understanding of the two higher senses, of which there are seven, ... pertains rather to the lower Yoga. The *hatha* so called was and still is discountenanced by the Arhats. It is injurious to the health and alone can never develop into Raj Yoga. *SD 1, pp. 94 - 95*

5. See the quarrel of the senses about their respective superiority and their taking the Brahman, the lord of all creatures, for their arbiter. "You are all greatest and not greatest," or superior to objects, as Arjuna Misra says, none being independent of the other. "You are all possessed of one another's qualities. All are greatest in their own spheres and all support one another. There is one unmoving (life-wind or breath, the 'Yoga inhalation,' so called, which is the breath of the *one* or Higher Self). That is the (or my) own Self, accumulated in noumenon (forms)."

The Breath, Voice, Self or "Wind"... is the Synthesis of the Seven Senses, *noumenally* all minor deities and esoterically - the *septenary* and the "Army of the Voice."
SD 1, p. 96

THE GREAT DAY OF BE-WITH-US

1. The "Great Day of BE-WITH-US," ... is an expression the only merit of which lies in its literal translation. Its significance is not so easily revealed to a public, unacquainted with the mystic tenets of Occultism, or rather of Esoteric Wisdom or "Budhism." It is an expression peculiar to the latter, and as hazy for the profane as that of the Egyptians who called the same the "Day of COME-TO-US," which is identical with the former, though the verb "be" in this sense, might be still better replaced with either of the two words "Remain" or "Rest-with-us," as it refers to that long period of REST which is called Paranirvana (also Mahapralaya - Ed.).

As in the exoteric interpretation of the Egyptian rites the soul of every defunct person ... became an Osiris, was Osirified, though the Secret Doctrine had always taught, that the real Osirification was the lot of every Monad (fragment or spark of the Divine - Ed.) only after 3,000 cycles of Existences; so in the present case. The "Monad," born of the nature and the very Essence of the "Seven" (its highest principle becoming immediately enshrined in the Seventh Cosmic Element), has to perform its septenary gyration throughout the Cycle of Being and forms, from the highest to the lowest; and then again from man to God. At the threshold of Paranirvana it reassumes its primeval Essence and becomes the Absolute once more. *SD 1, pp. 134 - 135*

2. As expressed by the *Bhagavadgita* lecturer (Subba Row - Ed.), "It must not be supposed that the Logos is but a single centre of energy manifested from Parabrahman (the Absolute - Ed.); there are innumerable other centres ... and their number is almost infinite in the bosom of Parabrahman." Hence the expression, "The Day of Come to Us" and "the Day of Be with Us," etc. Just as the square is the symbol of the Four sacred Forces or Powers ... so the Circle shows the boundary within the Infinity that no man can cross, even in spirit, nor Deva nor Dhyan Chohan (Archangel - Ed.). The Spirits of those who 'descend and ascend" during the course of cyclic evolution shall cross the "iron-bound world" only on the day of their approach to the threshold of Paranirvana. If they reach it - they will rest in the bosom of Parabrahman, or the "Unknown Darkness," which shall then become for all of them Light - during the whole period of Mahapralaya, the "Great Night," namely, 311,040,000,000,000 years of absorption in Brahm. The day of "Be-With-Us" is this period of rest or Paranirvana. See also for other data on this peculiar expression, the day of "Come-To-Us," *The Funeral Ritual of the Egyptians, by* Viscount de Rouge. It corresponds to the Day of the Last Judgment of the Christians, which has been sorely materialised by their religion. *SD 1, p. 134, foot-note*

3. Thou art Myself, My image and its shadow (said the Flame to the spark). I have clothed myself in thee, and thou art my vahan (vehicle) to the Day, "Be With Us," when thou shalt rebecome Myself and others, thyself and Me. *SD 1, Stanza VII, v.7*

The day when "the spark will re-become the Flame (man will merge into his Dhyan Chohan) Myself and others, thyself and Me," as the Stanza has it - means this: In Paranirvana - when Pralaya will have reduced not only material and psychical bodies, but even the spiritual Ego(s) to their original principle - the Past, Present, and even Future Humanities, like all things will be one and the same. Everything will have re-entered the Great Breath. In other words, everything will be "merged in Brahma" or the divine unity. ***SD 1, pp. 265 - 266***

HERMAPHRODITISM

1. An impenetrable veil of secrecy was thrown over the occult and religious mysteries taught, after the submersion of the last remnant of the Atlantean race, some 12,000 years ago, lest they should be shared by the unworthy, and so desecrated. Of these sciences several have now become exoteric - such as Astronomy, for instance, in its purely mathematical and physical aspect. Hence their dogmas and tenets, being all symbolised and left to the sole guardianship of parable and allegory, have been forgotten, and their meaning has become perverted. Nevertheless, one finds the hermaphrodite in the scriptures and traditions of almost every nation; and why such unanimous agreement if the statement is only a fiction?

It is this secrecy which led the Fifth (Roof) Race to the establishment, or rather the re-establishment of the religious mysteries, in which ancient truths might be taught to the coming generations under the veil of allegory and symbolism. Behold the imperishable witness to the evolution of the human races from the divine, and especially from the androgynous Race - the Egyptian Sphinx, the riddle of the Ages! Divine wisdom incarnating on earth, and forced to taste of the bitter fruit of personal experience of pain and suffering, generated under the shade of the tree of the knowledge of Good and Evil - a secret first known only to the

Elohim, the SELF-INITIATES, *"higher gods"* - on earth only.

In the Book of Enoch we have Adam, the first divine androgyne separating into man and woman, and becoming JAH-HEVA in one form, or *Race*, and Cain and Abel (male and female) in its other form or Race - the double-sexed Jehovah - an echo of its Aryan prototype, Brahma-Vach. After which comes the Third and Fourth Root-Races of mankind - that is to say, races of men and women, or individuals of opposite sexes, no longer sexless semi-spirits and androgynes, as were the two races which precede them. It is found in fable and allegory, in myth and revealed Scriptures in legend and tradition. Because of all the great Mysteries inherited by Initiates from hoary antiquity, this is *one of the greatest*. It accounts for the bi-sexual element found in every creative deity, in Brahma-Viraj-Vach, as in Adam-Jehovah-Eve, also in "Cain-Jehovah-Abel." For "The Book of Generations of Adam" does not even mention Cain and Abel, but says only: "Male and female created he them ... and called their name Adam" (ch.v.5). Then it proceeds to say: "And Adam begat a son *in his own likeness*, after his image, and called his name Seth" (v.3); after which he begets other sons and daughters, thus proving that Cain and Abel are his own allegorical permutations. Adam stands for the primitive human race, especially its cosmo-sidereal sense. Not so, however, in its theo-anthropological meaning. The compound name of Jehovah, or Jah-Hovah, meaning male life and female life - first androgynous, then separated into sexes - is used in this sense in *Genesis*

134

from ch.v onwards. As the author of "The Source of Measures" says (*p. 159*): "The two words of which Jehovah is composed make up the original idea of male-female, as the birth originates; for the Hebrew letter, *Jod* was the *membrum virile* and *Hovah* was Eve, the mother of all living, or the procreatix, Earth and Nature. The author believes, therefore, that "It is seen that the *perfect one*" (the perfect female circle or Yoni, 20162 numerically), "as *originator of measures*, takes also the form of *birth*-origin, as *Hermaphrodite one*; hence the phallic form and use."

Precisely; only the "phallic form and use" came long ages later; and the first and original meaning of Eros, the son of Seth, was the First born in the present usual way from, man and woman - for Seth is no man, but a *race*. Before him humanity was hermaphrodite. While Seth is the first result (physiologically) after the FALL, he is also the *first man*; hence his son Enos is referred to as the "Son of man." Seth represents the *later* Third (Root) Race. *SD 2, pp. 124 - 126*

2. Hence all the higher gods of antiquity are all "Sons of the Mother," before they become those of the Father." The Logoi, like Jupiter or Zeus, Son of Kronos-Saturn, "Infinite Time" (or Kala), in their origin were represented as male-female. Zeus is said to be the "beautiful Virgin," and Venus is made bearded. Apollo is originally bisexual, so is Brahma-Vach, in the Manu and the Puranas. Osiris is interchangeable with Isis, and Horus is of both sexes. Finally, St. John's vision in Revelation, that of the Logos, who is now connected with Jesus - is hermaphrodite, for he is described as having female breasts. *SD 1, p. 72, foot-note*

3. In Southern India, the writer has seen a converted native making pujah with offerings before a statue of Jesus clad in women's clothes and with a ring in his nose. When asking the meaning of the masquerade we were answered that it was Jesu-Maria blended in one, and that it was done by the permission of the Padri, as the zealous convert had no money to purchase two statues or "idols" as they, very properly are, were called by a witness - another but a non-converted Hindu. Blasphemous this will appear to a dogmatic Christian, but the Theosophist and the Occultist must award the palm of logic to the converted Hindu. The esoteric Christos in the gnosis is, of course, sexless, but in exoteric theology he is male and female. *SD 1, p. 72, foot-note*

THE HIGHER SELF

1. Remember ... the *Tabula Smaragdina* (*The Emerald Tablet* - Ed.) of Hermes, the esoteric meaning of which has seven keys to it.... The Astro-Chemical is well known to students, the anthropological may be given now. "One thing" mentioned in it is MAN. It is said: "The Father of THAT ONE ONLY THING is the Sun; its Mother the Moon; the Wind carries it in his bosom, and its nurse is the Spirituous Earth." In one occult rendering of the same it is added: "And Spiritual Fire is its instructor (Guru)."

This fire is the higher Self, the Spiritual Ego, or that which is eternally reincarnating under the influence of its lower personal Selves, changing with every re-birth, full of *Tanha* (thirst - Ed.) or desire to live. It is a strange law of nature that, on this plane, the higher (Spiritual) Nature should be, so to say, in bondage to the lower. Unless the Ego takes refuge in the Atman, the ALL-SPIRIT, and merges entirely into the essence thereof, the personal Ego may goad it to the bitter end. This cannot be thoroughly understood unless the student makes himself familiar with the mystery of evolution, which proceeds on triple lines - spiritual, psychic and physical.

That which propels towards, and forces evolution, *i.e.,* compels the growth and development of Man towards perfection, is (a) the MONAD, or that which acts in it unconsciously through a force inherent in itself and (b)

137

the lower astral body of the *personal* SELF. The former whether imprisoned in a vegetable or an animal body, is endowed with, is indeed itself, that force. Owing to its identity with the ALL-FORCE, which as said is inherent in the Monad, it is all potent on the Arupa or formless plane.

On our plane, its essence being too pure, it remains all-potential, but individually becomes inactive: e.g., the rays of the Sun, which contribute to the growth of vegetation, do not select this or that plant to shine upon. Uproot the plant and transfer it to a piece of soil where the sunbeam cannot reach it, and the latter will not follow it. So with the Atman: unless the higher Self or EGO gravitates towards the Sun - the Monad - the lower *Ego*, or *personal* Self, will have the upper hand in every case. For it is this Ego, with its fierce Selfishness and animal desire to live a Senseless life (*Tanha*), which is "the maker of the tabernacle," as Buddha calls it in the *Dhammapada* (153 and 154). Hence the expression, "the Spirits of the Earth clothed the shadows and expanded them." To these "Spirits" belong temporarily human astral selves; and it is they who give or build the physical tabernacle of man, for the Monad and its conscious principle, Manas, to dwell in.

But the "Solar" Lhas, Spirits, warm them, the shadows. This is physically and literally true; metaphysically, or on the psychic and spiritual plane, it is equally true that the Atman alone warms the inner man; *i.e.*, it enlightens it with the ray of divine life and alone is able to impart to the inner, or the reincarnating Ego, its immortality.

Thus, as we shall find, for the first three and a half Root-races, up to the middle or turning point, it is the astral shadows of the "progenitors," the lunar Pitiris, which are the formative powers in the Races, and which build and gradually force the evolution of the physical form towards perfection - this, at the cost of a proportionate loss of spirituality. Then, from the turning point, it is the Higher Ego, or incarnating principle, the *nous* or *Mind* which reigns over the animal Ego, and rules it whenever it is not carried down by the latter. ***SD 2, pp. 109 - 110***

2. Now what is a Ferrouer, or Farvarshi? In some Mazdean works (Zoroastrian) ... it is plainly implied that Farvarshi is the *inner*, immortal man (or that *Ego* which reincarnates); that it existed before its physical body and survives all such it happens to be clothed in. "Not only man was endowed with the Farvarshi, *but gods* too, and the sky, fire, waters, and plants." (Introduction to the *Vendidad*, by J. Darmsteter). This shows as plainly as can be shown that the *ferouer* is the "spiritual counterpart" of whether god, animal, plant, or even element, *i.e.*, the refined and the *purer* part of the grosser creation, the soul of the body, whatever the body may happen to be. Therefore does Ahura-Mazda recommend Zarathustra to invoke his *Farvarshi* and not himself (Ahura-Mazda); that is to say, the impersonal and *true* Essence of Deity, *one with Zoroaster's own Atman* (or Christos) not the *false* and personal appearance. This is quite clear. ***SD 2, p. 480***

KARMA AND DESTINY

1. The ONE LIFE is closely related to *the one* law which governs the World of Being - KARMA. Exoterically, this is simply and literally "action," or rather an "effect-producing cause." Esoterically it is quite a different thing in its far-fetching moral effects. It is the unerring LAW OF RETRIBUTION. To say to those ignorant of the real significance, characteristics and awful importance of this eternal immutable law, that no theological definition of a personal deity can give an idea of this impersonal, yet ever present and active Principle, is to speak in vain. Nor can it be called Providence. For Providence, with the Theists (the Christian Protestants, at any rate), rejoices in a personal male gender, while with the Roman Catholics it is a female potency. "Divine Providence tempers His blessings to secure their better effects." Wogan tells us. Indeed "He" tempers them, which Karma - a sexless principle - does not.

Throughout the first two Parts (of *The Secret Doctrine* - Ed.) it was shown that, at the first flutter of renascent life, Swabhavat (Mother-Father - Ed.), "the mutable radiance of the Immutable Darkness unconscious in Eternity," passes, at every new rebirth of Kosmos, from an inactive state into one of intense activity; that it differentiates, and then begins its work through that differentiation. This work is KARMA. *SD 1, p. 634*

140

2. Yes; "our destiny is written in the stars!" Only, the closer union between the mortal reflection MAN and his celestial PROTOTYPE, the less dangerous the external conditions and subsequent reincarnations - which neither Buddhas nor Christs can escape. This is not superstition, least of all is it *Fatalism*. The latter implies a blind course of some still blinder power, and man is a free agent during his stay on earth. He cannot escape his *ruling* Destiny, but he has the choice of two paths that lead him in that direction, and he can reach the goal of misery - if such is decreed to him, either in the snowy white robes of the Martyr, or in the soiled garments of a volunteer in the inquisitor course; for there are *external and internal* conditions which affect the determination of our will upon our actions, and it is in our power to follow either of the two.

Those who believe in *Karma* have to believe in *destiny*, which, from birth to death, every man is weaving thread by thread around himself, as a spider does his cobweb; and this destiny is guided either by the heavenly voice of the invisible prototype outside of us, or by our more intimate *astral*, or inner man, who is but, too often the evil genius of the embodied entity called man. Both these lead on the outward man, but one of them must prevail; and from the very beginning of the invisible affray the stern and implacable *law of compensation* steps and takes its course, faithfully following the fluctuations. When the last strand is woven, and man seemingly enwrapped in the net-work of his own doing, then he find himself completely under the empire of this *self-made* destiny. It then either fixes him like the inert shell against the immovable rock, or carries him away like a feather in a whirlwind raised by his own actions, and this is - KARMA. **SD 1, p. 639**

3. Nor would the ways of Karma be inscrutable were men to work in union and harmony, instead of disunion and strife. For our ignorance of those ways - which one portion of mankind calls the ways of Providence, dark and intricate; while another sees in them the action of blind Fatalism; and a third, simple chance, with neither gods nor devils to guide them - would surely disappear if we would but attribute all these to their correct cause. With right knowledge, or at any rate with a confident conviction that our neighbours will no more work to hurt us than we would think of harming them, the two-thirds of the World's evil would vanish into thin air.

Were no man to hurt his brother, Karma-nemesis would have neither cause to work for, nor weapons to act through. It is the constant presence in our midst of every element of strife and opposition, and the division of races, nations, tribes, societies and individuals into Cains and Abels, wolves and lambs, that is the chief cause of the "ways of Providence."

We cut these numerous windings in our destinies daily with our own hands, while we can imagine that we are pursuing a track on the royal high road of respectability and duty, and then complain of those ways being so intricate and so dark. We stand bewildered before the mystery of our own making, and the riddles of life that we *will not solve*, and then accuse the great Sphinx of devouring us. But truly there is not an accident in our lives, not a misshapen day, or a misfortune, that could not be traced back to our own doings in this or in another life. *SD 1, pp. 643 - 644*

KWAN-YIN AND KWAN-SHI-YIN

1. The Mother of Mercy and Knowledge is called "the triple" of Kwan-Shi-Yin because in her correlations, metaphysical and cosmical she is the "Mother, the Wife and the Daughter" of the *Logos,* just as in the later theological translations she became "the father, Son and (the female) Holy Ghost" - the Sakti or Energy - the Essence of the three. Thus in the Esotericism of the Vedantins, *Daiviprakriti,* the Light manifested through Eswara, the *Logos,* is at one and the same time the Mother and also the Daughter of the Logos or Verbum of Parabrahman; while in that of the trans-Himalayan teachings it is - in the hierarchy of allegorical and metaphysical theogony - "the MOTHER" or abstract, ideal matter, Mulaprakriti, the Root of Nature; - and from the metaphysical standpoint, a correlation of Adhi-Bhuta (the first Being - Ed.), manifested in the Logos, Avalokiteswara; and from the purely occult and Cosmical, Fohat, the ... androgyne energy resulting from the "Light of the Logos," and which manifests in the plane of the objective Universe as the hidden, as much as the revealed, Electricity - which is LIFE. *SD1, pp. 136 - 137*

2. *Kwan-Yin-Tien* means the "melodious heaven of Sound," the abode of Kwan-Yin, or the *"Divine Voice"* literally. This "Voice" is a synonym of the *Verbum* or the Word: "Speech," as the expression of thought. Thus may be traced the connection with, and even the origin of the Hebrew Bath-Kol, the "daughter of the Divine

Voice," or Verbum, or the male and female Logos, the "Heavenly Man" or Adam Kadmon.... The latter was surely anticipated by the Hindu Vach, the goddess of Speech, or of the Word. For Vach, the daughter and the female portion, as is stated, of Brahman, one "generated by the gods" - is in company with Kwan-Yin, with Isis (also the *daughter*, wife and *sister* of Osiris) and other goddesses, the female *Logos*, so to speak, the goddess of the active forces in nature, the Word, Voice, or Sound, and Speech.

If Kwan-Yin is the "melodious Voice," so is Vach; "the melodious cow who milked forth sustenance and water" (the female principle) - "who yields as nourishment and sustenance," as Mother Nature. She is associated with the work of creation.... She is male and female *ad libitum*, as Eve is with Adam. ....Thus Vach and Kwan-Yin are both the magic potency of Occult sound in nature and *Ether* -which "Voice" calls forth Sien-Tchan, the illusive form of the Universe out of Chaos and the Seven Elements. *SD 1, p. 137*

3. ... Kwan-shi-yin has passed through several transformations, but it is an error to say of him that he is a modern invention of the Northern Buddhists, for under another appellation he has been known from the earliest times. The Secret Doctrine teaches that "He who is the first to appear at Renovation will be the last to come before Re-absorption (pralaya)." Thus the logoi of all nations, from the Vedic Visvakarma of the Mysteries down to the Saviour of the present civilised nations, are the "Word" who was "in the beginning" (or the re-awakening of the energising powers of Nature) with the One ABSOLUTE.

Born of Fire and Water, before these became distinct elements, it was the "Maker" (fashioner or modeller) of all things; "without him was not anything made that was made"; "in whom was life, and the life was the light of men"; and who finally may be called, as he ever has been, the Alpha and the Omega of manifested Nature. The great Dragon of Wisdom is born of Fire and Water; and into Fire and Water will all be reabsorbed with him. As this Bodhisattva is said "to assume any form he pleases" from the beginning of a Manvantara to its end, though his special birthday (memorial day) is celebrated according to the Kin-kwang-ming-King ("Luminous Sutra of Golden Light") in the second month on the nineteenth day, and that of "Maitreya Buddha" in the first month on the first day, yet the two are one. He will appear as "Maitreya Buddha," the last of the Avatars and Buddhas in the seventh Race. This belief and expectations are universal throughout the East. *SD 1, p. 470*

4. Hence the ritual in the exoteric worship of this deity (Kwan-Shi-Yin) as founded on magic. The Mantras are all taken from special books kept secret by the priests, and each is said to work a magical effect; as the reciter or reader produces, by simply chanting them, a secret causation which results in immediate effects. Kwan-Shi-Yin is Avalokiteswara and both are forms of the seventh Universal principle; while in its highest metaphysical character this deity is the synthetic aggregation of all the planetary Spirits, Dhyan-Chohans. He is the "Self-manifested;" in short the "Son of the Father." Crowned with seven dragons, above his statue there appears the inscription Pu-Tsi-K'iun-ling, "the universal Saviour of all living beings." *SD 1, p. 471*

5. Of course the name given in the archaic volume of the Stanzas is quite different, but Kwan-Yin is a perfect equivalent (of Kwan-Shi-Yin - Ed.). In a temple of Pu'to, the sacred island of the Buddhists in China, Kwan-Shi-Yin is represented floating on a black aquatic bird (*Kala-hansa*), and pouring on the heads of mortals the elixir of life, which, as it flows, is transformed into one of the chief Dhyani-Buddhas - the Regent of a star called the "Star of Salvation." In his third transformation Kwan-Shi-Yin is the informing spirit or genius of Water. In China the Dalai Lama is believed to be an incarnation of Kwan-Shi-Yin, who in his third terrestrial appearance was a Bodhisattva, while the Teshu Lama (also called the Panchen Lama - Ed.) is an incarnation of Amitabha Buddha, or Gautama (the Buddha - Ed.). *SD 1, p. 471*

LEMURIA AND THE LEMURIANS

1. They (*the Lemurians*) built huge cities. Of rare earths and metals they built. Out of the fires (*lava*) vomited. Out of the white stone of the mountains (*marble*) and the black stone (*of the subterranean fires*) they cut their own images, in their size and likeness, and worshipped them. ***SD 2, p. 316, Stanza 43***

2. As the History of the first two human races - the last of the Lemurians and the first of the future Atlanteans - proceeds, we have at this point to blend the two, and speak of them for a time collectively.

Here reference is also made to the *divine* Dynasties, such as were claimed by the Egyptians, Chaldeans, Greeks, etc., to have preceded their *human* kings; they are still believed in by the modern Hindus, and are enumerated in their sacred books .... What remains to be shown is, that our modern geologists are now being driven into admitting the evident existence for submerged continents. But to confess their presence is not to accept that there were men on them during the early geological periods; - ay, men and civilized nations, not Paleolithic primitives only; who, under the guidance of their *divine* Rulers, built large cities, cultivated the arts and sciences, and knew astronomy, architecture and mathematics to perfection. This primeval civilization did not, as one may think, immediately follow their physiological transformation.

Between the final evolution and the first city built, many hundred thousands of years had passed. Yet, we find the Lemurians in their sixth sub-race building their first rock cities out of stone and lava.

One of such great cities of primitive structure was built entirely of lava, some thirty miles west from where Easter Island now stretches its narrow piece of sterile ground, and was entirely destroyed by a series of volcanic eruptions. The oldest remains of Cyclopean buildings were all the handiwork of the Lemurians of the last sub-races; and an occultist shows, therefore, no wonder on learning that the stone relics found on the small piece of land called Easter Island by Captain Cook, are "very much like the walls of the temple of Pachacamac or Tia-Huanuco in Peru," ("*The Countries of the World," by Robert Brown, Vol. 4, p.43*); and that they are in the CYCLOPEAN STYLE. The first large cities, however, appeared on that region of the continent which is now known as the island of Madagascar. There were civilized people and savages in those days as there are now. Evolution achieved its work by perfection with the former, and Karma - its work of destruction on the latter. *SD 2, pp. 316 - 318*

3. The earliest pioneers of the Fourth Race were not Atlanteans, nor yet the human Asuras and the Rakshasas which they became later. In those days large portions of the future continent of Atlantis were yet part and parcel of the Ocean floors. "Lemuria," as we have called the continent of the Third Race, was then a gigantic land. It covered the whole area of space from the foot of the Himalayas, which separated it from the inland sea rolling its waves over what is now Tibet, Mongolia, and the great desert of Schamo (Gobi); from Chittagong, westward to Hardwar, and eastward to Assam.

From thence, it stretched South across what is known to us as Southern India, Ceylon, and Sumatra; then embracing on its way, as we go South, Madagascar on its right hand and Australia and Tasmania on its left, it ran down to within a few degrees of the Antarctic Circle; when, from Australia, an inland region on the Mother Continent in those ages, it extended far into the Pacific ocean, not only beyond Rapa-nui (Tepay, or Easter Island) which now lies in latitude 26S., and longitude 110 W. This statement seems corroborated by Science, - if only partially; as, when discussing continental trends, and showing the infra-Arctic masses trending generally with the meridian, several ancient continents are generally mentioned, although inferentially. Among such the "Mascarene continent," which included Madagascar, stretching north and south, is spoken of, and the existence of another ancient continent running "from Spitzbergen to the Straits of Dover, while most of the other parts of Europe were sea bottom," is taught. The latter corroborates, then, the Occult teaching which shows the (now) polar regions as the earliest of the seven cradles of Humanity, and as the tomb of the bulk of the mankind of that region during the Third Race, when the gigantic continent of Lemuria began separating into smaller continents. *SD 2, pp. 323 - 324*

4. It must be noted that the Lemuria, which served as the cradle of the Third Root Race, not only embraced a vast area in the Pacific and Indian Oceans, but extended in the shape of a horse-shoe past Madagascar, round "South Africa" (then a mere fragment in process of formation), through the Atlantic up to Norway. The great *English fresh-water deposit called the Wealden - which every geologist regards as the mouth of a former great river - is the bed of the main stream which drained Northern Lemuria in the Secondary Age.* The former reality of this river is a fact of science - will its votaries acknowledge the necessity of accepting the Secondary-Age Northern Lemuria, which their data demand? Professor Berthold Seeman not only accepted the reality of such a mighty continent, but regarded *Australia and Europe as formerly portions of one continent*, thus corroborating the whole "Horse-shoe" doctrine already enunciated. *SD 2, p. 333*

5. The sinking and transformation of Lemuria beginning nearly at the Arctic Circle (Norway), the Third Race ended its career in Lanka, or rather on that which became Lanka with the Atlanteans. The small remnant now known as Ceylon is the Northern highland of ancient Lanka, while the enormous island of that name was, in the Lemurian period, the gigantic continent described a few pages back.

As a Master says (See *"Esoteric Buddhism,"* p. 65) : - "Why should not your geologists bear in mind that under the continents explored and fathomed by them ... there may be hidden, deep in the fathomless, or rather unfathomed ocean beds, other and far older continents whose strata have never been geologically explored; and that they may some day upset entirely their present theories? Why not admit that our present continents have, like Lemuria and Atlantis, been several times already submerged, and had the time to re-appear again and bear their groups of mankind and civilizations; and that at the first great geological cataclysms that occur from the beginning to the end of every Round, our already autopsized continents will go down and the Lemurias and Atlantises come up again?" Not the same identical continents, of course. *SD 2, pp. 332 - 333*

6. It is well worth noticing that most of the gigantic statues discovered on Easter Island, a portion of an undeniably submerged continent (Lemuria - Ed.) - as also those found on the outskirts of Gobi, a region which had been submerged for untold ages - are all between 20 and 30 feet high. The statues found by Cook on Easter Island measured almost all *twenty-seven* feet in height, and eight feet across the shoulders.

The writer is well aware that the modern archaeologists have decided now that "these statues are not very old," as declared by one of the high officials of the British Museum, where some of them now are. But this is one of those arbitrary decisions of modern science which does not carry much weight. We are told that after the destruction of "Lemuria" by subterranean fires that men went on steadily decreasing in stature - a process already commenced after their *physical* Fall - and that finally, some millions of years after they reached between six and seven feet, and are now dwindling down (as the older Asiatic races) to nearer five than six feet. **SD 2, pp. 331 - 332**

7. The most archaic Sanskrit and Tamil works teem with references to both Continents (Lemuria and Atlantis - Ed.). The seven sacred islands (Dwipas) are mentioned in the *Surya Siddhanta*, the oldest astronomical work in the whole world, and in the works of Asura Maya, the Atlantean astronomer whom Professor Weber has made out re-incarnated in Ptolemy. **SD 2, p. 326**

8. Science speaks of an ancient continent which stretched from Spitzbergen down to the Straits of Dover, The Secret Doctrine teaches that, in the earliest geological periods, these regions formed a horse-shoe-like continent, whose one end, the Eastern, far more Northward than North Cornwall, included Greenland, and the other contained the Behring Straits as an inland piece of ground and descended southward in its natural trend down to the British Isles, which in those days must have been right under the lower curve of the semi-circle. This continent was raised simultaneously with the submersion of the equatorial portions of Lemuria.

Ages later, some of the Lemurian remains reappeared again on the face of the oceans. Therefore, though it can be said without departing from truth that Atlantis is included in the seven great insular continents, since the Fourth Race Atlanteans got some of the Lemurian relics, and, settling on the islands, included them among their lands and continents, yet a difference should be made and an explanation given, once that a fuller and more accurate account is attempted, as in the present work. Easter Island was also taken possession of in this manner by some Atlanteans; who, having escaped from the cataclysm which befell their own land, settled on that remnant of Lemuria only to perish thereon, when destroyed in one day by its volcanic fires and lava. This may be regarded as fiction by certain geographers and geologists; to the occultist it is *history*. **SD 2, pp. 326 - 327**

LIGHT AND DARKNESS

1. "Darkness is Father-Mother: light their son," says an old Eastern proverb. Light is inconceivable except as coming from some source which is the cause of it; and as, in the instance of primordial light, that source is unknown, though as strongly demanded by reason and logic, therefore it is called "Darkness" by us, from an intellectual point of view. As to borrowed or secondary light, whatever its source, it can be but of a temporary mayavic nature.

Darkness, then, is the eternal matrix in which the sources of light appear and disappear. Nothing is added to darkness to make of it light, or to light to make it darkness, on this our plane. They are interchangeable, and scientifically light is but a mode of darkness and vice versa. Yet both are phenomena of the same noumenon - which is absolute darkness to the scientific mind, and but a gray twilight to the perception of the average mystic, though to that of the spiritual eye of the Initiate it is absolute light. How far we discern the light that shines in darkness depends upon our powers of vision. What is light to us is darkness to certain insects, and the eye of the clairvoyant sees illumination where the normal eye perceives only blackness. When the whole universe was plunged in sleep - had returned to its one primordial element - there was neither centre of luminosity, nor eye to perceive light, and darkness necessarily filled the boundless all. *SD 1, pp. 40-41*

2. The essence of darkness being absolute light, darkness is taken as the appropriate allegorical representation of the condition of the Universe during Pralaya, or the term of absolute rest, or non-being, as it appears to our finite minds.

.... According to the Rosicrucian tenets, "light and darkness are identical in themselves, being only divisible in the human mind," and according to Robert Fludd, "Darkness adopted illumination in order to make itself visible." According to the tenets of Eastern Occultism, DARKNESS is the one true actuality, the basis and the root of light, without which the latter could never manifest, nor even exist. Light is matter, and DARKNESS pure Spirit. Darkness in its radical, metaphysical basis is subjective and absolute light; while the latter in all its seeming effulgence and glory, is merely a mass of shadow, as it can never be eternal, and is simply an illusion or Maya.

Even the mind-baffling and science-harassing Genesis, light is created out of darkness "and darkness was upon the face of the deep" and not vice versa. "In him (in darkness) was life, and the life was the light of men" (John i.4). A day may come when the eyes of men will be opened; and when they may comprehend better than they do now, that verse in the Gospel of John that says, "And the light shineth in darkness, and the darkness comprehendeth it not." They will see then the word "darkness" does not apply to man's spiritual eyesight but indeed to "Darkness," the absolute, that comprehendeth not (cannot cognize) transient light, however transcendent in human eyes. *SD 1, pp. 69 - 70*

3. Now there are three kinds of light in Occultism, as in the Kabala. (1) The Abstract and Absolute Light, which is darkness; (2) The Light of the Manifested-Unmanifested, called by some the Logos: and (3) The latter light reflected in the Dhyan Chohans, the minor logoi (the Elohim collectively), who in their turn, shed it on the objective Universe ....

The Occultists call this light (of the Logos - Ed.) *Daiviprakriti* in the East and light of Christos in the West. It is the light of the LOGOS, the direct reflection of the ever Unknowable on the plane of Universal manifestation. ... Here is the interpretation given by the modern Christians from the Kabala: -

.... "First then the Sephiroth (in the Kabala - Ed.) are described as *Light*, that is, they themselves are a function of, indeed, the same as, the manifestation of Ain Soph (the Absolute - Ed.); and they are so from the fact that Light represents the ratio of 20612 to 6561.... *Light* is so much the burden of the Kabala, in explaining the Sephiroth, that the most famous book on the Kabala is called *Zohar* or *Light*. In this we find expressions of this kind:- 'The Infinite was entirely unknown and diffused no light before the luminous point violently broke through into vision.... When he first assumed the form (of the crown, or the first Sephira), he caused 9 splendid lights to emanate from it, which, shining through it, diffused a bright light in all directions': that is, these 9 with his one (which was the origin as above, of the nine), together made the 10, that is ... *the sacred ten* (numbers or Sephiroth), or *Jod* - and these numbers were *'the Light.'* Just as in the Gospel of St. John, God ... was that light ... by which (Light) all things were made." **SD 2, pp. 37-38**

4. In the catechism (commentary of the Himalayan Brotherhood), the Master is made to ask the pupil: -

"Lift thy head, oh Lanoo; dost thou see one, or countless lights above thee burning in the dark midnight sky?"

"I see one Flame, oh Gurudeva, I see countless undetached sparks shining in it."

"Thou sayest well. And now look around and into thyself. That light which burns inside thee, dost thou feel it different in anywise from the light that shines in thy Brother-men?"

"It is in no way different, though the prisoner is held in bondage by Karma, and though its outer garments delude the ignorant into saying, 'Thy Soul and My Soul.'" **SD 1, p. 120**

5. "There exists an universal agent unique of all forms and of life, that is called Od, Ob and Aour, active and passive, positive and negative, like day and night: it is the first light in Creation" (Eliphas Levi's Kabala): - the first Light of the primordial Elohim - the Adam, "male and female" - or (scientifically) ELECTRICITY AND LIFE. **SD 1, p. 76**

6. Od is the pure life-giving Light or magnetic fluid; Ob, the messenger of death used by the sorcerers, the nefarious evil fluid; Aour is the synthesis of the two, Astral Light proper. Can the Philologists tell why Od - a term used by Reichenbach to denominate the vital fluid - is also a Tibetan word meaning light, brightness, radiancy? It equally means "Sky" in an occult sense. **SD 1, p. 76, foot-note**

7. "And God said, Let there be a firmament ..." (Genesis, v. 6) and "God," the second (the Logos), obeyed and "made the firmament" (v. 7). "And God said let there be light," and "there was light." Now the latter does not mean light at all, but in the Kabala, the androgyne "Adam Kadmon" or Sephira (*Spiritual light*), for they are one; or, according to the Chaldean "*Book of Numbers*," the *secondary* angels, the first being the Elohim who are the *aggregate* of that fashioning god. For to whom are those words of command addressed? And who is it who commands? That which commands is the *eternal Law*, and he who obeys, the *Elohim*, the known quantity acting in and with ... the *Forces* of the one Force. All this is Occultism, and is found in the archaic STANZAS. It is perfectly immaterial whether we call these "Forces" the Dhyan Chohans or the *Ophanim*, as St. John does.

"The one Universal Light, which to Man is *Darkness*, is ever existence," says the Chaldean "Book of Numbers." From it proceeds periodically the ENERGY, which is reflected in the "Deep" or Chaos, the store-house of future worlds, and, once awakened, stirs up and fructifies the latent Forces, which are the ever present potentialities in it. Then awake anew the Brahmas and Buddhas - the co-eternal Forces - and a new Universe springs into being...." *SD 1, p. 337*

THE LOGOS AND UNIVERSAL MIND

1. It (The Secret Doctrine) admits a Logos or a collective "Creator" of the Universe; a *Demi-urgos* - in the sense implied when one speaks of an "Architect" as the" Creator" of an edifice, whereas the Architect has never touched one stone of it, but, while furnishing the plan, left all the manual labour to the masons; in our case the plan was furnished by the Ideation of the Universe, and the constructive labour was left to the Hosts of Intelligent Powers and Forces. But that *Demiurgos* is no *personal* deity, - *i.e.*, an imperfect *extra-cosmic god*, - but only the aggregate of the Dhyan-Chohans (Archangels - Ed.) and the other forces. *SD 1, pp. 279 - 280*

2. At the commencement of a great Manvantara (Manifestation - Ed.), Parabrahm manifests as Mulaprakriti (primordial Cosmic Substance - Ed.) and then as the Logos. This Logos is equivalent to the "Unconscious Universal Mind," etc., of Western Pantheists. It constitutes the Basis of the SUBJECT side of manifested Being, and is the source of all manifestations. Mulaprakriti or Primordial Cosmic Substance, is the foundation of the OBJECT side of things - the basis of all objective evolution and Cosmogenesis. Force, then, does not emerge with Primordial Substance from Parabrahmic latency. It is *the transformation into energy of the supra-consciousness thought of the Logos*, infused, so to speak, into the objectivation of the latter out of potential latency.... *SD 2, p. 24*

3." Every Universe (world or planet) has its own Logos," says the doctrine. The Sun was always called by the Egyptians "the eye of Osiris," and was himself the *Logos*, or the first begotten, or light made manifest in the world "which is the Mind and divine intellect of the Concealed." It is only by the sevenfold Ray of this light that we can become cognizant of the Logos through the Demiurge, regarding the latter as the *creator* of the planet and everything pertaining to it, and the former as the guiding Force of that "Creator" - good and bad at the same time, the origin of good and the origin of evil. This "creator" is neither good nor bad per se, but its differentiated aspects in nature make it assume one or the other character. *SD 2, p. 25*

4. It is a well-known fact - to learned Symbologists at all events - that in every great religion, of antiquity, it is the Logos Demiurge (the second logos) or the first emanation from the mind (Mahat), who is made to strike, so to say, the key-note of that which may be called the CORRELATION of individuality and personality in the subsequent scheme of evolution. The Logos, it is, who is shown in the mystic symbolism of cosmogony theology, theogony, and anthropogony, playing two parts in the drama of Creation and Being *i.e.*, that of the purely human personality and the divine impersonality of the so-called Avatars, or divine incarnations, and of the Universal Spirit, called Christos by the Gnostics, and the Farvarshi (or *Ferour*) of Ahura Mazda in the Mazdean phillosophy. *SD 2, p. 478*

5. That it is pretty well-established that Christ, the Logos, or the God in Space and the Saviour on Earth, is but one of the echoes of the same antediluvian and sorely misunderstood Wisdom. The history begins by the descent on Earth of the "Gods" who incarnate in mankind and this is the FALL. Whether Brahma hurled down on Earth in the allegory by Bhagavant, or Jupiter, by Kronos, all are the symbols of the human races. Once landed on and having touched this planet of dense matter, no snow-white wings of the highest angel can remain immaculate, or the *Avatar* (or incarnation) be perfect, as every such Avatar is the fall of God into generation. *SD 2, pp. 483 - 484*

6. Explaining some of the "heresies" of his day, Justin Martyr shows the identity of all the world religions at their starting point. The first *beginning* opens invariably with the *unknown* and PASSIVE deity, from which emanates a certain active power or virtue, the Mystery that is sometimes called WISDOM, sometimes the SON, very often God, Angel, Lord and LOGOS. The latter is sometimes applied to the very first emanation, but in several systems it proceeds from the first androgyne or double ray produced at the beginning by the unseen. Philo (Philo Judaeus - Ed.) depicts this wisdom as male and female. But though its first manifestation had a beginning, for it produced from *Oulon* (Aion, time), the highest of the Aeons when emitted from the Father, it had remained with him *before all creations*, for it is part of him (also called *Protogonos*, the "first-born" - Ed.). ***SD 2, pp. 489 - 490***

7. The "Heavenly Man" (Tetragrammaton - a term in the Kabala for the "Heavenly Man" - Ed.) who is the Protogonos, Tikkoun, the first born from the passive deity (the Absolute - Ed.) and the first manifestation of that deity's shadow, is the universal form and idea which engenders the manifested Logos, Adam Kadmon, or the four-lettered symbol in the Kabala, of the Universe itself, also called the second Logos. The second springs from the first and develops the third triangle (see the Sephirothal Tree); from the last of which (the lower host of Angels) MEN are generated. (There are three aspects to the Logos known as the first, second and third logos and they can be related esoterically to the Christian and Hindu Trinities - Ed.) ***SD 2, p. 25***

8. The esoteric meaning of the word Logos (speech or word, Verbum) is the rendering in objective expression, as in a photograph, of the concealed thought. The Logos is the mirror reflecting DIVINE MIND, and the Universe is the mirror of the Logos, though the latter is the esse of the Universe. As the Logos reflects all that he sees and finds in the Universe of Pleroma, so man reflects in himself all that he sees and finds in his Universe, the Earth. ***SD 2, p. 25***

9. It is said by Krishna, the *Logos*, incarnate, in the Bhagavat-gita, "The seven great Rishis, the four preceding Manus, partaking of my nature, were born from my mind: from them sprang (emanated or was born) the human race and the world," (*Ch. X, Verse 6*).... As Krishna truly says - the same words being repeated later by another *vehicle* of the Logos (Jesus - Ed.) - "I am the same to all beings .... those who worship me (the 6th principle of the intellectual divine Soul, *Buddhi*, made conscious by its union with the higher faculties of *Manas) are in me and I am in them.*" The Logos, being no personality but the universal principle, is represented by all the divine Powers *born of its mind* - the pure Flames, or as they are called in Occultism, the "Intellectual Breaths" - those angels who are said to "have *made themselves independent, i.e.,* passed from the passive and quiescent, into the active stage of Self-Consciousness. When this is recognised, the true meaning of Krishna becomes comprehensible. *SD 2, p. 318, foot-note*

10. The *Logos*, or both the unmanifested and the manifested WORD, is called by the Hindus, Iswara, "the Lord," though the Occultists give it another name. Iswara, say the Vedantins, is the highest consciousness in nature. "This highest consciousness," answer the Occultists, "is only a *synthetic* unit in the world of the manifested Logos - or on the *plane of illusion;* for it is the sum total of Dhyan-Chohanic *consciousness.*" *SD 1, p. 573*

THE LOTUS - A SPIRITUAL SYMBOL

1. One of the symbolical figures for the Dual creative power in nature (matter and force on the material plane) is *Padma, the water-lily of India.* The Lotus is the product of heat (fire) and water (vapour or Ether); fire standing in every philosophical and religious system as a representation of the Spirit of Deity, the active, male, generative principle; and Ether, or the Soul of matter, the light of the fire, for the passive female principle from which everything in this Universe emanated. Hence, Ether or Water is the Mother, and Fire is the Father. Sir W. Jones (and before him archaic botany) showed that the seeds of the Lotus contain - even before they germinate - perfectly formed leaves, the miniature shape of what one day, as perfect plants, they will become: nature thus giving us a specimen of the preformation of its production ... the seed of all phanerogamous plants bearing proper flowers containing an embryo plantlet ready formed....

The Lotus, or Padma, is moreover, a very ancient and favourite simile for the Kosmos itself, and also for man. The popular reasons given are, firstly, the fact just mentioned, that the Lotus-seed contains within itself a perfect miniature of the future plant which typifies the fact that the spiritual prototypes of all things exist in the immaterial world before those things become materialised on Earth. Secondly, the fact that the Lotus plant grows up through the water, having its root in the Ilus, or mud, and spreading its flower in the air above. The Lotus that typifies the life of man and also that of the Kosmos; for the Secret Doctrine teaches that the elements of both are the same and that both are developing in the same direction. The root of the Lotus sunk in the mud represents material life, the stalk passing through the water typifies existence in the astral world, and the flower floating on the water and opening to the sky is emblematical of spiritual being. *SD 1, pp. 57 - 58*

2. There are no ancient symbols, without a deep and philosophical meaning attached to them; their importance and significance increasing with their antiquity. Such is the Lotus. It is the flower sacred to nature and her Gods, and represents the abstract and the Concrete Universes, standing as the emblem of the productive powers of both spiritual and physical nature. It was held sacred from the remotest antiquity by the Aryan Hindu, the Egyptians, and the Buddhists after them; revered in China and Japan, and adopted as a Christian emblem by the Greek and Latin Churches, who made of it a messenger as the Christians do now, who replace it with the water lily.

It had and still has, its mystic meaning which is identical with every nation on the earth…. With the Hindus, the lotus is the emblem of the productive power of nature through the agency of fire and water (spirit and matter). "Eternal!" says a verse in the Bhagavad Gita, "I see Brahm in the creator enthroned in thee above the lotus!"; and Sir W. Jones (author of *Dissertations*

Relating to Asia - Ed.) shows, as noted in the Stanzas, that the seeds of the lotus contain even before they germinate, perfectly-formed leaves, the miniature shapes of what one day, as perfected plants, they will become. The lotus in India, is the symbol of prolific earth, and what is more, of Mount Meru. The four angels or genii of the four quarters of the heaven (the Maharajahs) stand each on a lotus. The lotus is the two-fold type of the Divine and human hermaphrodite, being of dual sex, so to say.

The Spirit of Fire (or Heat), which stirs up, fructifies, and develops into concrete form everything (from its ideal prototype) which is born of water or primordial Earth, evolved Brahma (the male Creator God - Ed.) with the Hindus. The lotus flower, represented as growing our of Vishnu's navel - that God resting on the waters of space and his Serpent of Infinity - is the most graphic allegory ever made: the Universe evolving from the central Sun, the POINT, the ever-concealed germ. Lakshmi, who is the female aspect of Vishnu, and who is also called Padma, the lotus, is likewise shown floating at "Creation," on a lotus flower, and during the "churning of the ocean" of space, springing from the "sea of milk," like Venus from the froth....

The underlying idea in this symbol is very beautiful, and it shows, furthermore, its identical parentage in all the religious systems. Whether in the lotus or water-lily shape it signifies one and the same philosophical idea - namely, the emanation of the objective from the subjective, divine Ideation passing from the abstract into the concrete or visible form. For as soon as DARKNESS - or rather that which is "darkness' or ignorance - has disappeared in its own realm of eternal Light, leaving behind itself only its divine manifested Ideation, the creative Logoi have their understanding opened, and they see in the ideal world (hitherto concealed in the divine thought) the archetypal forms of all, and proceed to copy and build or fashion upon these models forms evanescent and transcendent.

At this stage of action, the Demiurge is not yet the Architect. Born in the twilight of action, he has yet to first perceive the plan to realise the ideal forms which lie buried in the bosom of the Eternal Ideation, as the future lotus-leaves, the immaculate petals, are concealed within the seed of that plant....

In chapter lxxxi of the *Ritual* (*Book of the Dead*), called "Transformation into the Lotus," a head emerging from this flower, the god exclaims: "I am the pure lotus, emerging from the Luminous one..... I carry the messages of Horus. I am the pure lotus which comes from the Solar Fields...."

.... Such is the cosmic and ideal significance of this great symbol with the Eastern peoples. *SD 1, pp. 379 - 380*

3. In the Christian religion Gabriel, the Archangel, holding in his hand a spray of water lilies, appears to the Virgin Mary in every picture of the Annunciation. This spray typifying fire and water, or the idea of creation and generation, symbolizes *precisely the same idea as the lotus* in the hand of the Bodhisat

(Bodhisattva - Ed.) who announces to Maha-Maya, Gautama's mother, the birth of the world's Saviour, Buddha. Thus also Osiris and Horus were represented by the Egyptians constantly in association with the lotus-flower, the two being Sun-gods or Fire (the Holy Ghost being still typified by 'tongues of fire.'), (Acts). *SD 1, p. 379, foot-note*

Helena Petrovna Blavatsky (1831 - 1891)

Helena Petrovna Blavatsky in London (1887)

The Countess Constance Wachtmeister (1838 - 1910)

Archibald Keightley (1859 - 1930)

Bertram Keightley (1860 - 1945)

William Quan Judge (1851 - 1896)

Henry Steel Olcott (1832 - 1907)

Sir William Crookes (1822 - 1919)

THE LUNAR PITRIS

1. The Progenitors of Man, called in India "Fathers," Pitara or Pitris are the creators of our bodies and lower principles. They are ourselves, as the *first personalities*, and *we are they*. Primeval man would be "the bone of their bone and the flesh of their flesh," if they had body and flesh. As stated they were "lunar Beings." **SD 2, p. 88**

2. With the Brahmins the Pitris are very sacred, because they are the Progenitors, or ancestors of men - the first *Manushya* on this Earth - and offerings are made to them by the Brahmin when a son is born unto him They are more honoured and their ritual is more important than the worship of the gods. **SD 2, p. 91**

3. This was hinted at in *Isis Unveiled, Vol.I, p. xxxviii*, though the full explanation could not then be given: "The *Pitris* are not the ancestors of the present living men, but those of the first human kind or Adamic race; the spirits of human races, which on the great scale of descending evolution, preceded our races of man, and were physically as well as spiritually, far superior to our modern pigmies. In *Manava-Dharma-Sastra* they are called the *Lunar* ancestors." **SD 2, p. 91, footnote**

4. Exoteric Hindu books mention seven classes of Pitris, and among them two distinct kinds of Progenitors or Ancestors: the *Barhishad* and the *Agnishwatta*; or those possessed of the "sacred fire" and those devoid of it.

179

Hindu ritualism seems to connect them with sacrificial fires, and with *Grihasta* Brahmins in earlier incarnations: those who have, and those who have *not* attended as they should to their household sacred fires in their previous births. The distinction, as said, is derived from the *Vedas*. The first and highest class (esoterically) the *Agnishwatta*, are represented in the exoteric allegory as *Grihasta* (Brahman - householders) who, in their past births in other Manvantaras having failed to maintain their domestic fires and to offer burnt sacrifices, have lost every right to have oblations with fire presented to them. Whereas the Barhishad, being Brahmins who have kept up their household sacred fires, are thus honoured to this day. Thence the *Agnishwatta* are represented as devoid of, and the *Barhishad* as possessed of, fires.

But esoteric philosophy explains the original qualifications as being due to the difference between the natures of the two classes: the *Agnishwatta* Pitris are devoid of fire (*i.e.* creative passion), because too divine and pure; whereas the Barhishad, being the lunar spirits more closely connected with Earth, because the creative Elohim of form, of the Adam of dust. **SD 2, pp. 77 - 78**

5. The *Barhishad*, though possessed of creative fire, were devoid of the higher MAHAT-mic element (Divine Mind - Ed,). Being on a level with the lower principles - those which precede gross objective matter - they could only give birth to the outer man, or rather to the model of the physical, the astral man (etheric - Ed.). Thus, though we see them entrusted with the task by Brahma (the collective *Mahat* or Universal Divine Mind), the "Mystery of Creation" is repeated on Earth, only in an inverted sense, as in a *mirror*. It is those who are unable to create the spiritual immortal man, who project the senseless model (the Astral - now called the Etheric - Ed.) of the physical Being; and, as will be seen, it was those who could not multiply, who sacrificed themselves to the good and salvation of Spiritual Hierarchy. For, to complete the *septenary man*, to add to his three lower principles and cement them with the spiritual Monad - which could never dwell in such a form otherwise than in an *absolutely latent state* - two connecting principles are needed: *Manas* and *Kama* (mind and desire - Ed.). **SD. 2, p. 79**

6. The (Lunar) Pitris shoot out from their ethereal bodies, still more ethereal and shadowy similitudes of themselves, or what we should now call "doubles," or "astral forms," in their own likeness. This furnishes the Monad with its first dwelling, and blind matter with a model around and upon which to build from henceforth. But *Man is still incomplete.* From Swayambhuva Manu (in Manu, Book 1), from whom descended the seven primitive Manus or Prajapati, each of whom gave birth to a primitive race of men, down to the Codex Nazareus, in which Karabtonos or Fetahil (blind concupiscent matter) begets on his Mother, "Spiritus," seven figures, each of which stands as the progenitor of one of the primeval seven races - this doctrine has left its impress on every Archaic Scripture. **SD 1, p. 248**

7. Evolutionary law compelled the lunar "Fathers" to pass, in their monadic condition, through all the forms of life and being on this globe; but at the end of the Third Round, they were already human in their divine nature, and were thus called upon to become the creators of the forms destined to fashion the tabernacles of the less progressed Monads whose turn it was to incarnate. *SD 2, p. 115*

8. What, it may be asked, are the "Lunar Monads" (Lunar Pitris - Ed.) just spoken of? .... It must be plain to everyone that they are Monads, who, having ended their life-cycle on the lunar chain, which is inferior to the terrestrial chain, have incarnated on this one. But there are some further details which may be added, though they border too closely on forbidden ground to be treated fully. The last word of the mystery is divulged only to the adepts.... *SD 1, p. 179*

MAHAMAYA - THE GREAT ILLUSION

1. During the great mystery and drama of life known as the Manvantara, real Kosmos is like the object placed behind the white screen upon which are thrown the Chinese shadows, called forth by the magic lantern. The actual figures and things remain invisible, while the wires of evolution are pulled by the unseen hands; and men and things are thus but the reflections, *on* the white field, of the realities *behind* the snares of *Mahamaya* or the great illusion. This was taught in every philosophy, in every religion, ante as well as post diluvian in India and Chaldea, by the Chinese as by the Grecian sages. *SD 1, p. 278*

2. Just as milliards of bright sparks dance on the waters of an ocean above which one and the same moon is shining, so our evanescent personalities - the illusive envelopes of the immortal MONAD-EGO - twinkle and dance on the waves of Maya. They last and appear, as the thousand sparks produced by the moon-beams, only so long as the Queen of the Night radiates her lustre on the running waters of life: the period of a Manvantara; and then they disappear, the beams - symbols of our eternal spiritual Egos - alone surviving, re-merged in, and being, as they were before, one with the Mother-Source. *SD 1, p. 237*

3. Hermes Trismegistos: "Reality is not upon the earth, my son, and it cannot be thereon. ... Nothing on earth

183

is real, there are only appearances.... He (man) is not real, my son, as man. The real consists solely in itself and remains what it is.... Man is transient, therefore he is not real, he is but appearance, and appearance is the supreme illusion.

Tatios: Then the *celestial bodies themselves are not real, my father, since they also vary?*

Trismegistos: That which is subject to birth and to change is not real. .... There is in them a certain falsity, seeing that they too are variable ....

Tatios: And what then is the primordial Reality?

Trismegistos: That which is one and alone, O Tatios; That which is not made of matter, nor in any body. Which has neither colour nor form which changes not nor is transmitted but which always is."

This is quite consistent with the Vedanta teaching. The leading thought is Occult; and many are the passages in the Hermetic Fragments that belong bodily to the Secret Doctrine. *SD 1, p. 287*

4. Maya or illusion is an element which enters into all finite things, for everything that exists has only a relative, not an absolute, reality, since the appearance which the hidden noumenon assumes for any observer depends upon his power of recognition. To the untrained eye of the savage, a painting is at first an unmeaning confusion of streaks and daubs of colour, while an educated eye sees instantly a face or a landscape. Nothing is permanent except the one hidden absolute existence which contains in itself the noumena of all realities. The existences belonging to every plane of being, up to the highest Dhyan-Chohans, are, in degree, of the nature of shadow cast by a magic lantern on a colourless screen; but all things are relatively real, for the cogniser is also a reflection, and the things cognised are therefore as real to him as himself.

Whatever reality things possess must be looked for in them before or after they have passed like a flash through the material world; but we cannot cognise any such existence directly, so long as we have sense instruments which bring only material existence into the field of our consciousness. Whatever plane of consciousness may be acting in, both we and the things belonging to that plane are, for the time being, our only realities. As we rise in the scale of development we perceive that during the stages through which we have passed we mistook shadows for realities, and the upward progress of the Ego is a series of progressive awakenings, each advance bringing with it the idea that now, at last, we have reached "reality;" but only when we shall have reached the absolute Consciousness, and blended out own with it, shall we be free from the delusions produced by Maya. *SD 1, pp. 39 - 40*

MAN - THE HUMAN BEING

1. As the Commentary (part of the archives of the Himalayan Brotherhood - Ed.), broadly rendered says: - "Every form on earth, and every speck (atom) in Space, strives in its efforts towards self-formation to follow the model placed for it in the 'Heavenly MAN' (the Logos - Ed.).... Its (the atom's) involution and evolution, its external and internal growth and development, have all one and the same object - man; man, as the highest physical and ultimate form on this earth; the MONAD, in its absolute totality and awakened condition - as the culmination of the divine incarnations on Earth." *SD 1, p. 183*

2. It comes to this: Mankind in its first prototypal, shadowy form, is the offspring of the Elohim of Life (or Pitris); in its qualitative and physical aspect it is the direct progeny of the "Ancestors," the lowest Dhyanis, or Spirits of the Earth; for its moral, psychic, and spiritual nature, it is indebted to a group of divine Beings.... Collectively, men are the handiwork of hosts of various spirits; distributively, the tabernacles of those hosts; and occasionally and singly, the vehicles of some of them.

In our present all material Fifth (Root) Race, the earthly Spirit of the Fourth (Root Race) is still strong in us; but we are approaching the time when the pendulum of evolution will direct its swing decidedly upwards, bringing Humanity back on a parallel line with the primitive third Root-Race in Spirituality. During its childhood, mankind was composed wholly of that Angelic Host, who were the indwelling Spirits that animated the monstrous and gigantic tabernacles of clay of the Fourth race - built by (as they are now also) and composed of countless myriads of lives. ....The "tabernacles" have improved in texture and symmetry of form, growing and developing with the globe that bore them; but the physical improvement took place at the expense of the spiritual inner man and nature. The three middle principles in earth and man became with every race more material; the Soul stepping back to make room for the physical intellect; the essence of elements becoming the material and composite elements now known.

Man is not, nor could he ever be, the complete product of the "Lord God"; but he is the child of the *Elohim*, so arbitrarily changed into the singular masculine gender. The first Dhyanis, commissioned to "create" man in their image, could only throw off their shadows, like a delicate model for the Nature Spirits of matter to work upon. Man is, beyond any doubt, formed physically out of the dust of the Earth, but his creators and fashioners were many. Nor can it be said that the "Lord God breathed into his nostrils the breath of life," unless that God is identified with the "ONE LIFE," Omnipresent though invisible, and unless the same operation is attributed to "God" on behalf of every *living Soul* - or *Nephesch*, which is the vital Soul, not the divine Spirit or *Ruach*, which ensures to man alone a divine degree of immortality, that no animal, as such, could ever attain in this cycle of incarnation. *SD 1, pp. 224 - 225*

3. Between man and the animal - whose Monads (or Jivas) are fundamentally identical - there is the impassable abyss of Mentality and Self-consciousness. What is human mind in its higher aspect, whence comes it, if it is not a portion of the essence - and, in some rare cases of incarnation, the *very essence* - of a higher Being; one from a higher and divine plane? Can man - a god in the animal form - be the product of Material Nature by evolution alone, even as is the animal, which differs from man in external shape, but by no means in the materials of its physical fabric, and is informed by the same, though undeveloped, Monad - seeing that the intellectual potentialities of the two differ as the Sun does from the Glow-worm? And what is it that creates such difference, unless man is an animal plus a living god within his physical shell? Let us pause and ask ourselves seriously the question, regardless of the vagaries and sophisms of both the materialistic and the psychological modern sciences

To some extent, it is admitted that even the esoteric teaching is allegorical. To make the latter comprehensible to the average intelligence, requires the use of symbols cast in an intelligible form. Hence the allegorical and semi-mythical narratives in the exoteric, and the (only) semi-metaphysical and objective representations in the esoteric teachings. For the purely and transcendentally spiritual conceptions are adapted only to the perceptions of those who "see without eyes, hear without ears, and sense without organs," according to the graphic expression of the Commentary. The too puritan idealist is at liberty to spiritualise the tenet, whereas the modern psychologist would simply try to spirit away our "fallen," yet still divine, human Soul in its connection with *Buddhi* (the sixth principle, from whence spring intuition and compassion - Ed.).

The mystery attached to the highly spiritual ancestors of the divine man within the earthly man is very great. His dual creations hinted at in the Puranas, though its esoteric meaning can be approached only by collating together the many varying accounts, and reading them in their symbolical and allegorical character. So it is in the Bible, both in Genseis and even in the *Epistles* of Paul. For that *creator*, who is called in the second chapter of *Genesis*, the "Lord God," is in the original the Elohim, or Gods in the plural; and while one of them make the earthly Adam of dust, the other breathes into him the breath of life, and the third makes of him a *living soul*, all of which readings are implied in the plural number of the Elohim. "The first man is of the Earth, the second (the last or rather highest) is from heaven," says Paul in 1. *Corinthians* xv. 47. **SD 2, pp. 81 - 82**

4. Each class of Creators endows man with what it has to give: the one builds his external form; the other gives him its essence, which later on becomes the Human *Higher Self* owing to the *personal exertion of the individual*; but they could not make men as they were themselves - perfect, because sinless; sinless because having only the first, pale shadowy outlines of attributes, and these all perfect - from the human standpoint - white, pure and cold as the virgin snow. Where there is no struggle, there is no merit.

Humanity, "of the earth earthy," was not destined to be created by the angels of the first divine Breath; therefore they are said to *have refused* to do so, and man had to be formed by more material creators, who, in their turn, could give only what they had in their own natures, and no more. Subservient to eternal law, the pure gods could only project out of themselves *shadowy* men, a little less ethereal and spiritual less *divine and perfect* than themselves - shadows still. The first humanity, therefore, was a pale copy of its progenitors; too material, even in its etheriality, to be a hierarchy of gods; too spiritual and pure to be MEN, endowed as it is with every negative (Nirguana) perfection.

Perfection, to be fully such, must be born out of imperfection, the *incorruptible* must grow out of the corruptible, having the latter as its vehicle and basis and contrast. Absolute light is absolute darkness, and vice versa. In fact, there is neither light nor darkness in the realms of truth. Good and Evil are twins, the progeny of Space and Time, under the sway of Maya. Separate them, by cutting off one from the other, and they will both die. Neither exists, per se, since each has to be generated and created out of the other, in order to come into being; both must be known and appreciated before becoming objects of perception, hence in mortal mind, they must be divided. *SD 2, pp. 95 - 96*

5. ... that man was a kind of Cyclops in days of old - will all be contested. Yet, scientists will never be able to prove - except to their own satisfaction - that - *it was not so*. Nor can they admit that the first two (Root) races of men were too ethereal and phantom-like in their constitution, organism and *shape*, even to be called physical men. For, if they do, it will be found that this is one of the reasons why their relics can never be expected to be exhumed among other fossils. Nevertheless all this is maintained. Man was the store-house, so to speak, of *all the seeds of life* for this Round, vegetable and animal alike. As En-Soph (the Absolute - Ed.) is "One, *notwithstanding the innumerable forms which are in him*" (*Zohar*, i., 21a) so is man, on Earth the microcosm of the macrocosm. "As soon as man appeared, everything was complete ... for everything is comprised in man. He *unites in himself all forms* (*Ibid, iii, 48a*)." "The mystery of the earthly man is after the mystery of the Heavenly Man" (*ii, 76a*).

The human form - so called, because it is the vehicle (under whatever shape) of the divine man - is, as so intuitionally remarked by the author of "Esoteric Studies," (Visconde de Figaniere), the *new type*, at the beginning of every Round, "as man never can be, so he never has been, manifested in a shape belonging to the animal kingdom *in esse*." The author proceeds, "he never formed part of that kingdom. Derived, only derived, from the most finished class of the latter, a new human form must always have been the new type of the cycle. The human shape in one ring (Round - Ed.) as I imagine, becomes cast-off clothes in the next; it is then appropriated by the highest order in the servant kingdom below."

If the idea is what we understand it to mean ... then it is the correct esoteric teaching. having appeared at the very beginning, and at the head of sentient and conscious life, man (the astral, or the "Soul," for the Zohar, repeating the archaic teaching, distinctly says that "the real man is the Soul, and his material frame no part of him") - man became the living and animal UNIT, from which the "cast-off clothes" determined the shape of every life and animal in this Round. *SD 2, pp. 289 - 290*

6. Could men exist 18,000,000 years ago? To this Occultism answers in the affirmative, notwithstanding all scientific objectors. Moreover, this duration covers only the Vaivasvata-Manu *Man, i.e.,* the male and female entity already separated into distinct sexes. The two and a half Races that preceded that event may have lived 300,000,000 years ago for all that science can tell. For the geological and physical difficulties in the way of the theory could not exist for the primeval, *ethereal* man of the Occult teachings. *The whole issue of the quarrel between the profane and the esoteric science depends upon the belief in, and demonstration of, the existence of an astral body* (etheric - Ed.) *within the physical,* the former independent of the latter. Paul d'Assier, the Positivist, seems to have proven the fact plainly, not to speak of the accumulated testimony of the ages, and that of the modern spiritualists and mystics. It will be found difficult to reject this fact in our age of proofs, tests, and ocular demonstrations. *SD 2 pp. 148 - 149*

7. The Secret Doctrine maintains that, notwithstanding the general cataclysms and disturbances of our globe, which - owing to its being the period of the greatest physical development, for the Fourth Round is the middle point of the life allotted to it - were far more terrible and intense than during any of the three preceding Rounds (the cycles of its earlier psychic and spiritual life of its semi-ethereal conditions) physical Humanity has existed upon it for the last 18,000,000 years.

This period was preceded by 300,000,000 years of the mineral and vegetable development. To this, all those who refuse to accept the theory of a "boneless," purely ethereal, man, will object. Science, which knows only of physical organisms, will feel indignant; and materialistic theology still more so. The first will object on logical and reasonable grounds, based on the preconception that all animate organisms have always existed on the same plane of materiality in all the ages; the last on a tissue of most absurd fictions. *SD 2, p. 149*

8. Neither the form of man, nor that of any animal, plant or stone has ever been created, and it is only on this plane of ours that it commenced "becoming," *i.e.*, objectivising into its present materiality, or *expanding from within outwards*, from the most sublimated and supersensuous essence into its grossest appearance. Therefore, *our* human forms have existed in the Eternity as astral or ethereal prototypes; according to which models, the Spiritual Beings (or Gods) whose duty it was to bring them into objective being and terrestrial Life, evolved the protoplasmic forms of the future *Egos from their own essence.* After which, when this human Upandhi, or basic mould was ready, the natural terrestrial forces began to work on those supersensuous moulds *which contained, besides their own the* elements of all the past vegetable and future animal forms of this globe in them. Therefore, man's outward shell passed through every vegetable and animal body before it assumed the human shape. ***SD 1, p. 282***

THE MONAD

1. The well-known Kabalistic aphorism runs: - "A stone becomes a plant; a plant, a beast; the beast, a man; a man a spirit; and the spirit a god." The "spark" (the monad - Ed.) animates all the kingdoms in turn before it enters into and informs divine man, between whom and his predecessor, animal man, there is all the difference in the world. **SD 1, p. 246**

2. The Monad or Jiva, as said in "Isis Unveiled," vol. i, p. 302, is first of all shot down by the law of Evolution into the lowest form of matter - the mineral. After a sevenfold gyration encased in the stone (or that which will become mineral and stone in the Fourth Round), it creeps out of it, as a lichen. Passing thence, through all the forms of vegetable matter, into what is termed animal matter, it has now reached the point in which it has become the germ, so to speak, of the animal, that will become the physical man.

All this up to the Third Round, is formless, as matter, and senseless, as consciousness. For the Monad or Jiva per se cannot be even called spirit; it is a ray, a breath of the ABSOLUTE, or the Absoluteness, rather, and the Absolute Homogeneity, having no relations with the conditioned and relative finiteness, is unconscious on our plane. Therefore, besides the material which will be needed for its future human form, the monad requires (a) a spiritual model, or prototype, for that material to shape itself into; and (b) an intelligent consciousness to guide its evolution and progress, neither of which is possessed by the homogeneous monad, or by senseless though living matter.

The Adam of dust requires the *Soul of Life* to be breathed into him: the two middle principles which are the *sentient* life of the irrational animal and the Human Soul, for the former is irrational without the latter. It is only when, from a potential androgyne, man has become separated into male and female, that he will be endowed with this conscious, rational, individual Soul (Manas) "the principle, or the intelligence of the Elohim" to receive which, he has to eat of the fruit of knowledge from the Tree of Good and Evil.

The Occult doctrine teaches that while the monad is cycling on downward into matter, those very Elohim - or Pitris, the lower Dhyan-Chohans - are evolving pari passu with it on a higher and more spiritual plane, descending also relatively into matter on their own plane of consciousness, when, after reaching a certain point, they will meet the incarnating senseless monad, encased in the lowest matter, and blending the two potencies, Spirit and Matter, the union will produce that terrestrial symbol of the "Heavenly Man" in space - PERFECT MAN. *SD 1, pp. 246 - 247*

3. In reference to the Monads, the reader is asked to bear in mind that Eastern philosophy rejects the Western theological dogma of a newly-created soul for every baby born, as being as unphilosophical as it is impossible in the economy of nature. There must be a limited number of Monads evolving and growing more and more perfect through their assimilation of many successive personalities, in every new Manvantara. This is absolutely necessary in view of the doctrines of Rebirth, Karma, and the gradual return of the human Monad to its source - *absolute* Deity. Thus although the hosts of more or less progressed Monads are almost incalculable, they are still finite, as is everything in this Universe of differentiation and finiteness. *SD 1, p. 171*

4. The phrase "through the seven Worlds of Maya" refers ... to the seven globes of the planetary chain and the seven rounds, or the 49 stations of active existence that are before the "Spark" or Monad at the beginning of every "Great Life Cycle" or Manvantara....

This relates to the greatest problem of philosophy - the physical and substantial nature of life, the independent nature of which is denied by modern science because that science is unable to comprehend it. The reincarnationists and believers in Karma alone dimly perceive that the whole secret of Life is in the unbroken series of its manifestations: whether in, or apart from the physical body. Because if - "Life like a dome of many-coloured glass, Stains the white radiance of Eternity" - yet it is itself part and parcel of that Eternity for life alone can understand life.

What is that "Spark" which "hangs from the flame?" It is JIVA, the MONAD in conjunction with MANAS or rather its aroma - that which remains from each personality, when worthy, and hangs from Atma-Buddhi, the Flame, by the thread of life. In whatever way interpreted, and into whatever number of principles the human being is divided, it may easily be shown that this doctrine is supported by all the ancient religions, from the Vedic to the Egyptian, from the Zoroastrian to the Jewish. In the case of the last-mentioned, the Kabalistic works offer abundant proof of this statement. The entire system of the Kabalistic numerals is based on the divine septenary hanging from the Triad (the Divine Trinity of Father-Mother, and Son - Ed.) (thus forming the Decade) and its permutations 7, 5, 4, and 3, which finally all merge into the ONE itself: an endless and boundless Circle. *SD 1, p. 238*

5. The ... difficulty of language is met with in describing the "stages" through which the Monad passes. Metaphysically speaking it is of course an absurdity to talk of the "development" of a Monad, or to say it becomes "Man." But any attempt to preserve metaphysical accuracy of language in the use of such a tongue as English would necessitate at least three extra volumes of this work, and would entail an amount of verbal repetition which would be worrisome in the extreme. It stands to reason that a MONAD cannot either progress or develop, or even be affected by the changes of states it passes through. *It is not of this world or plane*, and may be compared only to an indestructible star of divine light and fire thrown down onto our Earth as a plank of salvation for the personalities in which it dwells. It is for the latter to cling to it; and thus partaking of its divine nature, obtain immortality. Left to itself the Monad still clings to no-one; but like the 'plank' be drifted away to another incarnation by the unresting current of evolution. *SD 1, pp. 174 - 175, foot-note*

6. ... it (the atom) is a concrete manifestation of the Universal Energy which itself has not yet become individualized; a sequential manifestation of the one Universal Monas (Monad - Ed.). The ocean of matter does not divide into its potential and constituent drops until the sweep of the life-impulse reaches the evolutionary stage of man-birth. The tendency towards segregation into individual Monads is gradual, and in the higher animals comes almost to the point. The Peripatetics applied the word Monas to the whole Kosmos, in the pantheistic sense; and the Occultists, while accepting this thought for convenience sake, distinguish the progressive stages of the evolution of the concrete from the abstract by terms of which the "Mineral, Vegetable, Animal, (etc.), Monad" are examples. The term merely means that the tidal wave of spiritual evolution is passing through that arc of its circuit. The "Monadic Essence" begins to imperceptibly differentiate towards individual consciousness in the Vegetable Kingdom. As the Monads are uncompounded things, as correctly defined by Leibnitz, it is the spiritual essence which vivifies them in their degrees of differentiation, which properly constitutes the Monad - not the atomic aggregation, which is only the vehicle, and the substance through which thrill the lower and the higher degrees of intelligence.

Leibnitz conceived of the Monads as elementary and indestructible units endowed with the power of *giving and receiving* with respect to other units, and thus of determining all spiritual and physical phenomena. It is he who invented the term apperception, which together with nerve (not perception, but rather) - sensation, expresses the state of the Monadic consciousness through all the Kingdoms up to Man.

Thus it may be wrong on strictly metaphysical lines to call Atma-Buddhi a MONAD, since in the materialistic view it is dual and therefore a compound. But as matter is Spirit, and vice versa; and since the Universe and the Deity which informs it are unthinkable apart from each other; so in the case of Atma-Buddhi. The latter being the vehicle of the former, Buddhi stands in the same relation to Atma, as Adam Kadmon, the Kabalistic Logos, does to En Soph, (the Absolute - Ed.), or Mulaprakriti (Root Matter - Ed.) to *Parabrahm. SD 1, pp. 178 - 179*

THE MOON AND ITS MYSTERIES

1. The last word of the mystery is divulged only to the adepts, but it may be stated that our satellite is only the gross body of its invisible principles. Seeing then that there are 7 Earths, so there are 7 Moons, the last one alone being visible; the same for the Sun, whose visible body is called a Maya, a reflection, just as man's body is. "The real Sun and the real Moon are as invisible as the real man," says an occult maxim.

And it may be remarked *en passant* that those ancients were not so foolish after all who first stated the idea of "the seven moons." For though this conception is now taken solely as an astronomical measure of time, in a very materialised form, yet underlying the husk there can still be recognised the traces of a profoundly philosophical idea. ***SD 1, p.p. 179 - 180***

2. In reality the Moon is only the satellite of the Earth in one respect, viz., that physically the Moon revolved round the Earth. But in every other respect it is the Earth which is the satellite of the Moon, and not vice versa. Startling as the statement may seem it is not without confirmation from scientific knowledge. It is evidenced by the tides, by the cyclic changes in many forms of disease which coincide with the lunar phases; it can be traced in the growth of plants, and is very marked in the phenomena of human gestation and conception.

The importance of the Moon and its influence on the Earth were recognised in every ancient religion, notably the Jewish, and have been remarked by many observers of psychical and physical phenomena. But so far as Science knows, the earth's action on the Moon is confined to the physical attraction, which causes her to circle in her orbit. And should an objector insist that this fact alone is sufficient evidence that the Moon is truly the Earth's satellite on other planes of action, one may reply by asking whether a mother, who walks round and round her child's cradle keeping watch over the infant, is the subordinate of her child or dependent upon it; though in one sense she is its satellite, yet she is certainly older and more fully developed than the child she watches. *SD p. 180*

3. The Moon is far older than the Earth; and as explained in Book I, it is the latter which owes its being to the former, however astronomy and geology may explain the fact. Hence the tides and the attraction to the Moon, as shown by the liquid portion of the Globe ever striving to raise itself towards its parent. This is the meaning of the sentence (*Stanza II, v. 9*) that "the Mother-Water arose and disappeared in the Moon, which had lifted her, which had given her birth." *SD 2, p. 64*

4. For the present it may be as well to remind the reader that while the Moon-goddesses were connected in every mythology, especially the Grecian, with child-birth, because of the lunar influence on women and conception, the occult and actual connection of our satellite with fecundation is to this day unknown to physiology, which regards every popular practice in this reference as gross superstition. As it is useless to discuss them in detail, we may only stop at present to discuss the lunar symbology casually, to show that the said superstition belongs to the most ancient beliefs, and even to Judaism - the basis of Christianity. With the Israelites, the chief function of Jehovah was child-giving, and the esotericism of the Bible, interpreted Kabalistically, shows undeniably the Holy of Holies in the temple to be only the symbol of the womb. This is now proven beyond a doubt and cavil, by the numerical reading of the Bible in general, and of Genesis especially.

This idea must certainly have been borrowed by the Jews from the Egyptians and Indians, whose Holy of Holies was, and with the latter is to this day, symbolised by the King's chamber in the Great Pyramid ... and the Yoni symbols of exoteric Hindusim. *SD 1, p. 264*

5. When a planetary chain is in its last Round, its Globe 1 or A before finally dying *out* sends all its energy and "principles" into a neutral centre of latent force, a "laya centre," and thereby informs a new nucleus of undifferentiated substance or matter, *i.e*, calls it into activity or gives it life. Suppose such a process to have taken place in the lunar "planetary" chain....

Imagine the six fellow-globes of the moon - aeons before the first globe of our seven was evolved - just in the same position in relation to each other as the fellow-globes of our chain occupy in regard to our Earth now. And now it will be easy to imagine further Globe A of the lunar chain informing Globe A of the terrestrial chain and - dying; Globe B of the former sending that its energy into Globe B of the new chain; then Globe C of the lunar, creating its progeny sphere C of the terrene chain; then the Moon (our Satellite) pouring forth into the lowest globe of our planetary ring - Globe D, our Earth - all its life, energy and powers; and having transferred them to a new centre becoming virtually a dead planet, in which rotation has almost ceased since the birth of our globe.

The Moon is now the cold residual quantity, the shadow dragged after the new body, into which her living powers and "principles" are transfused. She now is doomed for long ages to be ever pursuing the Earth, to be attracted by and to attract her progeny. Constantly vampirised by her child, she revenges herself on it by soaking it through and through with the nefarious, invisible, and poisoned influence which emanates from the occult side of her nature. For she is a dead, yet a living body.

The particles of her decaying corpse are full of active and destructive life, although the body which they had formed is soulless and lifeless. Therefore its emanations are at the same time beneficent and maleficent - this circumstance finding its parallel on earth in the fact that the grass and plants are nowhere more juicy and thriving than on the graves; while at the same time it is the graveyard or corpse-emanations which kill. And like all ghouls and vampires, the moon is the friend of the sorcerers and the foe of the unwary. From the archaic aeons and the later times of the witches of Thessaly, down to some of the present tantrikas of Bengal, her nature and properties were known to every occultist, but have remained a closed book for physicists. *SD 1, pp. 155 - 156*

6. This (the transfer of the Moon's seven principles to the Earth - Ed.) is one of the "seven mysteries of the Moon," and it is now revealed. The seven "mysteries" are called by the Japanese Yamaboosis, the mystics of the Lao-Tze sect and the ascetic monks of Kioto, the Dzenodoo - the "seven jewels." Only the Japanese and the Chinese Buddhist ascetics and Initiates are, if possible, even more reticent in giving out their "Knowledge" than are the Hindus. *SD 1, pp. 173 - 174*

THE MUNDANE EGG

1. Whence this universal symbol? The Egg was incorporated as a sacred sign in the cosmogony of every people on the Earth, and was revered both on account of its form and its inner mystery. From the earliest mental conceptions of man, it was known as that which represented most successfully the origin and secret of being. The gradual development of the imperceptible germ within the closed shell; the inward working, without any apparent outward interference of force, which from a latent *nothing* produced an active *something*, needing naught save heat; and which, having gradually evolved into a concrete, living creature, broke its shell, appearing to the outward senses of all a self-generated, and self-created being - must have been a standing miracle from the beginning.

The secret teaching explains the reason for this reverence by the Symbolism of the prehistoric races. The "First Cause" had no name in the beginnings. Later it was pictured in the fancy of the thinkers as an ever invisible, mysterious Bird that dropped an Egg into Chaos, which Egg becomes the Universe. Hence Brahma was called Kalahansa, "the swan in (Space and) Time." He became the "Swan of Eternity," who lays at the beginning of each Mahamanvantara a "Golden Egg." it typifies the great Circle, or O, itself a symbol for the universe and its spherical bodies. *SD 1, p. 359*

2. The second reason for its having been chosen as the symbolical representation of the Universe and of our Earth, was its form. It was a Circle and a Sphere; and the ovi-form shape of our globe must have been known from the beginning of symbology, since it was so universally adopted. The first manifestation of the Kosmos in the form of an egg was the most widely diffused belief of antiquity. As Bryant shows ... it was a symbol adopted among the Greeks, the Syrians, Persians, and Egyptians. In chap. liv. of the Egyptian Ritual, Seb, the god of Time and of the Earth, is spoken of as having laid an egg, or the Universe, "an egg conceived at the hour of the great one of Dual Force."

Ra is shown like Brahma gestating in the Egg of the Universe. The deceased is "resplendent in the Egg of the land of mysteries." For, this is "the Egg to which is given life among the gods." "It is the Egg of the great clucking hen, the Egg of Seb, who issues from it like a hawk." *SD 1, p. 359*

3. The "Mundane Egg" is, perhaps, one of the most universally adopted symbols, highly suggestive as it is, equally in the spiritual, physiological, and cosmological sense. Therefore, it is found in every world theogony, where it is largely associated with the serpent symbol; the latter being everywhere in philosophy as in religious symbolism, an emblem of eternity, infinitude, regeneration, and rejuvenation, as well as of wisdom. The mystery of apparent self-generation and evolution through its own creative power repeating in miniature the process of Cosmic evolution in the egg, both being due to heat and moisture under the efflux of the unseen creative spirit, justified fully the selection of this graphic symbol.

The "Virgin Egg" is the microcosmic symbol of the macrocosmic - the "Virgin Mother" - Chaos or the Primeval Deep. The male Creator (under whatever name) springs forth from the Virgin female, the immaculate root fructified by the Ray. Who, if versed in astronomy and natural sciences, can fail to see its suggestiveness? Cosmos as receptive Nature is an Egg fructified - yet left immaculate; once regarded as boundless, it could have no other representation than a spheroid. The Golden Egg was surrounded by seven natural elements (ether, fire, air, water), "four ready, three secret." It may be found stated in the Vishnu Purana where elements are translated as "Envelopes".... *SD 1, p. 65*

4. With the Greeks the Orphic Egg is described by Aristophanes, and was part of the Dionysiac and other mysteries, during which the Mundane Egg was consecrated and its significance explained; Porphyry showing it a representation of the world .... Faber and Bryant have tried to show that the egg typified the ark of Noah, which, unless the latter is accepted as purely allegorical and symbolical, is a wild belief. It can have typified the ark only as a synonym of the moon, the argha which carries the seed of life; but had surely nothing to do with the ark of the Bible.

Anyhow, the belief that the universe existed in the beginning in the shape of an egg was general. And as

Wilson has it: "A similar account of the first aggregation of the elements in the form of an egg is given in all the (Indian) Puranas, with the usual epithet Maima or Hiranya, 'golden' as it occurs in Manu." Hiranya, however, means "resplendent," "shining," rather than "golden," as proven by the great Indian scholar, the late Swami Dayanand Sarasvati, in his unpublished polemics with Professor Max Muller. As said in the Vishnu Purana: "Intellect (Mahat) ... the (unmanifested) gross elements inclusive, formed an egg ... and the lord of the universe himself abided in it, in the character of Brahma. In that egg, O Brahman, were the continents, and seas and mountains, the planets and divisions of the universe, the gods, the demons and mankind." *SD 1, pp. 359 - 360*

5. In view of this circular form, the "1" issuing from the "O" or the egg, or the male from the female in the androgyne, it is strange to find a scholar saying - on the ground that the most ancient Indian MSS, show no trace of it - that the ancient Aryans were ignorant of the decimal notation. The 10, being the sacred number of the universe was secret and esoteric, both as the unit and cipher, or zero, the circle. Moreover, Professor Max Muller says that "the two words cipher and zero, which are one, are sufficient to prove that our figures are borrowed from the Arabs. Cipher is the Arabic 'cifron,' and means empty, a translation of the Sanscrit name of nought....."

The Arabs had their figures from Hindustan, and never claimed the discovery for themselves. As to the Pythagoreans, we need but turn to the ancient manuscripts of Boethius's Geometry, composed in the sixth century, to find among the Pythagorean numerals the 1 and the nought, as the first and final ciphers. And Porphyry, who quotes from the Pythagorean Moderatus, says that the numerals of Pythagoras were "heiroglyphical symbols, by means whereof he explained ideas concerning the nature of things," or the origin of the universe. *SD 1, pp. 360 - 361*

6. The simile of an egg also expresses the fact taught in occultism that the primordial form of everything manifested from atom to globe, from man to angel, is spheroidal, the sphere having been with all nations the emblem of eternity and infinity - a serpent swallowing its tail. To realize the meaning, however, the sphere must be thought of as seen from its center. The field of vision or of thought is like a sphere whose radii proceed from one's self in every direction, and extend out into space, opening up boundless vistas all around. It is the symbolical circle of Pascal and the Kabalists "whose center is everywhere and circumference nowhere," a conception which enters into the compound idea of this emblem. *SD 1, p. 65*

NUMBERS AND SACRED GEOMETRY

1. From the very beginning of Aeons - in time and space in our Round and Globe - the Mysteries of Nature (at any rate, those which it is lawful for our races to know) were recorded by the pupils of those same now invisible "heavenly men," in geometrical figures and symbols. The keys thereto passed from one generation of "wise men" to the other. Some of the symbols thus passed from the east to the west, were brought therefrom by Pythagoras, who was not the inventor of his famous "Triangle." The latter figure, along with the plane, cube and circle, are more eloquent and scientific descriptions of the order of the evolution of the Universe, spiritual and psychic, as well as physical, than volumes of descriptive Cosmogonies and revealed "*Geneses.*"

The *ten points* inscribed within that "Pythagorean triangle" (the "tetraktys" - Ed.) are worth all the theogonies and angelologies ever emanated from the theological brain. For he who interprets them - on their very face, and in the order given - will find in these seventeen points (the seven Mathematical Points hidden) the uninterrupted series of the genealogies from the first *Heavenly* to *terrestrial* man. And as they give the order of Beings, so they reveal the order in which were evolved the Kosmos, our earth, and the primordial elements which the latter was generated. Begotten in the invisible Depths, and in the womb of the same

"Mother" as its fellow-globes - he who will master the mysteries of our Earth, will have mastered those of all others. **SD 1, pp. 612 - 613**

2. "Listen, ye Sons of the Earth to your Instructors - the Sons of the Fire. Learn there is neither first nor last; for all is One Number, issued from No Number." **SD 1, p. 86, Stanza 1V, v.1**

3. ... The sacred science of the Numerals: so sacred, indeed and so important in the study of Occultism that the subject can hardly be skimmed.... It is on the Hierarchies (of Angels - Ed.) and correct numbers of these beings invisible (to us) except upon very rare occasions, that the mystery of the whole Universe is built. The Kumaras (the "Seven Rays", and in Hindusim - the "seven sons of Brahma" - Ed.) for instance, are called the "Four" though in reality seven in number, because Sanka, Sananda, Sanatana and Sanat Kumara are the chief Vaidhatra (their patronymic name), as they spring from the "four-fold mystery" (the Logos, called "Brahma" in Hinduism - Ed.). **SD 1, p. 89**

4. The Three, the One, the Four, the One, the Five" (in their totality - twice seven) represent 31415 - the numerical hierarchy of the Dhyan Chohans of various orders, and of the inner or circumscribed world. When placed on the boundary of the great circle of "Pass not," called also the Dhyanipass, the "rope of the Angels," the rope that hedges off the phenomenal world from the noumenal Kosmos, (not falling within the range of our present objective consciousness); the number, when not enlarged by permutation and expansion, is ever 31415 anagrammatically and Kabalistically, being ... the number of the circle, the twice seven once more; for whatever way the two sets of figures are counted, when added separately, one figure after another, whether crossways, from right or from left, they will always yield fourteen.

Mathematically they represent the well-known calculation, namely, that the ratio of the diameter to the circumference of a circle is as 1 to 3.1415, or the value of pi, as this ratio is called - the symbol ... being always used in mathematical formulae to express it. This set of figures must have the same meaning, since the 1: 314,159 and then again 1: 3: 1,415,927 are worked out in the secret calculations to express the various cycles and ages of the "first born" (the Logos), or 311,040,000, 000 with fractions (the age of Brahma - "Day" or "Night of Brama"), and yield the same 13.415 by a process we are not concerned with at present. **SD 1, pp. 90 - 91**

5. ... We see Cosmic matter scattering and forming itself into elements; grouped into the mystic four within the fifth element - Ether - the lining of Akasha, the Anima Mundi or Mother of Kosmos. "Dots, Lines, Triangles, Cubes, Circles" and finally "Spheres" - why or how? Because says the Commentary (of the Himalayan Brotherhood - Ed), such is the first law of Nature, and because nature geometrizes universally in all her manifestations. There is an inherent law - not only in the primordial, but also in the manifested matter of our phenomenal plane - by which Nature correlates her geometrical forms, and later, also, her compound elements; and in which there is no place for accident or chance. *SD 1, p. 97*

6. "The number seven," says the Kabala, "is the great number of the Divine Mysteries;" number ten is that of all human knowledge (Pythagorean decade); 1,000 is the number ten to the third power, and therefore the number 7,000 is also symbolical. In the Secret Doctrine the figure and number 4 are the male symbol only on the higher plane of abstraction; on the plane of matter the 3 is the masculine and the 4 the female: the upright and the horizontal in the fourth stage of symbolism, when the symbols became the glyphs of the generative powers on the physical plane. *SD 1, p. 36*

7. The "First is the Second," because the "First" cannot really be numbered or regarded as the First, as that is the realm of noumena in its primary manifestation; the threshold to the World of Truth, or SAT, through which the direct energy that radiates from the ONE REALITY - Nameless Deity - reaches us. Here again, the untranslateable term SAT (*Be-ness*) is likely to lead into an erroneous conception since that which is manifested cannot be SAT, but is something phenomenal, not everlasting, nor, in truth, even sempiternal. It is coeval and coexistent with the One Life, "Secondless," but as a manifestation it is still a Maya - like the rest. This "World of Truth" can be described only in the words of the Commentary as "A bright star dropped from the heart of Eternity; the beacon of hope on whose Seven Rays hang the

Seven Worlds of being." Truly so; since these are the Seven Lights whose reflections are the human immortal Monads - the Atma or irradiating Spirit of every creature of the human family. *SD 1, p. 119*

THE PLANETS

1. The occult Doctrine rejects the hypothesis born out of the Nebular Theory, that the (seven) great planets have evolved from the Sun's central mass, not of this our visible Sun, at any rate. The first condensation of Cosmic matter of course took place about a central nucleus, its parent Sun; but our Sun, it is taught, merely detached itself earlier than all the others, as the rotating mass contracted, and is their elder, bigger brother therefore, not their father. The eight Adityas "the gods," are all formed from the eternal substance or the "World-Stuff" which is both the fifth cosmic Principle (Manas - Ed.), the Upadhi or basis of the Universal Soul, just as in man, the Microcosm, Manas (mind) is the Upahdhi (vehicle) of Buddhi (spiritual soul). *SD 1, p. 101*

2. The "Breath" of all the "seven" is said to be Bhaskara (light-making), because they (the planets) were all comets and suns in their origin. They evolve into Manvantaric life from primeval Chaos (now the noumenon of irresolvable nebulae) by aggregation and accumulation of the primary differentiation of the eternal matter, according to the beautiful expression in the Commentary, "Thus the Sons of Light clothe themselves in the fabric of Darkness." They are called allegorically "the Heavenly Snails," on account of their (to us) formless INTELLIGENCES inhabiting unseen their starry and planetary homes, and, so to speak, carrying them as the snails do along with themselves in their revolution.

The doctrine of a common origin for all the heavenly bodies and planets, was, as we see inculcated by the Archaic astronomers, before Kepler, Newton, Leibnitz, Kant, Herschel and Laplace. Heat (the Breath), attraction and repulsion - the three great factors of Motion - are the conditions under which all the members of all this primitive family are born, developed, and die, to be reborn after a "Night of Brahma," during which eternal matter relapses periodically into its primary undifferentiated state. The most attenuated gases can give no idea of its nature to the modern physicist. Centres of Forces at first, the invisible sparks of primordial atoms differentiate into molecules, and become Suns - passing gradually into objectivity - gaseous, radiant, cosmic, the one "Whirlwind" (or motion) finally giving the impulse to the form, and the initial motion regulated and sustained by the never-resting breaths - the Dhyan Chohans. *SD 1, p. 103*

3. The ... Commentary (of the Himalayan Brotherhood - Ed.) explains ... "that Mercury receives seven times more light and heat from the Sun than Earth, or even the beautiful Venus, which receives but twice the amount more than our insignificant Globe." Whether the fact was known in antiquity may be inferred from the prayer of the "Earth Spirit" to the Sun as given in the text (See *SD 2, Stanza I, v. 2* - Ed).

Mercury is, as an astrological planet, still more occult and mysterious than Venus. It is identical with the Mazdean Mithra, the genius, or god, "established between the Sun and the Moon, the perpetual companion of the 'Sun' of Wisdom." Pausanias shows him as having an altar in common with Jupiter. He had wings to express his attendance upon the Sun in its course, and he was called the *Nuntis*, or Sun-wolf, *"solaris luminis particeps."* He was the leader of the evocator of Souls, the "great Magician" and the Hierophant. .... He is the golden-coloured Mercury, ... whom the Hierophants forbade to name.

He is symbolised in Grecian mythology by one of the *dogs* (vigilance), which watch over the celestial flock (occult wisdom), or Hermes Anubis, or again Agathodaemon. He is the Argus watching over the Earth, and which the latter mistakes for the Sun itself. It is through the intercession of Mercury that the Emperor Julian prayed to the Occult Sun every night; for as says Vossius: "All the theologians agree to say that *Mercury and the Sun are one....* He was the most eloquent and the most wise of all the gods, which is not to be wondered at, since *Mercury is in such close proximity to the Wisdom and the Word of God* (the Sun) *that he was confused with both.* Vossius utters here a greater occult truth than he suspected. The *Hermes-Sarameyas* of the Greeks is closely related to the Hindu *Saram and Sarmeya*, the divine watchman, "who watches over the golden flock of stars and solar rays." *SD 2, pp. 27 - 28*

4. In the clearer words of the Commentary: - "The Globe propelled onward by the Spirit of the Earth ... gets all its vital forces, life, and powers through the medium of the seven Planetary Dhyanis (the Planetary

Spirits) from the Spirit of the Sun. They are his messengers of Light and life."

"Like each of the seven regions of the Earth, each of the seven First born (the primordial human groups) receives its light and life from its own especial Dhyani - spiritually, and from the palace (house, the planet), of that Dhyani physically; so with the seven great Races to be born in it. The first is born under the Sun; the second under Brihaspati (Jupiter); the third under Lohitanga (the 'fiery-bodied,' Venus or Sukra); the fourth under Soma (the Moon, our globe also, the Fourth Sphere being born under and from the Moon) and Sani, Saturn, the Karuna-lochana (evil-eyed) and the Asita (the dark); the fifth, under Budha (Mercury).

So also with man.... Each gets its specific quality from its primary (the planetary spirit), therefore every man is a septenate (or a combination of principles, each having its origin in a quality of that special Dhyani). Every active power or force of the earth comes to her from one of the seven Lords (the seven sacred planets -Ed.). Light comes through Sukra (Venus), who receives a triple supply, and gives one-third of it to the Earth. Therefore the two are called 'Twin-sisters,' but the Spirit of the Earth is subservient to the 'Lord' of Sukra. Our wise men represent the two Globes, one over the other under the double sign (the astrological sign for Venus - Ed.)." *SD 2, pp. 28 - 29*

5. Plato represented the planets as moved by an *intrinsic* Rector, one with his dwelling, like "A Boatman in his boat." As for Aristotle, he called those rulers "immaterial substances;" though as one who had never been initiated, he rejected the gods as *Entities*. But this did not prevent him from recognising the fact that the stars and planets "were not inanimate masses but *acting* and *living* bodies indeed ...." As if *"sidereal spirits were the divine* portion of their phenomena ...." **SD 1, p. 493**

6. If we look for corroboration in more modern and Scientific times, we find Tycho Brahe recognising in the stars a triple force, *divine, spiritual, and vital.* Kepler, putting together the Pythagorean sentence, "The Sun, guardian of Jupiter," and the verses of David, "He placed his throne in the Sun" and "The Lord is the Sun," etc., said that he understood perfectly how the Pythagoreans could believe that all the globes disseminated through Space were rational Intelligences ... circulating round the Sun, "in which resides *a pure spirit of fire*; the source of the general harmony." **SD 1, p. 493**

PLATO ON GOD

1. Plato having been initiated could not believe in a personal God - a gigantic Shadow of Man. His epithets of "monarch" and "Law-giver of the Universe" bear an abstract meaning well understood by every Occultist, who, no less than any Christian, believes in the One Law that governs the Universe, recognizing it at the same time as immutable. "Beyond all *finite* existence" he says, "and secondary causes, all laws, ideas and principles, there is an INTELLIGENCE OF MIND, the first principle of all principles, the Supreme Idea on which all other ideas are grounded ... the *ultimate* substance *from which all things derive their being and essence*, the first and efficient cause of all the order and harmony, and beauty and excellency, and goodness, which pervades the Universe" - who is called, by way of preeminence and excellence, the Supreme good "the god" and "the god over all."

These words apply, as Plato himself shows, neither to the "Creator" nor to the "Father" of our modern Monotheist, but to the *ideal* and abstract cause. For, as he says, "this the god over all, *is not the truth or the intelligence* but the Father of it" and its Primal cause.

Is it Plato, the greatest pupil of the archaic Sages, a sage himself, for whom there was but a single object of attainment in this life - REAL KNOWLEDGE - who would have ever believed in a deity that curses and damns men for ever, on the slightest provocation? Not he, who considered only those to be genuine philosophers and students of truth who possessed the knowledge of the *really existing* in opposition to mere seeming; of the *always* existing in opposition to the transitory; and of that which exists *permanently* in opposition to that which waxes, wanes, and is developed and destroyed alternately. Speusippus and Xenocrates followed in his footsteps. The ONE, the original, had no existence, in the sense applied to it by mortal men. "The honoured one dwells in the centre as in the circumference, but *it is only the reflection of the Deity - the world Soul"* - the plane of the surface of the circle. *SD 2, pp. 554 - 555*

2. It is to avoid anthropomorphic conceptions that the Initiates never use the epithet "God" to designate the One and Secondless Principle in the Universe; and that - faithful in this to the oldest traditions of the Secret Doctrine the world over - they deny that such imperfect and often not very clean work could ever be produced by Absolute Perfection. There is no need to mention here other still greater metaphysical details between speculative Atheism and idiotic anthropomorphism there must be a philosophical mean, and a reconciliation. The presence of the Unseen Principle throughout all nature, and the highest manifestation of it on Earth - MAN, can alone help to solve the Problem, which is that of the mathematician whose x must ever elude the gasp of our terrestrial algebra. The Hindus have tried to solve it by their *avatars*, the Christians think they did it - by their one divine Incarnation. Exoterically - both are wrong; *esoterically* both of them are very near the truth. **SD 2, pp. 555 - 556**

REINCARNATION

1. The twelve Nidanas or causes of being ... a doctrine especially characteristic of the Hinayana System (of Buddhism - Ed.) is based upon the great truth that re-incarnation is to be dreaded, as existence in this world only entails upon man suffering, misery and pain.

Death itself being unable to deliver man from it, since death is merely the door through which he passes to another life on earth after a little rest on its threshold - Devachan (an illusory heaven - Ed.). The Hinayana the System or School of the "Little Vehicle," is of very ancient growth; while the Mahayana is of a later period, having originated after the death of Buddha.

Yet the tenets of the latter are as old as the hills that have contained such schools from time immemorial, and the Hinayana and Mahayana Schools (the latter, that of the "Great Vehicle") both teach the same doctrine in reality. *Yama*, or Vehicle (in Sanskrit, Vahan) is a mystic expression, both "vehicles" inculcating that man may escape the sufferings of rebirths and even the false bliss of Devachan, by obtaining Wisdom and Knowledge, which alone can dispel the Fruits of Illusion and ignorance. *SD 1, p. 39*

2. Moreover the Secret Doctrine teaches: - The fundamental identity of all Souls with the Universal Over-Soul, the latter being itself an aspect of the Unknown Root (the Absolute - Ed.); and the

224

obligatory pilgrimage for every Soul - a spark of the former - through the Cycle of Incarnation (or "Necessity") in accordance with Cyclic and Karmic law, during the whole term. In other words, no purely spiritual Buddhi (divine Soul) can have an independent (conscious) existence before the spark which issued from the pure Essence of the Universal Sixth principle, - or the OVER-SOUL, - has (a) passed through every elemental form of the phenomenal world of that Manvantara, (b) acquired individuality, first by natural impulse, and then by self-induced efforts (checked by its Karma), thus ascending through all the degrees of intelligence, from the lowest to the highest Manas, from mineral and plant, up to the holiest archangel (Dhyani-Buddha). The pivotal doctrine of the esoteric philosophy admits no privileges or special gifts in man, save those won by his own Ego through personal effort and merit throughout a long series of metempsychoses and reincarnations. **SD 1, p. 17**

3. There is an eternal cyclic law of re-births, and the series is headed at every new Manvantaric dawn by those who had enjoyed their rest from re-incarnations and in previous Kalpas for incalculable *Aeons* - by the highest and the earliest *Nirvanees* (those returning from Nirvana). It was the turn of those "Gods" to incarnate in the present Manvantara; hence their presence on Earth and the ensuing allegories; hence, also the perversion of the original meaning. The Gods who had *fallen* into generation, whose mission it was to complete *divine* man, are found represented later on as Demons, evil Spirits, and fiends, at feud and war with Gods, or the irresponsible agents of the one Eternal law. But no conception of such creatures as the devils of the Christian, Jewish, and Mahommedan religions was ever intended under those thousand and one Aryan allegories. *SD 2, p. 232*

RELIGION AND ANCIENT RACES

1. What was the religion of the Third and Fourth (Root) Races? In the common acceptance of the term, neither the Lemurians nor yet their progeny, the Lemuro-Atlanteans, had any, as they knew no dogma, nor had they to believe *on faith*. No sooner had the mental eye of man been opened to understanding, than the Third Race felt itself one with the ever-present as the ever to be unknown and invisible ALL, the One Universal Deity. Endowed with divine powers, and feeling in himself his *inner* God, each felt he was a Man-God in his nature, though an animal in his physical Self. The struggle between the two began from the very day they tasted of the fruit of the Tree of Wisdom; a struggle for life between the spiritual and the psychic, the psychic and the physical. Those who conquered the lower principles by obtaining mastery over the body, joined the "Sons of Light." Those who fell victims to their lower natures, became the slaves of Matter. From "Sons of Light and Wisdom" they ended by becoming the "Sons of Darkness." They had fallen in the battle of mortal life with Life immortal, and all those so fallen became the seed of the future generations of Atlanteans. *SD 2, p. 272*

2. At the dawn of his consciousness, the man of the Third Root Race had thus no beliefs that could be called *religion*. That is to say, he was equally as ignorant of "religions, full of pomp and gold" as any system of faith

227

or outward worship. But if the term is to be defined as the binding together of the masses in one form of reverence paid to those we feel higher than ourselves, of piety - as a feeling expressed by a child toward a loved parent - then even the earliest Lemurians had a religion - and a most beautiful one - from the very beginning of their intellectual life.

Had they not their bright gods of the elements around them, and even within themselves? Was not their childhood passed with, nursed and tendered by those who had given them life and called them forth to intelligent, conscious life? We are assured it was so, and we believe it. For the evolution of Spirit into matter could never have been achieved; nor would it have received its first impulse, had not the bright Spirits sacrificed their own respective super-ethereal essences to animate the man of clay, by endowing each of his inner principles with a portion, or rather, a reflection of that essence. The Dhyanis of the Seven heavens (the seven planes of being) are the NOUMENOI of the actual and the future Elements, just as the Angels of the Seven Powers of nature - the grosser effects of which are perceived by us in what Science is pleased to call the "modes of motion" - the imponderable forces and what not - are the still higher noumenoi of still higher Hierarchies. *SD 2, pp. 272 - 273*

3. In treating of Cosmogony and then of the Anthropogenesis of mankind, it was necessary to show that no religion, since the very earliest, has ever been entirely based on fiction, as none was the object of special revelation; and that it is dogma alone which has ever been killing primeval truth. Finally, no human-born doctrine, no creed, however sanctified by custom and antiquity, can compare in sacredness with the religion of Nature. The Key of Wisdom that unlocks the massive gates leading to the arcana of the innermost sanctuaries can be found hidden in her bosom only; and that bosom is in the countries pointed to by the great seer of the past century Emmanuel Swedenborg. There lies the heart of nature, that shrine whence issued the early races of primeval Humanity, and which is the cradle of *physical* man. **SD 2, p. 797**

THE ROOT RACES

1. Man's organism was adapted in every race to its surroundings. The first Root-Race was as ethereal as ours is material. The progeny of the seven Creators, who evolved the seven primordial Adams, surely required no purified gases to breathe and live upon. Therefore, however strongly the impossibility of this teaching may be urged by the devotees of modern science, the Occultist maintains that the case was as stated *aeons of years* before even the evolution of the Lemurian, the first physical man, which itself took place 18,000,000 years ago! *SD 2, p. 46*

2. The first race of men were, then, simply the images, the astral doubles (etheric doubles - Ed.) of their Fathers, who were the pioneers, or the most progressed Entities from a preceding though *lower* sphere, the shell of which is now our Moon. But even this shell is all-potential, for, having generated the Earth, it is the *phantom* of the Moon which, attracted by magnetic affinity, sought to form its first inhabitants, the pre-human monsters. *SD 2, p. 115*

3. ... Occult philosophy steps in. It teaches that the first human stock was projected by higher and semi-divine Beings out of their own essences. If the latter process is to be considered as abnormal or even inconceivable - because obsolete in Nature at this point of evolution - it is yet proven possible on the authority of certain

"Spiritualistic" FACTS (e.g. the oozing of ectoplasm from the medium - Ed.). **SD 2, p. 87**

4. The First Root-Race, the "Shadows" of the Progenitors, could not be injured, or destroyed by death. Being so ethereal and so little human in constitution, they could not be affected by any element - flood or fire. But their "Sons," the Second Root-Race, could be and were so destroyed. As the "progenitors" merged wholly in their own astral bodies, which were their progeny; so that progeny was absorbed in its descendants, the "Sweat-born." These were the second Humanity - composed of the most heterogeneous gigantic semi-human monsters - the first attempts of material nature at building human bodies. ... the bulk of the Second Race perished in this first great throe of the evolution and consolidation of the globe during the human period. Of such great cataclysms there have already been four. (The first occurred when what is now the North Pole was separated from the later Continents - *foot-note - SD 2, p. 138*). And we may expect a fifth for ourselves in due course of time. **SD 2, p. 138**

5. They (the lunar pitris/fathers/gods - Ed.) threw off their "shadows" or astral bodies - if such an ethereal being as a "lunar Spirit" may be supposed to rejoice in an astral, besides a hardly tangible body. In another Commentary it is said that the "Ancestors" *breathed* out the first man, as Brahma (*i.e.* Brahma the Creator) is explained to have breathed out the *Suras* (Gods), when they became *Asuras* (from *Asu, breath*). In a third

(Commentary) it is said that they, the newly-created men, "were the shadows of the Shadows." **SD 2, pp. 86 - 87**

6. Now Kandu (in Hindu mythology a sage and Yogi eminent in holy wisdom and pious austerities - Ed.) stands ... for the *First Race.* He is a son of the Pitris, hence one *devoid of mind,* which is hinted at by his being unable to discern a period of nearly one thousand years from one day; therefore he is shown to be so easily deluded and blinded. Here is a variant of the allegory in *Genesis* of Adam, born an image of clay, into which the "Lord-god" breathes the *breath of life* but not of intellect and discrimination, which are developed only after he had tasted of the fruit of the Tree of Knowledge; in other words when he has acquired the first development of Mind, and had implanted in him, *Manas,*whose terrestrial aspect is of the Earth earthy, though its highest faculties connect it with Spirit and the *divine soul.* Pamlocha (the nymph in Hindu mythology who seduces the sage, Kandu) is the Hindu Lilith of the Aryan Adam; and Marisha, the daughter born of the perspiration from her pores, is the "sweat-born," and stands as a symbol for the Second Race of Mankind. **SD 2, p. 175**

7. (a) The old (primitive) Race merged in the second race, and became one with it.

(b) This is the mysterious process of transformation and evolution of mankind. The material of the first forms - shadowy, ethereal, and negative - was drawn or absorbed into, and thus became the complement of the forms of the Second Race.

The *Commentary* (part of the archives of the Himalayan Brotherhood - Ed.) explains this by saying that, as the First Race was simply composed of the astral shadows of the creative progenitors (the lunar pitris - Ed.), having of course neither astral nor physical bodies of their own - this Race *never died*. Its "men" melted gradually away, becoming absorbed in the bodies of their own "sweat-born" progeny, more solid than their own. The old form vanished and was absorbed by, disappeared in, the new form, more human and physical. There was no death in those days of a period more blissful than the Golden Age; but the first, or parent material was used for the formation of the new being, to form the body and even the inner or *lower* principles or bodies of their progeny.

(c) When the shadow retires, *i.e.* when the astral body becomes covered with more solid flesh, man develops a physical body. The "wing," or the ethereal form that produced its shadow and image, became the shadow of the astral body and its own progeny. The expression is queer but original. *SD 2, p. 121*

8. ... it is as well to point out ... the dual meaning contained in the Greek myth bearing upon this particular phase of evolution (the development of the Second and Third Root Races - Ed). It is found in the several variants of the allegory of Leda and her sons Castor and Pollux, which variants have a special meaning. Thus in Book XI, of the *Odyssey*, Leda is spoken of as the spouse of Tyndarus, who gave birth by her husband "to two sons of valiant heart" - Castor and Pollux. Jupiter endows them with a marvelous gift and privilege. They are semi-immortal ; they live and die, each in turn, and every alternate day. ... in the allegory where Zeus is shown as the father of the two heroes - born from the egg to which Leda gives birth - the myth is entirely theogonical. It relates to that group of cosmic allegories in which the world is described as born from an egg. For Leda assumes in it the shape of a white swan when uniting herself to the Divine Swan.

Leda is the mystical bird, then, to which, in the traditions of various people of the Aryan race, are attributed various ornithological forms of birds which all lay golden eggs.... But the variant of the Leda allegory which has a direct reference to mystic man is found in Pinda, only with a slight reference to it in the Homeric hymns. Castor and Pollux ... become the highly significant symbol of the Third Race, and its transformation from the animal man into a god-man with only an animal body. *SD 2, pp. 121 - 122*

9. What will be most contested by scientific authorities is this a-sexual Race, the Second, the fathers of the "Sweat-born" so-called, and perhaps still more the Third Race, the "Egg-born" androgynes. These two modes of procreation are the most difficult to comprehend especially for the Western mind. It is evident that no explanation can be attempted for those who are not students of Occult metaphysics. European language has no words to express things which Nature repeats no more at this stage of evolution, things which therefore can have no meaning for the materialist. But there are analogies.

It is not denied that in the beginning of physical evolution there must have been processes in nature, spontaneous generation, for instance, now extinct, which are repeated in other forms. Thus we are told that microscopic research shows no permanence of any particular mode of reproducing life. For "it shows that the same organism may run through various metamorphoses in the course of its life-cycle, during some of which it may be *sexual*, and in others *a-sexual; i.e.,* it may reproduce itself alternately by the co-operation of two beings of opposite sex, and also by fissure or *budding* from one being only, which is of no sex."

"Budding" is the very word used in the Stanza. How could these Chhayas reproduce themselves otherwise; viz., procreate the Second Race, since they were ethereal, a-sexual, and even devoid, as yet, of the vehicle of desire, or Kama Rupa, which evolved only in the Third Race? They evolved the Second Race unconsciously, as do some plants. Or perhaps, as *Amoeba*, only on a more ethereal, impressive, and larger scale. If, indeed, the cell-theory applies equally to Botany and Zoology, and extends to Morphology, as well as to the Physiology of organisms, and if the microscopic cells are looked upon by physical science as independent living beings - just as Occultism regards the "fiery lives" - there is no difficulty in the conception of the primitive process of procreation.

Consider the first stages of the development of a germ-cell. Its *nucleus* grows, changes, and forms a double cone or spindle, thus ... *within* the cell. This spindle approaches the surface of the cell, and one half of it is *extended* in the form of what are called the *"polar cells."* These polar cells *now* die, and the embryo develops from the growth and segmentation of the remaining part of the nucleus which is *nourished* by the substance of the cell. Then why could not beings have lived thus, and been created in *this* way - at the very beginning of *human and mammalian evolution*?

This may serve as an analogy to give some idea of the process by which the Second Race was formed from the First.

The astral form clothing the monad was surrounded, as it still is, by its egg-shaped sphere of *aura*, which here corresponds to the substance of the germ-cell or *ovum*. The astral form itself is the nucleus, now, as then, instinct with the principle of life.

When the season of reproduction arrives, the *sub-astral "extrudes"* a miniature of itself from the egg of surrounding area. This germ grows and feeds on the aura till it becomes fully developed, when it gradually separates from its parent, carrying with it its own sphere of aura; just as we see living cells reproducing their like by growth and subsequent division into two.

The analogy with the *"polar cells"* would seem to hold good, since their death would *now* correspond to the change introduced by the separation of the sexes, when gestation *in utero, i.e., within the cell,* became the rule.

"The early Second (Root) *Race were the Fathers of the 'Sweat -born'; the later Second* (Root) *Race were 'Sweat-born' themselves."*

This passage from the Commentary refers to the work of evolution from the beginning of a Race to its close. The "Sons of Yoga," or the primitive astral race (ethereal race - Ed.), had seven stages of evolution *racially,* or collectively; as every individual Being in it had, and has now. It is not Shakespeare only who divided the ages of man into a series of seven, but Nature itself.

Thus the first sub-races of the Second Race were born at first by the process described in the law of analogy; while the last began gradually, *pari passu* with the evolution of the human body, to be formed otherwise. The process of reproduction had seven stages also in each (Root) Race, each covering aeons of time. What physiologist or biologist could tell whether the present mode of generation, with all its phases of gestation, is older than half a million, or at most one million of years, since their cycle of observation began hardly half a century ago. *SD 2, pp. 116 - 118*

10. ... the "Egg-born," *Third* Race; the first half of which is mortal, i.e., unconscious in its personality; and having nothing within itself to survive; and the latter half of which becomes immortal in its individuality, by reason of its fifth principle (mind - Ed.) being called to life by the *informing gods* (the solar angels - Ed.) and thus connecting the Monad with this Earth. This is Pollux; while Castor represents the *personal,* mortal man, an animal of not even a superior kind when unlinked from the divine individuality. "Twins," truly; yet divorced by death, unless Pollux moved by the voice of twinship, bestows on his less favoured mortal brother, a share of his own divine nature, thus associating him with his own immortality. *SD 2, pp. 122 - 123*

11. The text of the Stanza (*Stanza VI, v. 22*) implies that the human embryo was furnished *ab extra* by Cosmic forces, and the "Father-Mother" furnished apparently the germ that ripened: in all probability a "sweat-born egg," to be hatched out, in some mysterious way, disconnected from the "double" parent. It is comparatively easy to conceive of an oviparous humanity, since even now man is, in one sense, "egg-born." *SD 2, p. 131*

12. The early Third Race, then, is formed from drops of "sweat," which, after many a transformation, grow into human bodies. This is not more difficult to imagine or realise than the growth of the foetus from an imperceptible germ which foetus develops into a child, and then into a strong, heavy man. But this race again changes its mode of procreation according to the Commentaries.

It is said to have emanated a *vis formativa*, which changed the drops of perspiration into greater drops, which grew, expanded, and became ovoid bodies - huge eggs. In these the human foetus gestated for several years. In the Puranas, Marisha, the daughter of Kandu, the sage, becomes the wife of the *Prachetasa* and the mother of Daksha. Now Daksha is the father of the first *human-like* progenitors, having been born in this way. He is mentioned later on. The evolution of man, the microcosm, is analogous to that of the Universe, the macrocosm. His evolution stands between that of the latter and that of the animal, for which man, in his turn, is a macrocosm.

Then the race becomes androgyne, or hermaphrodite. This process of men-bearing explains, perhaps, why Aristophanes describes the nature of the old race as *androgynous* .... **SD 2, p. 177**

13. What say the old sages, the philosopher teachers of antiquity? Aristophanes speaks thus on the subject in Plato's *"Banquet "*: "our nature of old was not the same as it is now. It was *androynous*, the form and name partaking of, and being common to both the male and female.... Their bodies were round, and the manner of their running circular. They were terrible in force and strength and had prodigious ambition. Hence Zeus *divided each of them into two,* making them weaker; Apollo under his direction, closed up the skin." **SD 2, pp. 133 - 134**

14. Thus the pristine bi-sexual unity of the human *Third* Root race is an axiom in the Secret Doctrine. Its virgin individuals were raised to "Gods," because the Race represented their "divine Dynasty." The moderns are satisfied with worshipping the male heroes of the

Fourth Race, who created gods after their own sexual image, whereas the gods of primeval mankind were "male and female." **SD 2, p. 135**

15. It is of course impossible to attempt, within the compass of even several volumes, a consecutive and detailed account of the evolution and progress of the first three races - except so far as to give a general view of it.... Race the first had no history of its own. Of race the second the same may be said. We shall have, therefore, to pay careful attention only to the Lemurians and the Atlanteans before the history of our own race (the Fifth) can be attempted. **SD 2, p. 264**

16. The ape is sacred in India because its origin is well known to the Initiates, though concealed under a thick veil of allegory. Hanuman is the son of Pavana (Vayu, "the god of the wind") by Anjana, a monster called Kesari, though his geneology varies. The reader who bears this in mind will find in Book II ... the whole explanation of this ingenious allegory. The "Men" of the third Race, who separated were "gods" by their spirituality and purity, though senseless and as yet destitute of mind, as men.

These "Men" of the Third Race - the ancestors of the Atlanteans - were just such ape-like, intellectually senseless giants as were those beings, who during the Third Round, represented Humanity. Morally irresponsible, it was these third Race "men" who, through promiscuous connection with animal species lower than themselves, created that missing link which became ages later (in the tertiary period only) the remote ancestor of the real ape as we find it now in the pithecoid family.

Thus the earlier teachings, however unsatisfactory, vague and fragmentary, did not teach the evolution of "man" from the "ape." Nor does the author of "Esoteric Buddhism" (A.P. Sinnett) assert it anywhere in his work in so many words; but, owing to his inclination towards science, he used language, which might perhaps justify such an inference. The man, who preceded the Fourth, the Atlantean race, however much he may have looked physically like a "gigantic ape" - "the counterfeit of man who hath not the like of a man" - was still a thinking and already a speaking man. The "Lemuro-Atlantean" was a highly civilized race, and if one accepts tradition, which is better history than speculative fiction which now passes under that name, he was higher than we are with all our sciences and the degraded civilization of the day: at any rate, the Lemuro-Atlantean of the closing Third race was so. *SD 1, pp. 190 - 191*

17. As stated in Book 1, the humanities developed coordinately, and on parallel lines with the four Elements, every new Race being physiologically adapted to meet the additional element. Our Fifth Race is rapidly approaching the Fifth Element - call it interstellar ether, if you will - which has more to do, however, with psychology than with physics. We men have learned to live in every climate, whether frigid or tropical, but the first two races had naught to do with climate, nor were they subservient to any temperature or change therein. And thus, we are taught, men lived down to the close of the Third Root-Race, when eternal spring reigned over the whole globe.... *SD 2, p. 135*

18. It was the Atlanteans, the first progeny of *semi-divine* man after his separation into sexes - hence the first-begotten and humanly-born mortals - who became the first "Sacrificers" to the *god of matter*. They stand in the far-way distant past, in ages more than pre-historic, as the prototype on which the great symbol of Cain was built, as the first anthropomorphist who worshipped form and matter. That worship regenerated very soon into "self-worship", thence led to phallicism, or that which reigns supreme to this day in the symbolism of every exotic religion of ritual, dogma, and form. *SD 2, 273*

19. History does not begin with it (the fifth root race - Ed.), but living and ever-recurring tradition does. History - or what is called history - does not go further back than the fantastic origins of our fifth sub-race, a "few thousands" of years. It is the sub-divisions of this first sub-race of the Fifth Root-Race which are referred to in the sentence, "Some yellow, some brown and black, and some red, remained." The "moon coloured" (*i.e.*, the First and the Second Races) were gone for ever - ay, without leaving any traces whatever; and that, so far back as the third "Deluge" of the Third Lemurian race, that "Great Dragon," whose tail sweeps whole nations out of existence in the twinkling of an eye. And this is the true meaning of the Verse in the COMMENTARY which says:

"The GREAT DRAGON *has respect but for the* 'SERPENTS' *of* WISDOM, the Serpents whose holes are now under the triangular stones." *i.e.,* "the Pyramids, at the four corners of the world."

This tells us ... that which is mentioned elsewhere in the Commentaries; namely that the Adepts or "Wise" men of the three Races (the Third, Fourth and the Fifth) dwelt in subterranean habitats, generally under some kind of pyramidal structure, if not actually under a pyramid. For such "pyramids" existed in the four corners of the world, and were never the monopoly of the land of the Pharoahs, though until found scattered all over the two Americas, under and over ground, beneath and amidst virgin forests, as in plain and vale, they were supposed to be the exclusive property of Egypt. *SD 2, p. 351*

ROUNDS, GLOBES AND CHAINS

1. a. Everything in the metaphysical as in the physical Universe is septenary. Hence every sidereal body, every planet, whether visible or invisible is credited with six companion globes. The evolution of life proceeds on these seven globes or bodies from the 1st to the 7th in Seven Rounds or Seven Cycles.

b. These globes are formed by a process which the Occultists call the "rebirth of planetary chains (or rings). When the seventh and last Round of one of such rings has been entered upon, the highest or first globe "A," followed by all the others down to the last, instead of entering upon a certain time of rest - or "obscuration," as in their previous Rounds - begins to die out. The "planetary" dissolution (*pralaya*) is at hand, and its hour has struck; each globe has to transfer its life and energy to another planet.

c. Our Earth, as the visible representative of its invisible superior fellow globes (called the Earth chain - Ed.), its "lords," or "principles" has to live, as others, through seven Rounds. During the first three, it forms and consolidates; during the fourth (the Earth is currently about half-way through the fourth Round - Ed.) it settles and hardens; during the last three it gradually returns to its first ethereal form; it is spiritualised, so to say.

d. Its Humanity develops fully only in the Fourth - our present Round. Up to the fourth Life Cycle, it is referred to as "humanity" only for lack of a more appropriate term. Like the grub which becomes chrysalis and butterfly, Man, or rather that which becomes man, passes through all the forms and kingdoms during the first Round and through all the human shapes during the two following Rounds. Arrived on our Earth at the commencement of the Fourth in the present series of life-cycles and races, MAN is the first form that appears thereon, being preceded only by the mineral and vegetable kingdoms - even the latter *having to develop and continue its further evolution through man....* During the three Rounds to come, Humanity, like the globe on which it lives, will be ever tending to reassume its primeval form, that of a Dhyan Chohanic Host (consisting of very advanced god-like Intelligences - Ed.). Man tends to become a God and then - GOD, like every atom in the Universe

"Beginning so early as with the 2nd round, Evolution proceeds already on quite a different plan. It is only during the 1st round that (heavenly) man becomes a human being on globe A, (rebecomes) a mineral, a plant, an animal on globe B and C, etc. The process changes entirely from the second round; but you have learned prudence ... and I advise you *to say nothing before the time for saying it has come....*" (Extract from the Teacher's letters on various topics.)

e. Every life-cycle on Globe D (our Earth) is composed of seven root races. They commence with the Ethereal and end with the spiritual on the double line of physical and moral evolution - from the beginning of the terrestrial round to its close. (One is a "planetary round" from Globe A to Globe G, the seventh; the other is the "globe round" or the *terrestrial* - pertaining just to our globe, the Earth, which is the fourth in the Earth planetary chain of 7 globes, and the only visible globe of the chain. - Ed.).

f. The first root-race, *i.e.,* the first "men" on earth (irrespective of form) were the progeny of the "celestial men," called rightly in Indian philosophy, the "Lunar Ancestors" or the Pitris of which there are seven classes or Hierarchies. *SD 1, pp. 158 - 160*

2. From the doctrine (of the Rounds, and Globes - Ed.) - rather incomprehensible to western minds - which deals with the periodical "obscurations" (pralayas - Ed.) and successive "Rounds" of the Globes along their circular chains, were born the first perplexities and misconceptions. One of such has reference to the *"Fifth-"* and even *"Sixth*-Rounders." Those who knew that a Round was preceded and followed by a long *Pralaya,* a pause for rest which created an impassable gulf between the two Rounds until the time came for a renewed cycle of life, could not understand the "fallacy" of talking about *"fifth* and *sixth*-Rounders" in our *Fourth* Round. Gautama Buddha, it was held, was a Sixth-Rounder, Plato and some other great philosophers and minds, "Fifth Rounders." How could it be?

One Master taught and affirmed that there were such "Fifth-Rounders" even now on our Earth; and though *understood to say* that mankind was yet "in the Fourth Round," in another place he *seemed* to say that we were in the Fifth. To this an "apocalyptic answer" was returned by another Teacher; - "A few drops of rain do not make a Monsoon, though they presage it," ... "No, we are not in the Fifth Round but Fifth Round men have been coming in for the last few thousand years."

This was worse than the riddle of the Sphinx! Students of occultism subjected their brains to the wildest work of speculation. For a considerable time they tried to outvie Oedipus and reconcile the two statements. And as the Masters (Koot Hoomi and Morya - Ed.) kept as silent as the stony Sphinx herself, they were accused of inconsistency, "contradiction," and "discrepancies." But they were simply allowing the speculations to go on, in order *to teach a lesson* which the Western mind sorely needs. In their conceit and arrogance, as in their habit of materializing every metaphysical conception and term without allowing any margin for Eastern metaphor and allegory, the Orientalists have made a jumble of the Hindu exoteric philosophy and the Theosophists were now doing the same with regard to esoteric teachings. To this day it is evident that the latter have utterly failed to understand the meaning of the term "Fifth and Sixth Rounders."

But it is simply this: every "Round" brings about a new development and even an entire change in the mental, psychic, spiritual and physical constitution of man, all these principles evoluting on an ever ascending scale. Thence it follows that those persons who, like Confucius and Plato, belonged psychically, mentally, and spiritually to the higher planes of evolution, were in our Fourth Round as the average man will be in the Fifth Round, whose mankind is destined to find itself, on this scale of Evolution, immensely higher than is our present humanity. Similarly Gautama Buddha - Wisdom incarnate - was still higher and greater than all the men we have mentioned, who are called Fifth Rounders, while Buddha and Sankaracharya are termed Sixth Rounders, allegorically. Thence again the concealed wisdom of the remark, pronounced at the time "evasive" - that "a few drops of rain do not make the Monsoon, *though they presage it.*" ***SD pp. 161 - 162***

3. "Our Globe, as taught from the first, is at the bottom of the arc of descent, where the matter of our perceptions exhibits itself in its grossest form .... Hence it only stands to reason that the globes which overshadow our Earth (the 6 companion globes part of the Earth planetary chain - Ed.) must be on different and superior planes. In short, as Globes, they are in CO-ADUNITION but not IN CONSUBSTANTIALITY WITH OUR EARTH and thus pertain to quite another state of consciousness. Our planet (like all those we see) is adapted to the peculiar state of its human stock, that state which enables us to see with our naked eye the sidereal bodies which are co-essential with our terrene plane and substances, just as their respective inhabitants, the Jovians, Martians and others can perceive our little world; because our planes of consciousness, differing as they do in degree but being the same in kind, are on the same layer of differentiated matter...." (Comments by the Master Koot-Hoomi in answer to some objections - Ed.) ***SD 1, p. 166***

4. For, as will repeatedly be shown, it (our Earth - Ed.) is the fourth Sphere (of the seven globes of the Earth's Planetary Chain - Ed.) on the ... lowest plane of material life. And it so happens that we are in the Fourth Round, at the middle point of which the perfect equilibrium between Spirit and Matter had to take place. *SD 1, p. 192*

5. To present further misconceptions, some further details may be offered which will also throw light on the history of humanity on our own chain (the Planetary Chain of the Earth - Ed) the progeny of that of the Moon....

Now, it must be remembered that the monads cycling round any septenary chain are divided into seven classes or hierarchies according to their respective stages of evolution, consciousness, and merit. Let us follow, then, the order of their appearance on planet A, in the first Round. The time spaces between the appearances of these hierarchies on any one Globe are so adjusted that when Class 7, the last, appears on Globe A, Class 1, the first, has passed on to Globe B, and so on, step by step, all round the chain.

Again, in the seventh Round on the Lunar chain (the Moon Planetary Chain - Ed.), when Class 7, the last quit Globe A (on the Moon chain), that Globe instead of falling asleep, as it had done in previous Rounds, begins to die (to go into its planetary pralaya), and in dying it transfers successively ... its "principles," or life-elements and energy, etc., one after the other to a new "laya-centre," which commences the formation of Globe A of the Earth Chain.

A similar process takes place for each of the Globes of the "lunar chain" one after the other, each forming a fresh Globe of the "earth-chain." Our Moon was the fourth Globe of the series and was on the same plane of perception as our Earth. But Globe A of the lunar chain is not fully "dead" till the first Monads of the first class have passed from Globe G, the last of the "lunar-chain," into the Nirvana which awaits them between the two chains; and similarly for all the other Globes as stated, each giving birth to the corresponding globe of the "earth-chain."

Further, when Globe A of the new chain is ready, the first class of Hierarchy of Monads from the Lunar chain incarnate upon it in the lowest kingdom, and so on successively. The result of this is, that it is only the first class of Monads which attain the human state of development during the first Round, since the second class, on each planet, arriving later, has not time to reach that stage. Thus the Monads of Class 2 reach the incipient human stage only in the Second Round, and so on up to the middle of the Fourth Round in which the human stage will be fully developed - the "Door" into the human kingdom closes; and henceforward the number of "human" Monads, i.e., Monads of the human stage of development, is complete. For the Monads which had not reached the human stage by this point, will, owing to the evolution of humanity itself, find themselves so far behind that they will reach the

human stage only at the close of the seventh and last Round. They will, therefore, not be men on this chain, but will form the humanity of a future Manvantara and be rewarded by becoming "Men" on a higher chain altogether, thus receiving their karmic compensation....
SD 1, pp. 171 - 173

THE SACRED SEVENFOLD PRINCIPLE

1. Even the teaching about the Septenary constitution of the sidereal bodies and of the macrocosm - from which the septenary division of the microcosm, or Man - has until now been among the most esoteric. In olden times it used to be divulged only at the Initiation and along with the most sacred figures of the cycles. *SD 1, p. 168*

2. Number Seven, the fundamental figure among all other figures in every national religious system, from Cosmogony down to man, must have its *raison d'etre*. It is found among the ancient Americans, as prominently as among the archaic Aryans and Egyptians. ... Says the author (Augustus Le Plogean) of the *"Sacred Mysteries among the Mayas and Quiches, 11,500 years ago"* : -

"Seven seems to have been the sacred number *par excellence* among all civilized nations of antiquity. Why? Each separate people has given a different explanation, according to the peculiar tenets of their *(exoteric)* religion. That it was the *number of numbers for those initiated into the sacred mysteries, there can be no doubt.* Pythagoras ... calls it the 'Vehicle of Life' containing body and soul, since it is formed of a Quaternary, that is Wisdom and intellect, and of a *Trinity or action* and *matter*. The Emperor Julian, *'In matrem, etc.,'* expresses himself thus: 'Were I to touch upon the initiation into our Sacred Mysteries, which the

Chaldees Bacchized, respecting the *seven-rayed* god, lighting up the soul through him, I should say things unknown to the rabble, very unknown, but well known to the blessed Theurgists.'" (p. 141).

And who acquainted with the Puranas, the Book of the Dead, the Zendavesta, the Assyrian tiles, and finally the Bible, and who has observed the constant occurrence of the number seven, in these records of people, living from the remotest times unconnected and so far apart, can regard as a coincidence the following fact, given by the same explorer of ancient Mysteries? Speaking of the prevalence of seven as a mystic number, among the inhabitants of the "Western continent" (of America), he adds that it not less remarkable. For : -

"It frequently occurs in the *Popul-vuh* (the creation story of the Maya - Ed.) ... we find it besides in the *seven families* said by Sahagun and Clavigero to have accompanied the mystical personage named *Votan*, the reputed founder of the great city of Nachan, identified by some with Palenque. In the *seven caves* from which the ancestors of the Nahuatl are reported to have emerged.... In the seven *Antilles*; in the *seven heroes* who, we are told, escaped the Deluge...."

"Heroes," moreover whose number is found the same in every "Deluge" story - from the seven Rishis who were saved with Vaivasvata Manu, down to Noah's ark, unto which beasts, fowls, and living creatures were taken by "Sevens." Thus we see the figures 1, 3, 5, 7, as perfect, because thoroughly mystic, numbers playing a prominent part in every Cosmogony and evolution of living Beings. In China, 1, 3, 5, 7, are called "celestial numbers," in the canonical *"Book of Changes." SD 2, pp. 34 - 35*

3. Whether we count the principles in Kosmos and man as seven or only as four, the forces of, and in physical Nature are Seven; and it is stated (by Subba Row - Ed.) that *"Pragna,* or the capacity of perception, exists in seven different aspects corresponding to the seven conditions of matter." For "just as a human being is composed of seven principles, differentiated matter in the Solar System exists in seven different conditions." *SD 1, p. 139*

4. Thus the philosophy of psychic, spiritual and mental relations with man's physical functions is in almost inextricable confusion. Neither the old Aryan, nor the Egyptian psychology are now properly understood. Nor can they be assimilated without accepting the esoteric septenary, or, at any rate, the Vedantic quinquepartite division of the human inner principles. Failing which, it will be for ever impossible to understand the metaphysical and purely psychic and even physiological relations between the Dhyan-Chohans, or Angels, on the one plane, and humanity on the other. No Eastern (Aryan) esoteric works are so far published, but we possess the Egyptian papyri which speak clearly of the seven principles or the "Seven Souls of Man." The Book of the Dead gives a complete list of the "transformations" that every defunct undergoes, while divesting one by one, of all those principles - materialised for the sake of clearness into ethereal entities or bodies. *SD 1, pp. 226 - 227*

5. Through Hippolytus, an early Church father, we learn what Marcus - a Pythagorean rather than a Christian Gnostic, and a Kabalist most certainly - had received in mystic revelation. It is said that "Marcus had it revealed unto him that 'the *seven heavens*' (foot-note: the heavens are identical with "Angels").... sounded each one vowel, which, all combined together formed a complete doxology" ; in clearer words:"the *Sound* whereof being carried down (from these seven heavens) to earth, became the creator and parent of all things that be on earth." (See Hippolytus and King's *Gnostics*.) Translated from the Occult phraseology into still plainer language this would read: "The Sevenfold Logos having differentiated into seven *Logoi,* or creative potencies these (the second logos, or "Sound") created all on earth."

Assuredly one who is acquainted with Gnostic literature can hardly help seeing in St. John's "Apocalypse", a work of the same school of thought. For we find John saying (Chap. x. 3, 4), "Seven thunders uttered their voices ... and I was about to write ... (but) I heard a voice from heaven saying unto me, 'Seal up those things which the seven thunders uttered, and write them not.'" The same injunction is given to Marcus, the same to all other *semi* and *full* Initiates. Yet the sameness of equivalent expressions used, and of the underlying ideas always betrays a portion of the mysteries.

We must always seek for more than one meaning in every mystery allegorically revealed, especially in those in which the number seven and its multiplication seven by seven, or forty-nine, appear. Now when the Rabbi Jesus is requested (in *Pistis Sophia)* by his disciples to reveal to them, "the mysteries of the Light of thy (his) Father," (*i.e.,* of the higher Self enlightened by Initiation and Divine Knowledge), Jesus answers: "Do ye seek after these mysteries? No mystery is more excellent than they which shall bring your souls unto the Light of Lights, unto the place of truth and Goodness, unto the place where, there is neither male nor female, neither form in that place but Light, everlasting not to be uttered. Nothing therefore is more excellent than the mysteries which ye seek after *saving only THE MYSTERY of the seven vowels and their* FORTY AND NINE POWERS and their numbers thereof; and no name is more excellent *than all these vowels.*" "The Seven fathers and the Forty-nine Sons blaze in DARKNESS, but they are the LIFE and LIGHT and the continuation thereof through the Great Age"- says the Commentary speaking of the "Fires." *SD 2, pp. 563 - 564*

SAKTI - THE FORCES OF NATURE

It may be interesting ... to remind the reader of what Mr. Subba Row said of the Forces mystically defined. See *"Five Years of Theosophy"* and "The Twelve Signs of the Zodiac." Thus he says:

"Kanya (the sixth sign of the Zodiac, or *Virgo*) means a Virgin, and represents *Sakti* or *Mahamaya* (the "Great Illusion" - Ed.). The sign ... is the 6th *Rasi* or division and indicated that there are six primary forces in Nature (synthesized by the Seventh)." ... These Sakti stand as follows:

(1.) Parasakti. Literally the great or Supreme Force or power. It means and includes the powers of *light and heat.*

(2.) Jnanasakti.... The power of intellect, of real Wisdom or Knowledge. It has two aspects:

The following are *some* of its manifestations *when placed under the influences or control of material conditions.* (a) The power of the mind in interpreting our sensations. (b) Its power in recalling past ideas (memory) and raising future expectation. (c) Its power as exhibited in what are called by modern psychologists "the laws of association," which enables it to form persisting connections between various groups of sensations and possibilities of sensations, and thus generate the notion or idea of an external object. (d)

Its power in connecting our ideas together by the mysterious link of memory, and thus generating the notion of self or individuality; *some* of its manifestations when liberated *from the bonds of matter* are - (a) Clairvoyance, (b) Psychometry.

(3.) Itchasakti - the *power of the Will*. Its most ordinary manifestation is the generation of certain nerve currents which set in motion such muscles as required for the accomplishment of the desired object.

(4.) Kriyasakti. The mysterious power of thought which enables it to produce external, perceptible, phenomenal results by its own inherent energy. The ancients held that *any idea will manifest itself externally if one's attention is deeply concentrated upon it*. Similarly, *an intense volition will be followed by the desired result.*

A Yogi generally performs his wonders by means of Itchasakti and Kriyasakti.

(5) Kundalini Sakti. The power or Force which moves in a curved path. It is the Universal life-Principle manifesting everywhere in nature. This force includes the two great forces of attraction and repulsion. Electricity and magnetism are but manifestations of it. This is the power which brings about that "continuous adjustment of *internal relations to external relations*" which is the essence of life according to Herbert Spencer, and that "*continuous adjustment of external relations to internal relations*" which is the basis of ... *punar jaman* (re-birth) in the doctrines of the ancient Hindu philosophers. A Yogi must thoroughly

subjugate this power before he can attain Moksham (liberation - Ed.)....

(6) Mantra-Sakti. The force or power of letters, speech or music. The *Mantra Shastra* (Brahmanical writings on esoteric science of incantations) has for its subject-matter this force in all its manifestations.... The influence of melody is one of its ordinary manifestations. The power of the ineffable name is the crown of this Sakti.

Modern Science has but partly investigated the first, second and fifth of the forces above named, but is altogether in the dark as regards the remaining powers. The six forces are in their unity represented by the "*Daiviprakriti*" (the Seventh, the light of the LOGOS).

The above is quoted to show the real Hindu ideas on the same. It is all esoteric, though not covering the tenth part of *what might be said*. For one, the six names of the Six Forces mentioned are those of *the six Hierarchies* of Dhyan Chohans synthesized by their *Primary*, the seventh ... the "Mother" in its mystical Sense. The enumeration alone of the *yogi* Powers would require ten volumes. Each of these Forces has a *living Conscious Entity* at its head, of which entity it is an emanation. ***SD 1, pp. 292 - 293***

SCIENCE AND SCIENTISTS

1. Science is, undeniably, ultra-materialistic in our days; but it finds, in one sense, its justification. Nature, behaving *in actu* ever esoterically, and being, as the Kabalists say, *in abscondite*, can only be judged by the profane, through her appearance, and that appearance is always deceitful on the physical plane.

On the other hand, the naturalists refuse to blend physics with metaphysics, the body with its informing soul and spirit, which they prefer ignoring. This is a matter of choice with some, while the minority strive very sensibly to enlarge the domain of physical science by trespassing on the forbidden grounds of metaphysics, so distasteful to some materialists. These scientists are wise in their generation. For all their wonderful discoveries would go for nothing, and remain for ever headless bodies, unless they lift the veil of matter and strain their eyes to see *beyond*. Now that they have studied nature in the length, breadth, and thickness of her physical frame, it is time to remove the skeleton to the second plane and search within the unknown depths for the living and real entity, for its sub-stance - the noumenon of evanescent matter. **SD 1, p. 610**

2. The exact extent, depth, breadth, and length of the mysteries of nature are to be found only in Eastern esoteric sciences. So vast and so profound are these that hardly a few, a very few of the highest

Initiates - those *whose very existence is known but to a small number of Adepts* - are capable of assimilating the knowledge. Yet, it is all there, and one by one facts and processes in nature's workshops are permitted to find their way into the exact Sciences, while mysterious help is given to rare individuals in unravelling its arcana. It is at the close of great Cycles, in connection with racial development, that such events generally take place. We are at the very close of the cycle of 5,000 years of the present Aryan Kaliyuga; and between this time and 1897 (written in 1888) there will be a large rent made in the Veil of nature, and materialistic science will receive a death blow. *SD 1, pp. 611 - 612*

3. Whatever ignorance, pride or fanatacism may suggest to the contrary, Esoteric Cosmology can be shown inseparably connected with both philosophy and modern science. The gods of the ancients, the monads - from Pythagoras down to Leibnitz - and the atoms of the present materialistic schools (as borrowed by them from the theories of the old Greek Atomists) are only a compound unit, or a graduated unity like the human frame, which begins with body and ends with spirit. In the occult sciences they can be studied separately, but never mastered unless viewed in their mutual correlations during their life-cycle, and as a Universal Unity during *Pralayas. SD 1, p. 613*

4. To make of Science an integral *whole* necessitates, indeed, the study of spiritual and psychic, as well as physical Nature. Otherwise it will ever be like the anatomy of man, discussed of old by the profane from the point of view of his shell-side and in ignorance of the interior work. Even Plato, the greatest philosopher of his country, became guilty, before his initiation, of such statements as that liquids pass into the stomach through the lungs. Without metaphysics as Mr. H.J. Slack says, *real* science is inadmissable. *SD 1, p. 588*

5. The duty of the Occultist lies with the *Soul and Spirit* of Cosmic Space, not merely with its illusive appearance and behaviour. That of official physical science is to analyze and study its *shell* - the *Ultima Thule* - of the Universe and man, in the opinion of Materialism.

With the latter, Occultism has naught to do. It is only with the theories of such men of learning as Kepler, Kant, Oersted, and Sir W. Herschell, who believed in a Spiritual world, that Occult Cosmogony might treat, and attempt a satisfactory compromise. But the views of those scientists differed vastly from the latest modern speculations. Kant and Herschell had in their mind's eye speculations upon the origin and *the final destiny,* as well as the present aspect of the Universe, from a far more philosophical and psychic standpoint; whereas modern Cosmology and Astronomy now repudiate anything like research into the mysteries of being. The result is what might be expected: complete failure and inextricable contradictions in the thousand and one varieties of so-called scientific theories and in this theory as in all others. *SD 1, p. 589*

6. That matter - the real primordial substance, the noumenon of all the "matter" we know of - even some of the astronomers have been led to believe in, and to despair of the possibility of ever accounting for rotation, gravitation, and the origin of any mechanical, physical laws - unless ... *Intelligences* (Dhyan-Chohans - Ed.) be admitted by Science. In the ... work upon astronomy by Wolf (*i.e., Les Hypotheses Cosmogoniques*) the author endorses fully the theory of Kant, and the latter, if not in its general aspect, at any rate in some of its features, reminds one strongly of certain esoteric teachings. Here we have the world's system *reborn from its ashes*, through a nebula; the emanation from the bodies dead and dissolved in Space - resultant of the *incandescence* of the solar centre reanimated by the combustible matter of the planets.

In this theory, generated and developed in the brain of a young man barely twenty-five years of age, who had never left his native place, a small town of Northern Prussia (Konigsburg) one can hardly fail to recognise whether an inspiring external power, or the *reincarnation* which the occultists see in it.

It fills a gap which Newton, with all his genius, failed to bridge. And surely it is our primeval matter, Akasha, that Kant had in view, when proposing to solve Newton's difficulty and his failure to explain, by the natural forces, the primitive impulse imparted to the planets, by the postulation of a universally pervading primordial substance. For, as he remarks ... if it is at once admitted that the perfect harmony of the stars and planets and the coincidence of their orbital planets prove the existence of a natural cause, which would thus be the primal cause, "that cause *cannot really be the matter which fills today the heavenly spaces.*" It must be that which filled space - was space - originally....

In other words, it is that same matter of which are now composed the planets, comets, and the Sun himself, which, having in the origin formed itself into those bodies, has preserved its inherent quality of motion; which quality, now centred in their nuclei, directs all motion. A very slight alteration of words is needed, and a few additions, to make of this our Esoteric Doctrine.

The latter teaches that it is this original, primordial *prima materia*, divine and intelligent, the direct emanation of the Universal Mind - the *Daiviprakriti* (the divine light emanating from the *Logos*) - which formed the nuclei of all the "self-moving" orbs in Kosmos. It is the informing, ever-present moving power and life-principle, the vital soul of the suns, moons, planets, and even of our Earth. The former latent: the last one active - the invisible Ruler and guide of the gross body attached to, and connected with its Soul which is the spiritual emanation, after all, of these respective planetary Spirits.

.... From this Kantian mind and soul of Suns and Stars to the MAHAT (mind) and Prakriti (matter - Ed.) of the Puranas, there is but one step. After all, the admission of this by Science would be only the admission of a natural cause, whether it would or would not stretch its belief to such metaphysical heights. But then *Mahat*, the MIND is a "God," and physiology admits "mind" only as a temporary function of the material brain and no more.

The Satan of Materialism now laughs at all alike and denies the visible as well as the invisible Seeing in light, heat, electricity, and even in the *phenomenon of life*, only properties inherent in matter, it laughs whenever life is called VITAL PRINCIPLE, and derides the idea of its being independent of and distinct from the organism.

But here again scientific opinions differ as in everything else, and there are several men of science who accept views very similar to ours. Consider, for instance, what Dr. Richardson, F.R.S. says of that "Vital principle," which he calls "nervous ether." .... There are men of science who take the same views about "things occult" as theosophists and occultists do. These recognise a distinct, vital principle independent of the organism - material of course, *as physical force cannot be divorced from matter,* but of a substance existing in a state unknown to Science. *Life for them is something more than the mere interaction of molecules and atoms.* There is a vital principle without which no molecular combinations could ever have resulted in a living organism, least of all in the so-called "inorganic" matter of our plane of consciousness. ***SD 1, pp. 601 - 603***

7. But Chemistry is now on its ascending plane, thanks to one of its highest European representatives (Sir William Crookes - Ed.). It is impossible for it to go back to that day when materialism regarded its *sub*-elements as absolutely simple and homogenous bodies, which it had raised, in its blindness, to the rank of elements.

The mask has been snatched off by too clever a hand for there to be any fear of a new disguise. And after years of pseudology, of bastard molecules parading under the name of elements, behind and beyond which there could be naught but void, a great professor of chemistry asks once more: "What are these elements, whence do they come, what is their signification? .... These elements perplex us in our researches, baffle us in our speculations, and haunt us in our very dreams. They stretch like an unknown sea before us, mocking, mystifying, and murmuring strange revelations and possibilities." (*Genesis of Elements,* p. 1)

Those who are heirs to primeval revelations have taught these "possibilities" in every century, but have never found a fair hearing. The truths inspired to Kepler, Leibnitz, Gassendi, Swendenborg, etc., were ever alloyed with their own speculations in one or another predetermined direction - hence distorted. But now one of the great truths has dawned upon an eminent professor of modern exact science, and he fearlessly proclaims as a fundamental axiom that Science has not made itself acquainted, so far, with real simple elements (written in 1888 - Ed). For Prof. Crookes tells his audience:

"If I venture to say *that our commonly received elements are* NOT *simple and primordial,* that they have *not* arisen by chance or have *not* been created in a desultory and mechanical manner, but have been evolved from simpler matters - or perhaps, indeed from one sole kind of matter - I do but give formal utterance to an idea which has been, so to speak, for some time 'in the air' of science. Chemists, physicists, philosophers of the highest merit, declare explicitly their belief that the seventy (or thereabouts) elements of our text-books are not the pillars of Hercules which we must never hope to pass" ... "Philosophers in the present as in the past - men who certainly have not worked in the laboratory - have reached the same view from another side." Thus Herbert Spencer records his conviction that "the chemical atoms are produced from the true or physical atoms by process of evolution under conditions which chemistry has not yet been able to produce."

Nevertheless, the idea would have remained crystallized "in the air of Silence," and never have descended into the thick atmosphere of materialism and profane mortals for years to come perhaps, had not Professor Crookes bravely and fearlessly reduced it to its simple elements and thus publicly forced it on Scientific notice. .... The revolution produced in old chemistry by Avogadro was the first page in the Volume of *New Chemistry*. Mr. Crookes has now turned the second page, and is boldly pointing *to what may be the last*. ... it will reappear in its reincarnation as *New Alchemy* or *Metachemistry*. The discoverer of radiant matter will have vindicated in time the Archaic Aryan works on Occultism and even the Vedas and Puranas. For what are the manifested "Mother," the "Father-Son-Husband" (Aditi and Daksha, a form of Brahma, as creators) and the "Son," - the three "First-born" - but simply *Hydrogen, Oxygen,* and that which in its terrestrial manifestation is called Nitrogen.

Yet all the ancient, medieval, and modern poets and philosophers have been anticipated even in the exoteric Hindu books. Descartes' *plenum* of matter differentiated into particles; Leibnitz's *Ethereal Fluid*, and Kant's "primitive fluid" dissolved into its elements; Kepler's Solar Vortex and Systematic Vortices; in short, from the Elemental Vortices inaugurated by the universal mind - through Anaxagoras down to Galileo, Toricelli, and Swendenborg, and after them to the latest speculations by European mystics - all this is found in the Hindu hymns and mantras ... in their fullness, for they are inseparable.

In esoteric teachings, the most transcendental conceptions of the universe and its mysteries, as the most (seemingly) materialistic speculations are found reconciled, because those sciences embrace the whole scope of evolution from Spirit to matter. As declared by an American Theosophist (W.Q. Judge - Ed.), "The Monads (of Leibnitz) may from one point of view be called *force*, from another *matter*. To occult Science, *force* and *matter* are *only two sides of the same* SUBSTANCE." ("The Path," No. 10, p. 297)

Let the reader remember these "Monads" of Leibnitz, every one of which is a living mirror of the universe, every monad reflecting every other, and compare this view and definition with certain Sanskrit stanzas translated by Sir William Jones, in which it is said that the creative source of the Divine Mind ...."Hidden in a veil of thick darkness, formed *mirrors of the atoms* of the world, and *cast reflection from its own face on every atom....*"

When, therefore, Professor Crookes declares that "If we can show how the so-called chemical elements might have been generated we shall be able to fill up a formidable gap in our knowledge of the universe ...." the answer is ready. The theoretical knowledge is contained in the esoteric meaning of every Hindu cosmogony in the *Puranas;* the practical demonstration thereof - is in the hands of those who will not be recognised *in this* century, save by the very few. The scientific possibilities of various discoveries, that must inexorably lead exact Science into the acceptation of Eastern occult views, which contain all the requisite material for the filling of those "gaps," are, so far, at the mercy of modern materialism. It is only by working in the direction taken by Professor Crookes that there is any hope for the recognition of a few, hitherto, Occult, truths. *SD 1, pp.621 - 624*

8. Esoteric doctrines teach the existence of "an antecedent form of energy having periodic cycles of ebb and swell, rest and activity" - and behold a great scholar in Science (Crookes) now asking the world to accept this as one of the postulates. We have shown the "Mother", fiery and hot, becoming gradually cool and radiant, and that same Scientist claims as his second postulate, a *scientific necessity*, it would seem - "an internal action akin to cooling, operating slowly in the prototyle." Occult Science teaches that "Mother" lies stretched in infinity (during *Pralaya*) as the great

Deep, the *"dry* Waters of Space,"* according to the quaint expression in the *Catechism* (the commentary of the Himalayan Brotherhood - Ed.), and becomes wet only after the separation and the moving over its face of *Narayana*, the Spirit which is invisible Flame, which never burns, but sets on fire all that it touches, and gives it life and generation." ***SD 1, pp. 625 - 626***

9. Leibnitz was a philosopher; and as such he had certain primary principles, which biassed him in favour of certain conclusions, and his discovery that external things were substances endowed with force was at once used for the purpose of applying those principles. One of these laws was the law of continuity, the conviction that all the world was connected, that there were no gaps and chasms which could not be bridged over.

The divisions made by Leibnitz, however incomplete and faulty from the standpoint of Occultism, show a spirit of metaphysical intuition to which no man of science, not Descartes - not even Kant - has ever reached. With him there existed ever an infinite gradation of thought. Only a small portion of the contents of our thoughts, he said, rises into the clearness of apperception, "into the light of perfect consciousness." Many remain in a confused or obscure state, in the state of perceptions; "but they are there; ... Descartes denied soul to the animal, Leibnitz endowed, as the Occultists do, "the whole of creation with mental life, this being, according to him, capable of infinite gradations." ***SD 1, p. 627***

10. Spinoza recognised but one universal indivisible substance and Absolute ALL, like Parabrahman. Leibnitz, on the contrary perceived the existence of a plurality of substances. There was but ONE for Spinoza; for Leibnitz an infinitude of Beings, *from* and *in,* the One. Hence, though both admitted but *one real Entity,* while Spinoza made it impersonal and indivisible, Leibnitz divided his *personal* Deity into a number of divine and semi-divine Beings. Spinoza was a *subjective,* Leibnitz an *objective* Pantheist, yet both were great philosophers in their intuitive perception.

Now, if these two teachings were blended together and each corrected by the other - and foremost of the One Reality weeded of its personality - there would remain as sum total a true spirit of esoteric philosophy in them; the impersonal, attributeless, absolute divine essence which is *no* "Being," but the root of all being. *SD 1, p. 629*

THE SERPENT AND DRAGON SYMBOLS

1. The primitive symbol of the serpent symbolised divine Wisdom and Perfection, and had always stood for psychical Regeneration and Immortality. Hence - Hermes, calling the serpent the most spiritual of all beings; Moses, initiated in the wisdom of Hermes, following suit in Genesis; the Gnostic's Serpent with the seven vowels over its head, being the emblem of the seven hierarchies of the Septenary or Planetary Creators. Hence, also, the Hindu serpent Sesha or Ananta, "the Infinite," a name of Vishnu whose first Vahan or vehicle on the primordial waters is this serpent. Yet they all made a difference between the good and the bad Serpent (the Astral Light of the Kabalists) - between the former, the embodiment of divine Wisdom in the region of the Spiritual, and the latter, Evil, on the plane of matter. Jesus accepted the serpent as a synonym of Wisdom, and this formed part of his teachings: "Be ye wise as serpents," he says.

"In the beginning, before Mother became Father-Mother, the fiery dragon moved in the infinitudes alone" (Book of Sarpajni). The Aitareya Brahmana calls the Earth Sarparajni, "the Serpent Queen," and "the Mother of all that moves." Before our globe became egg-shaped (and the Universe also) "a long trail of Cosmic dust (or fire mist) moved and writhed like a serpent in Space."

The "Spirit of God moving on Chaos" was symbolized by every nation in the shape of a fiery serpent breathing fire and light upon the primordial waters, until it had incubated cosmic matter and made it assume the annular shape of a serpent with its tail in its mouth - which symbolizes not only Eternity and Infinitude, but also the the globular shape of all the bodies formed within the Universe from that fiery mist. The Universe, as well as the Earth and Man, cast off periodically, serpent-like, their old skins, to assume new ones after a time of rest. The serpent is, surely, a not less graceful or a more unpoetical image than the caterpillar and chrysalis from which springs the butterfly, the Greek emblem of Psyche, the human soul. *SD1, p.73*

2. Like the *logoi* and the Hierarchies of Powers, however, the "Serpents" have to be distinguished one from the other. Sesha or Ananta, "the couch of Vishnu," is an allegorical abstraction, symbolizing infinite Time in Space, which contains the germ and throws off periodically the efflorescence of this germ, the *manifested* Universe; whereas, the gnostic *Ophis* contained the mass triple symbolism in its seven vowels as the One, Three and Seven-syllabled *Oeaohoo* of the Archaic doctrine; *i.e.,* the One Unmanifested Logos, the Second manifested, the triangle concreting into the Quaternary or Tetragrammaton, and the rays of the matter on the material plane. *SD1, p.73, footnote*

3. *"The Serpents who redescended ... who taught and instructed"* the Fifth Race. What sane man is capable of believing in our day that *real* serpents are hereby meant? Hence the rough guess, now becomes almost an axiom with the men of science, that those who wrote in antiquity about various sacred Dragons and Serpents either were superstitious and credulous people, or were bent upon deceiving those more ignorant than themselves. Yet, from Homer downwards, the term implied something hidden from the profane.

"Terrible are the gods when they manifest themselves" - those *gods* whom men call *Dragons*. And Aelianus, treating in his *"De Natura Animalium"* of these Ophidian symbols, makes certain remarks which show that he understood well the nature of this most ancient of symbols. Thus he most pertinently explains with regard to the above Homeric verse - "For the Dragon, while sacred and to be worshipped, *has within himself something still more of the divine nature* of which it is better (for others?) to remain in ignorance." (Book xi., ch. 17) **SD 2, p. 355**

4. A specimen of Dragons, "winged and scaled," may be seen in the British Museum. Representing the events of the Fall according to the same authority, there are also two figures sitting on each side of a tree, and holding out their hands to the "apple," while at the back of the "Tree" is the Dragon-Serpent. Esoterically, the two figures are two "Chaldees" ready for initiation, the Serpent symbolising the "Initiator"; while the jealous gods, who curse the three, are the exoteric profane clergy. Not much of the literal "Biblical event" there, as any occultist can see. "The Great Dragon has respect but for the Serpents of Wisdom," says the Stanza (*SD*

2, p. 351 - Ed.); thus proving the correctness of our explanation of the two figures and the "Serpent." **SD 2, pp. 354 - 355**

5. The "Dragon" was also the symbol of the Logos with the Egyptians, as with the Gnostics. In the "Book of Hermes," Pymander, the oldest and the most spiritual of the Logoi of the Western Continent, appears to Hermes in the shape of a Fiery Dragon of "Light, Fire, and Flame." Pymander, the "Thought Divine" personified, says: "The Light is me, I am the Nous (the mind or Manu), I am they God and I am far older than the human principle which escapes from the shadow (*"Darkness,"* or the concealed Deity). I am the germ of thought, the resplendent *Word,* the *Son* of God. All that thus sees and hears in thee is the *Verbum* of the Master, it is the Thought (*Mahat*) which is God, the Father." (By "God the Father," the seventh principle in Man and Kosmos are here unmistakably meant, this principle being inseperable in its Esse and Nature from the seventh Cosmic principle. In one sense it is the Logos of the Greeks and the Avalokiteswara of the esoteric Buddhists.) (*from the footnote, p. 74)* The celestial Ocean, the Aether ... is the Breath of the father, the life-giving principle, the *Mother,* the Holy Spirit ... for these are not separated, and their union is LIFE." **SD 1, pp. 74 - 75**

6. The tradition of the Dragon and the Sun is echoed in every part of the world, both in its civilized and semi-savage regions. It took rise in the whisperings about secret initiations among the profane, and was

THE SERPENT AND DRAGON SYMBOLS

established universally through the once universal heliolatrous religion. There was a time when the four parts of the world were covered with the temples sacred to the Sun and the Dragon; but the cult is now preserved mostly in China and the Buddhist countries....

In the religions of the past, it is in Egypt we have to seek for its Western origin. The Ophites adopted their rites from Hermes Trismegistus, and heliolatrous worship crossed over with its Sun-gods into the land of the Pharaohs from India. In the gods of Stonehenge we recognise the divinities of Delphi and Babylon, and in those of the latter the devas of the Vedic nations. Bel and the Dragon, Apollo and Python, Krishna and Kaliya, Osiris and Typhon are all one under many names - the latest of which are Michael and the Red Dragon, and St. George and his Dragon. As Michael is "one as God," or his "Double," for terrestrial purposes, and is one of the Elohim, the fighting angel, he is thus simply a permutation of Jehovah. Whatever the Cosmic or astronomical event that first gave rise to the allegory of the "War in Heaven," its earthly origin has to be sought in the temples of Initiation and archaic crypts. The following are the proofs:-

We find (a) the priests assuming the name of the gods they served; (b) the "Dragons" held throughout all antiquity as the symbols of Immortality and Wisdom, of secret Knowledge and of Eternity; and (c) the hierophants of Egypt, of Babylon, and India, styling themselves generally the "Sons of the Dragon" and

"Serpents"; thus the teachings of the Secret Doctrine are thereby corroborated.

There were numerous catacombs in Egypt and Chaldea, some of them of a very vast extent. The most renowned of them were the subterranean crypts of Thebes and Memphis. The former, beginning on the western side of the Nile, extended towards the Lybian desert, and were known as the *Serpent's* catacombs, or passages. It was there that were performed the sacred mysteries of the ... "Unavoidable Cycle," more generally known as "the circle of necessity"; the inexorable doom imposed upon every soul after the bodily death, and when it had been judged in the Amenthian region.

In de Bourbourg's book, *Votan*, the Mexican demi-god, in narrating his expedition, describes a subterranean passage which ran underground, and terminated at the root of the heavens, adding that this passage was a snake's hole ...; and that he was admitted to it because he was himself "a son of the snakes," or a serpent.

This is, indeed, very suggestive; for his description of the *snake's hole* is that of the ancient Egyptian crypt, as above mentioned. The hierophants, moreover, of Egypt, as of Babylon, generally styled themselves the "Sons of the Serpent-god," or "Sons of the Dragon," during the mysteries. *SD2, pp. 378 - 380*

7. These few lines alone indicate the dual and even the triple character of the Amshaspends, our Dhyan-Chohans (high angels - Ed.) or the "Serpents of Wisdom." They are identical with, and yet separate from Ormazd (Ahura-Mazda - in Zoroastrianism - Ed.). They are also the Angels of the Stars of the Christians - the Star-yazatas of the Zoroastrians - or again the seven planets (including the sun) of every religion. The epithet - "the shining having efficacious eyes" - proves it. This on the physical and sidereal planes. On the spiritual, they are the divine powers of Ahura-Mazda; but on the astral or psychic plane again, they are the "Builders," the "watchers," the *Pitar* (fathers), and the first Preceptors of mankind. *SD 2, p. 358*

8. ... the Serpents were ever the emblems of wisdom and prudence is again shown by the caduceus of Mercury, one with Thot, the god of wisdom, with Hermes, and so on. The two serpents, entwined around the rod, are phallic symbols of Jupiter and other gods who transformed themselves into snakes for purposes of seducing goddesses - but only in the unclean fancies of profane symbologists. The serpent has ever been the symbol of the adept, and of his powers of immortality and divine knowledge. Mercury in his psychopompic character conducting and guiding with the caduceus the souls of the dead to Hades and even raising the dead to life with it, is simply a very transparent allegory. It shows the dual power of the Secret Wisdom.... It shows the personified Wisdom guiding the Soul after death, and its power to call to life that which is dead - a very deep metaphor if one thinks over its meaning. Every people of antiquity reverenced this symbol with the exception of Christians, who chose to forget the brazen Serpent of Moses, and even the implied acknowledgment of the great wisdom and prudence of the Serpent by Jesus himself. "Be ye wise as serpents and harmless as doves."

The Chinese, one of the oldest nations of our Fifth Race, made of it, the emblem of their Emperors, who are thus the degenerate successors of the "Serpents" or Initiates, who ruled the early races of the Fifth Humanity. The Emperor's throne is the "Dragon's Seat," and his dresses of State are embroidered with the likeness of the dragon. The aphorisms in the oldest books of China, moreover, say plainly that the "Dragon" is a human, albeit, *divine*, Being.

Speaking of the "Yellow dragon," the chief of the others, the *Twan-ying-t'u*, says: "His wisdom and virtue are unfathomable ... he does not go in company and does not live in herds (he is an ascetic). He wanders in the wilds beyond the heavens. He goes and comes, fulfilling the decree (Karma); at the proper seasons if there is perfection, he comes forth. If not he remains (invisible)." ... And Kon-fu-tyu is made to say by Lu-lan, "The dragon feeds in the pure water of Wisdom and sports in the clear waters of Life." *SD 2, pp. 364 - 365*

9. Then come the Nagas, the *Sarpa* (serpents or Seraphs). These again, show their character by the hidden meaning of their glyph. In Mythology they are *semi-divine* beings with a human face and the tail of a Dragon. They are therefore, undeniably, the Jewish *seraphim* (from *Serapis* and *Sarpa*, Serpent); the plural being *seraph*, "burning, fiery" (See Isaiah, vi. 23). Christian and Jewish angelology distinguishes between the Seraphim and the *Cherubim* or Cherubs, who come second in order; esoterically, and Kabalistically, they are identical; the *cherubim* being simply the name for the images or likenesses of any of the divisions of the celestial hosts. Now, as said before, the Dragons and *Nagas* were the names given to the Initiates-hermits, on account of their great Wisdom and Spirituality and their living in caves. *SD 2, p. 501*

10. So is the Dragon a mystery. Truly says Rabbi Simeon Ben-Iochai, that to understand the meaning of the Dragon is not given to the "Companions" (students, or *chelas*), but only to "the little ones," *i.e.*, the *perfect Initiates.* "The work of the beginning the companions understand; but it is only the little ones who understand the parable in the work in the *Precipium* by *the mystery of the serpent of the Great Sea.*" And those Christians who may happen to read this will also understand by the light of the above sentence who their "Christ" was. For Jesus states repeatedly that he who "shall not receive the Kingdom of God as a *little child,* he shall not enter therein"; and if some of his sayings have been meant to apply to children without any metaphor, most of what relates to the "little ones" in the Gospels, related to the *Initiates, of whom Jesus was one.* Paul (Saul) is referred to in the Talmud as "the little one."

That "Mystery of the Serpent" was this: Our Earth, *or rather terrestrial life,* is often referred to in the Secret teachings as the great Sea, "the sea of life" having remained to this day a favourite metaphor. The *Sephir Dzeniouta* (Kabalistic work - Ed.) speaks of primeval chaos and the evolution of the Universe after the destruction (*pralaya*), comparing it to an uncoiling serpent: - "Extending, hither and thither, its tail in its mouth, the head twisting on its neck, it is enraged and angry ... It watches and conceals itself. Every thousand Days *it is manifested.*" ***SD 2, p. 504***

11. Such was the name given in ancient Judea to the Initiates, called also the "Innocents" and the "Infants," *i.e.,* once more reborn. This *key* opens a vista into one of the New Testament mysteries; the slaughter by Herod of the 40,000 "Innocents." There is a legend to this effect, and the event which took place almost a century B.C., show the origin of the tradition blended at the same time with that of Krishna and his uncle Kansa. In the case of the N.T., Herod stands for Alexander Janneus (of Lyda), whose persecution and murder of hundreds and thousands of Initiates led to the adoption of the Bible story. ***SD 2, p. 504 - footnote***

12. "The whole world of thought is reproached by the Church with having adored the serpent. The whole of humanity 'incensed and at the same time stoned it.' The Zend Avesta speaks of it as the Kings and Vedas do, as the Edda and the Bible....

Everywhere the sacred serpent, the naga, and its shrine and its priest; in Rome it is the Vestal (virgin) who prepares its meal with the same care as she bestows on the sacred fire. In Greece, Aesculapius cannot cure without its assistance, and delegates to it his powers. Everyone has heard of the famous Roman embassy sent by the Senate to the god of medicine and its return with the not less famous serpent, which proceeded of its own will and by itself toward its Master's temple on one of the islands of the Tiber. Not a Bacchante that did not wind it (the serpent) in her hair, not an Augur but questioned it oracularly, not a necromancer whose tomb is free from its presence!" ("Sacred Serpents" of De Mirville's *"Memoirs"* - Ed.)

Yes, the author (De Mirville) is right, and if one would have a complete idea of the prestige which the serpent enjoys to our own day, one ought to study the matter in India and learn all that is believed about, and still attributed to, the *Nagas* (Cobras) in that country; .... But why wonder that the serpent is "adored" and at the same time cursed, since we know that from the beginning it was a symbol?

In every ancient language the word *dragon* signified what it now does in Chinese - *i.e.*, *"the being who excels in intelligence"* and in Greek ..., or *"he who sees and watches."* And is it to the animal of that name that any of these epithets can apply? Is it not evident, whenever superstition and oblivion of the primitive meaning may have led savages now, that the said qualifications were intended to apply to the human originals, who were symbolised by serpents and dragons? These originals - called to this day in China "the Dragons of Wisdom" - were the first disciples of the Dhyanis, who were their instructors; in short, the primitive adepts of the Third (Root), and later, of the Fourth and Fifth (Root) Races. The name became universal, and no sane man before the Christian era would ever have confounded the man and the symbol. *SD 2, pp 209 - 210*

THE SEVEN RAYS AND TWIN SOULS

1. There are seven chief groups of ... Dhyan Chohans, which groups will be found and recognised in every religion, for they are the primeval SEVEN RAYS. Humanity, occultism teaches us, is divided into seven distinct groups and their sub-divisions, mental, spiritual, and physical. *SD 1, p. 573*

2. The "triads" (the divine monads - Ed.) born under the same Parent-planet, or rather the *radiations* of one and the same Planetary Spirit (Dhyani Buddhas) are, in all their after lives and rebirths, sister, or "*twin*-souls," on this Earth.

This was known to every high Initiate in every age, and in every country: "I and my Father are one," said Jesus (John x, 30). When He is made to say elsewhere (xx, 17): "I ascend to *my* Father and your Father," it meant that which has just been stated. It was simply to show that the group of his disciples and followers attracted to Him belonged to the same Dhyani Buddha, "Star," or "Father," again of the same planetary realm and division as He did. It is the *knowledge* of this occult doctrine that found expression in the review of *"The Idyll of the White Lotus,"* when Mr. T. Subba Row wrote: "Every Buddha meets at his last initiation all the great adepts who reached Buddhahood during the preceding ages ... every class of adepts has its own bond of spiritual communion which knits them together. .... The only possible and effectual way of entering into such brotherhood ... is by bringing oneself within the influence of the Spiritual light which radiates *from one's own Logos.* I may point out here ... that such communion is only possible *between persons whose souls derive their life and sustenance from the same divine* RAY, and that, as seven distinct rays radiate from the "Central Spiritual Sun," *all adepts and Dhyan Chohans are divisible into seven classes,* each of which is guided, controlled, and overshadowed *by one of the seven forms* or manifestations of the divine Wisdom." (*"Theosophist,"* Aug., 1886) **SD 1, p. 574**

3. Hence the seven chief planets, the *spheres* of the indwelling seven spirits under each of which is born one of the human groups which is guided and influenced thereby. There are only seven planets specially connected with earth and twelve houses (astrological) but the possible combinations of their aspects are countless. As each planet can stand to each of the others in twelve different aspects, their combinations must, therefore, be almost infinite; as infinite, in fact, as the spiritual, psychic, mental and physical capacities in the numberless varieties of the *genus homo,* each of which varieties is born under one of the seven planets and one of the said countless planetary combinations. **SD 1, p, 573, foot-note**

4. The now universal error of attributing to the ancients the knowledge of only seven planets simply because they mentioned no others, is based on the same general ignorance of their occult doctrines The question is not whether the reverence paid by them to the four esoteric and three secret great gods - the star-angels, had not some special reason. The writer ventures to say there was such a reason, and it is this. Had they known of as many planets as we do now ... "they would have still connected with their religious worship only the seven, because these seven are directly and specially connected with our earth, or, using esoteric phraseology, with our septenary ring of spheres." **SD 1, p. 574, foot-note**

THE SHIFTING OF THE WORLD AXIS

1. The commentary (in the Archives of the Himalayan Brotherhood - Ed.) tells us that the Third Race was only about the middle point of its development when: -

"The axle of the Wheel tilted. The Sun and Moon shone no longer over the heads of that portion of the SWEAT BORN; people knew snow, ice, and frost, and men, plants, and animals were dwarfed in their growth. Those that did not perish REMAINED AS HALF-GROWN BABES IN SIZE AND INTELLECT (in comparison with their giant brethren on other zones - foot-note). *This was the third pralaya of the races.*

Which means again, that our globe is subject to seven periodical *entire* changes which go *pari passu* with the races. For the Secret Doctrine teaches that, during this Round, there must be seven terrestrial *pralayas,* three occasioned by the changes in the inclination of the earth's axis. It is a *law* which acts at its appointed time, and not at all blindly, as science may think, but in strict accordance and harmony with *Karmic* law. In Occultism this inexorable law is referred to as "the great ADJUSTER."

Science confesses its ignorance of the causes producing climate vicissitudes and such changes in the axial direction, which are always followed by these vicissitudes; nor does it seem so sure of the axial changes. And being unable to account for them, it is prepared rather to deny the axial phenomena altogether, than admit the intelligent Karmic hand and law, which alone could reasonably explain such sudden changes and their results. It has tried to account for them by various modes or less fantastic speculations; one of which would be the sudden and as imaginary, collision of our Earth with a comet. But we prefer holding to our esoteric explanation since FOHAT is as good as any comet, having, in addition, universal intelligence to guide him. *SD 2, pp. 329 - 330*

2. Thus since Vaivasvata Manu's Humanity appeared on this Earth, there have already been four such axial disturbances; when the old continents - save the first one - were sucked in by the oceans, other lands appeared, and huge mountain chains arose where there had been none before. The face of the Globe was completely changed each time; the *survival of the fittest* nations and races was secured through timely help; and the unfit ones - the failures - were disposed of by being swept off the earth. Such sorting and shifting does not happen between sunset and sunrise, as one may think, but required several thousands of years before the new house is set in order. *SD 2, p. 330*

3. The *Sub*-races are subject to the same cleansing process, as also the side branchlets (the family Races). Let one, well-acquainted with astronomy and mathematics, throw a retrospective glance into the twilight and shadows of the Past. Let him observe, take notes of what he knows of the history of peoples and nations, and collate their respective rises and falls with what is known of astronomical cycles - especially with the *Sidereal year,* equal to 25,868 of our solar years. If the observer is gifted with the faintest intuition, then will he find how the weal and woe of nations is intimately connected with the beginning and close of this sidereal cycle.

True, the non-occultist has the disadvantage that he has no such far distant times to rely upon. He knows nothing, through exact Science, of what took place nearly 10,000 years ago; yet he may find consolation in the knowledge or - if he so prefers - speculation on the fate of every one of the modern nations he knows of - about 16,000 years hence. Our meaning is clear. Every sidereal year, the tropics recede from the pole *four degrees* in each revolution from the equinoctial points, as the equator rounds through the Zodiacal constellations. Now, as every astronomer knows, at present the tropic is only twenty three degrees and a fraction less than half a degree from the equator. Hence it has still 2 and a half degrees to run before the end of the Sidereal year; which gives humanity in general and our civilized races in *particular,* a reprieve of about 16,000 years. *SD 2, pp 330 - 331*

THE SILENT WATCHER

1. This "Wondrous Being" descended from a "high region" they say, in the early part of the Third Age, before the separation of the sexes of the Third (Root) Race. .... In the first or earlier portion of the existence of this third race, while it was yet in its state of purity, the "Sons of Wisdom," who as will be seen, incarnated in this Third Race produced by Kriyashakti, a progeny called the "Sons of Ad" or "of the Fire Mist," "the Sons of Will and Yoga," etc. They were a conscious production, as a portion of the race was always animated with the divine spark of spiritual, superior intelligence.

It was not a Race, this progeny. It was at first a Wondrous Being called "the Initiator," and after him a group of semi-divine and semi-human beings. "Set apart" in Archaic *genesis* for certain purposes, they are those in whom are said to have incarnated the highest Dhyanis, "Munis and Rishis from previous Manvantaras" - *to form the nursery for future human adepts*, on this earth and during the present cycle. These "Sons of Will and Yoga" born, so to speak, in an immaculate way, remained, it is explained, entirely apart from the rest of mankind.

The "BEING" just referred to, which has to remain nameless, is the *Tree* from which in subsequent ages, all the great *historically* known Sages and Hierophants, such as the Rishi Kapila, Hermes, Enoch, Orpheus, etc. etc., have branched off. As objective *man*, he is the mysterious (to the profane) yet ever present Personage about whom legends are rife in the East, especially among the Occultists and the students of the sacred Science. And it is he who changes form, yet remains ever the same. And it is he again who holds spiritual sway over the *initiated* Adepts throughout the whole world. He is, as said, the "Nameless One" who has so many names, and yet whose names and whose very nature are unknown. He is *the "Initiator," called the* "GREAT SACRIFICE." For, sitting at the threshold of LIGHT, he looks into it from within the circle of Darkness, which he will not cross; nor will he quit his post till the last day of this life-cycle.

Why does the solitary Watcher remain at his self-chosen post? Why does he sit by the fountain of primeval Wisdom, of which he drinks no longer, as he has naught to learn which he does not know - aye, neither on this Earth, nor in its heaven? Because the lonely, sore-footed pilgrims on their way back to their *home* are never sure to the last moment of not losing their way in this limitless desert of illusion and matter called Earth-Life. Because he would fain show the way to that region of freedom and light, from which he is a voluntary exile himself from the bonds of flesh and illusion. Because, in short, he has sacrificed himself for the sake of mankind, though but a few Elect may profit by the GREAT SACRIFICE.

It is under the direct, silent guidance of this MAHA - (great) - GURU that all the other less divine Teachers and instructors of mankind became, from the first awakening of human consciousness, the guides of early humanity. It is through these "Sons of God" that infant humanity got its first notions of all the arts and sciences as well as of spiritual knowledge; and it is they who have laid the first foundation-stone of those ancient civilizations that puzzle so sorely our modern generation of students and scholars. *SD 1, pp. 207 - 208*

THE SOLAR ANGELS (PITRIS)

1. The Endowers of Man with his conscious, immortal EGO, are the "Solar Angels" - whether so regarded metaphorically or literally. The mysteries of the Conscious EGO or human Soul are great. The esoteric name of these "Solar Angels" is, literally, the "Lords" ... of "persevering ceaseless devotion" (*pranidhana*). Therefore they of the *fifth* principle (*Manas*) seem to be connected with, or to have originated the system of the Yogis.... It has already been explained why the trans-Himalayan Occultists regard them as evidently identical with those who in India are termed *Kumaras, Agnishwattas,....* **SD 2, p. 88**

2. Now, with regard to the seven classes of Pitris, each of which is again divided into seven, a word to students.... That class of the "Fire Dhyanis," which we identify on undeniable grounds with the Agnishwattas (Solar Angels/Pitris - Ed.), is called in our school the "Heart" of the Dhyan-Chohanic Body (high angelic hosts - Ed.); and it is said to have incarnated in the third race men and made them perfect. The esoteric Mystagogy speaks of the mysterious relations existing between the hebdomanic essence or substance of this angelic Heart and that of man, whose every physical organ and psychic, and spiritual function, is a reflection, so to say, a copy on the terrestrial plane of the model or prototype *above.* **SD 2, pp. 91-92**

3. It thus becomes clear why the *Agniswatta*, devoid of the grosser *creative fire*, or astral body, to protect, since they were without any *form*, are shown in exoteric allegories as Yogis, Kumaras (chaste youths), who became "rebels," *Asuras*, fighting and opposing gods, etc. etc. Yet it is they who could complete man, *i.e.*, make of him a self-conscious, almost divine being - a god on Earth. *SD 2, pp. 78 - 79*

4. ... as the allegory shows, the Gods who had no personal merit of their own, dreading the sanctity of those self-striving incarnated Beings who had become *ascetics* and Yogis (the Solar Angels - Ed.), and thus threatened to upset the power of the former by their *self-acquired* powers - denounced them. All this has a deep philosophical meaning and refers to the evolution and acquirement of divine powers through *self-exertion*. Some Rishi-Yogis are shown in the Puranas to be far more powerful than the gods. Secondary gods or temporary powers in Nature (the Forces) are doomed to disappear; it is only the spiritual potentiality in man which can lead him to become one with the INFINITE and the ABSOLUTE. *SD 2, pp. 78 - 79, foot-note*

5. *"The Sons of* MAHAT *are the quickeners of the human Plant* (man - Ed.). *They are the waters falling upon the arid soil of latent life, and the Spark that vivifies the human animal. They are the Lords of Spiritual Life eternal."....* "*In the beginning* (in the Second Race) *some* (of the Lords) *only breathed of their essence into Manushya* (men); *and some took in man their abode."*

This shows that not all men became incarnations of the "divine *Rebels*" but only a few among them. The remainder had their fifth principle (mind - Ed.) simply quickened by the spark thrown into it, which accounts for the great difference between the intellectual capacities of men and races. Had not the "sons of Mahat," speaking allegorically, skipped the intermediate worlds, in their impulse toward intellectual freedom, the animal man would never have been able to reach upward from this earth, and attain through self-exertion his ultimate goal. The cyclic pilgrimage would have to be performed through all the planes of existence half unconsciously, if not entirely so, as in the case of the animals. It is owing to this rebellion of intellectual life against the morbid inactivity of pure spirit, that we are what we think we are - self-conscious, thinking men, with the capabilities and attributes of God in us for good as much as for evil. Hence the REBELS are our Saviours.

Let the philosopher ponder well over this, and more than one mystery will become clear to him. It is only by the attractive force of the contrasts that the two opposites - Spirit and Matter - can be cemented on Earth, and, smelted in the fire of self-conscious experience and suffering, find themselves wedded in Eternity. This will reveal the meaning of many hitherto incomprehensible allegories, foolishly called "fables." *SD 2, p. 103*

6. For, to complete the *septenary man*, to add to his three lower principles (physical, etheric/pranic body, and prana - Ed.) and cement with the spiritual Monad (atma-buddhi) - which could never dwell in such a form otherwise than in an *absolutely latent state* - two connecting principles are needed: *Manas* (mind) and *Kama* (desire). This requires a living *Spiritual Fire* of the middle principle from the fifth and third states of Pleroma. But this fire is the possession of the *Triangles* which symbolize ... the Angelic beings (the Agniswatta/Solar Angels - Ed.). These are the active and therefore - in Heaven - no longer "pure" Beings. They have become the independent and free Intelligences, shown in every Theogony as fighting for that independence and freedom and hence - in the ordinary sense - "rebellious to the divine passive law."

These are then those "Flames" (the *Agniswatta*) who, ... "remain behind" instead of going along with the others to create men on Earth. But the true esoteric meaning is that most of them were destined to incarnate as the *Egos* (higher Egos/Souls) of the forthcoming crop of Mankind. The human Ego is neither Atman nor Buddhi, but the higher *Manas*; the intellectual fruition and the efflorescence of the intellectual self-conscious *Egotism* - in the higher spiritual sense. The ancient works refer to it as *Karana Sarira* on the plane of *Sutratma*, which is the golden thread on which, like beads, the various personalities of this higher *Ego* are strung.

If the reader were told, as in the *semi-esoteric* allegories, that these Beings were returning *Nirvanees*, from preceding *Maha-Manvantaras* - ages of incalculable duration which have rolled away in the Eternity, a still more incalculable time ago - he would hardly understand the text correctly; while some Vedantins might say: "This is not so; the Nirvanee can never return"; which is true during the Manvantara he belongs to, and erroneous where Eternity is concerned. For it is said in the Sacred Slokas: *"The thread of radiance which is imperishable and dissolves, only in Nirvana, re-emerges from it in its integrity on the day when the Great Law calls all things back into action...."* **SD 2, pp. 79 - 80**

THE THIRD EYE AND SEERSHIP

1. "There were four-armed human creatures in those early days of the male-females (hermaphrodites); with one head, yet three eyes. They could see before them and behind them. A KALPA (a long cycle of time - Ed.) later (after the separation of the sexes) men having fallen into matter, their spiritual vision became dim; and coordinately the third eye commenced to lose its power.... When the Fourth (Root Race) arrived at its middle age, the inner vision had to be awakened, and acquired by artificial stimuli, the process of which was known to the old sages.

... The third eye, likewise, getting gradually PETRIFIED, soon disappeared. The double-faced became the one-faced, and the eye was drawn deep into the head and is now buried under the hair. During the activity of the inner man (during trances and spiritual vision) the eye swells and expands. The Arhat (Adept - Ed.) sees and feels it, and regulates his action accordingly.... The undefiled Lanoo (disciple, chela) need fear no danger; he who keeps himself not in purity (who is not chaste) will receive no help from the 'deva eye'." (A passage from the *Commentaries* of the Himalayan Brotherhood - Ed.)

Unfortunately not. The "deva-eye" exists no more for the majority of mankind. The *third-eye is dead*, and acts no longer; but it had left behind a witness to its existence. The witness is now the PINEAL GLAND. As for the "four-armed" men, it is they who become the prototypes of the four-armed Hindu gods.... *SD pp. 294 - 295*

2. ... The third eye was at the back of the head. The statement that the latest hermaphrodite humanity was "four-armed," unriddles probably the mystery of all the representations and idols of the exoteric gods of India. On the Acropolis of Argos, there was a rudely carved wooden statue (attributed to Daedalus) representing a three-eyed colossus, which was consecrated to *Zeus Triopas* (three-eyed). The head of the "god" has two eyes in its face and one above on the top of the forehead. It is considered the most archaic of all the ancient statues. *SD 2 p. 294, foot-note*

3. The *Inner sight* could henceforth be acquired (after the withdrawl of the third eye deep into the head - Ed.) only though training and initiation, save in the cases of "natural and born magicians," sensitives and mediums, as they are called now. *SD 2, pp. 294, foot-note*

4. Such is the mystery of the human eye that, in their vain endeavours to explain and account for all the difficulties surrounding its action, some scientists have been forced to resort to occult explanations. The development of the *Human eye* gives more support to the occult anthropology than to that of the materialistic physiologists. "The eyes in the human embryo *grow from within* without" out of the brain, instead of being part of the skin, as in the insects and cuttlefish. Professor Lankester, thinking the brain a queer place for the eye, and attempting to explain the phenomenon on *Darwinian lines*, suggests the curious view that "our" earliest vertebrate ancestor was a *transparent* creature and hence did not mind where the eye was! And so was man "a transparent creature" (ethereal - Ed.) once upon a time, we are taught, hence our theory holds good. .... This seems to be proved by embryology. .... Occultism with its teaching as to the gradual development of senses "FROM WITHIN WITHOUT," from astral prototypes, is far more satisfactory. The *third eye retreated inwards* when its course was run - another point in favour of Occultism. *SD 2, p. 295*

5. The allegorical expression of the Hindu mystics when speaking of the "eye of Siva," the *Tri-bochana* ("three-eyed"), thus receives its justification and *rasion d'etre* - the transference of the pineal gland (once that "third eye") to the forehead, being an exoteric licence. This throws also a light on the mystery - incomprehensible to some - of the connection between *abnormal*, or Spiritual Seership, and the physiological purity of the Seer.

The question is often asked, "Why should celibacy and chastity be a *sine qua non* rule and condition of regular *chelaship*, or the development of psychic and occult powers?" The answer is contained in the Commentary (of the Himalayan Brotherhood - Ed.). When we learn that the "third-eye" was once a physiological organ, and that later on, owing to the gradual disappearance of spirituality and increase of materiality (spiritual nature being extinguished by the physical), it became an atrophied organ, as little understood now by physiologists as the spleen is - when we learn this, the connection will become clear.

During human life, the greatest impediment in the way of spiritual development, and especially to the acquirement of Yoga powers, is the activity of our physiological senses. Sexual action being closely connected, by interaction, with the spinal cord and the grey matter of the brain, it is useless to give any longer explanation. Of course, the normal and abnormal state of the brain, and the degree of active work in the *medulla oblongata*, reacts powerfully on the pineal gland, for, owing to the number of "centres" in that region, which controls by far the greater majority of the physiological actions of the animal economy, and also owing to the close and intimate neighbourhood of the two, there must be exerted a very powerful "inductive" action by the medulla on the pineal gland. *SD 2, pp. 295 - 296*

6. All this is quite plain to the Occultist, but is very vague in the sight of the general reader. The latter must then be shown the possibility of a three-eyed man in nature, in those periods when his formation was yet in a comparatively chaotic state. Such a possibility may be inferred from anatomical and zoological knowledge, first of all; then it may rest on the assumptions of materialistic science itself.

It is asserted upon the authority of Science, and upon evidence which is not merely a fiction of theoretical speculation this time, that many animals - especially among the lower orders of the vertebrates - have a *third* eye, now atrophied, but necessarily active in its origin. The Hatteria species, a lizard of the order Lacertilia, recently discovered in New Zealand (*a part of ancient Lemuria so called, mark well*) presents this peculiarity in a most extraordinary manner; and not only the *Hatteria punctata*, but the chameleon, certain reptiles, and even fishes. It was thought, at first, that it was no more than this. It offered - as its development and anatomical structure showed - such an analogy with that of the third eye, that it was found impossible to see in it anything else. There were and are paleontologists who feel convinced to this day that this "third eye" has functioned in its origin, and they are certainly right. *SD 2, pp. 296 - 29*

TIME AND DURATION

1. *Time was not, for it lay asleep in the infinite bosom of duration. SD 1, p. 36, Stanza 1, v.2*

Time is only an illusion produced by the succession of our states of consciousness as we travel though eternal duration, and it does not exist where no consciousness exists in which the illusion can be produced; but "lies asleep." The present is only a mathematical line which divides that part of eternal duration which we call the future, from that part which we call the past.

Nothing on earth has real duration, for nothing remains without change - or the same - for the billionth part of a second; and the sensation we have of the actuality of the division of "time" known as the present, comes from the blurring of that momentary glimpse, or succession of glimpses, of things that our senses give us, as those things pass from the region of ideals which we call the future, to the region of memories that we name the past. In the same way we experience a sensation of duration in the case of the instantaneous electric spark, by reason of the blurred and continuing impression on the retina. The real person or thing does not consist solely of what is seen at any particular moment, but is composed of the sum of all its various and changing conditions from its appearance in the material form to its disappearance from the earth. It is these "sum-totals" that exist from eternity in the "future," and pass by degrees through matter, to exist for eternity in the "past."

No one could say that a bar of metal dropped into the sea came into existence as it left the air, and ceased to exist as it entered the water, and that the bar itself consisted only of that cross-section thereof which at any given moment coincided with the mathematical plane that separates, and, at the same time, joins the atmosphere and the ocean. Even so of persons and things, which, dropping out of the to-be into the has-been, out of the future into the past - present momentarily to our senses a cross-section, as it were of their total selves, as they pass through time and space (as matter) on their way from one eternity to another; and these two constitute that "duration" in which alone anything has true existence, were our senses but able to cognize it there. *SD 1, p. 37*

3. The three periods - the Present, the Past, and the Future - are in the esoteric philosophy a compound time; for the three are a composite number only in relation to the phenomenal plane, but in the realm of noumena have no abstract validity.

As said in the Scriptures: "The Past time is the Present time, as also the Future, which, though it has not come into existence, still is"; according to a precept in the Prasanga Madhyamika teaching, whose dogmas have been known ever since it broke away from the purely esoteric schools. Our ideas, in short, on duration and time are all derived from our sensations according to the laws of Association. Inextricably bound up with the relativity of human knowledge, they nevertheless can have no existence except in the experience of the individual ego and perish when its evolutionary march dispels the Maya of phenomenal existence. What is Time, for instance, but the panoramic succession of our states of consciousness? In the words of a Master, "I feel irritated at having to use these three clumsy words- Past, Present, and Future - miserable concepts of the objective phases of the subjective whole, they are about as ill-adapted for the purpose as an axe for fine carving." One has to acquire *Paramartha* lest one should become too easy prey to *Samvriti* - is a philosophical axiom. *SD 1, pp. 43 - 44*

In clearer words, "One has to acquire true Self-Consciousness in order to understand *Samvriti*, or the 'origin of delusion'" *Paramartha* is the synonym of the Sanskrit term *Svasam-vedana*, or "the reflection which analyzes itself." *SD 1, p. 44, foot-note*

TWO ASTRONOMERS
OF ANCIENT TIMES

1. To the mind of the Eastern student of Occultism, two figures are indissolubly connected with mystic astronomy, chronology, and their cycles. Two grand and mysterious figures, towering like two giants of the Archaic Past, emerge before him, whenever he has to refer to Yugas and Kalpas. When, at what period of pre-history they lived, none save a few men in the world know, or ever know with that certainty which is required by exact chronology. It may have been 100,000 years ago, it may have been 1,000,000, for all that the outside world will ever know. The mystic West and Freemasonry talk loudly of Enoch and Hermes. The mystic East speaks of NARADA, the old Vedic Rishi, and of ASURAMAYA, the Atlantean.

It has already been hinted that of all the incomprehensible characters in the Mahabharata and the Puranas, Narada, the son of Brahma in Matsya Purana, the progeny of Kasyapa and the daughter of Daksha in the Vishnu Purana, is the most mysterious. He is referred to by the honourable title of Deva Rishi (divine Rishi, more than a demi-god) by Parasara, and yet he is cursed by Daksha and even Brahma. He informs Kansa (the Indian Herod - Ed.) that Bhagavat (Vishnu in exotericism) would incarnate in the eighth child of Devaki, and thus brings the wrath of the Indian *Herod* upon Krishna's mother; and then, from the cloud on which he is seated - invisible as a true *Manasaputra* (Solar Angel - Ed.) - he lauds Krishna, in delight at the Avatar's feat of killing the monster Kesim.

Narada is here, there, and everywhere; and yet none of the Puranas gives the true characteristics of this great enemy of physical procreation. Whatever those characteristics may be in Hindu Esotericism, Narada - who is in Cis-Himalayan Occultism *Pesh-Hun*, the "Messenger," or the Greek *Angelos* - is the sole confidant and the executor of the universal decrees of Karma and *Adi-Budh* (primeval intelligence or wisdom - Ed.): a kind of active and ever incarnating logos, who leads and guides human affairs from the beginning to the end of the Kalpa.

"Pesh-Hun" is a general not a special Hindu possession. He is the mysterious guiding intelligent power, which gives the impulse to, and regulates the impetus of cycles, Kalpas and universal events. He is Karma's visible adjuster on a general scale; the *inspirer* and the leader of the greatest heroes of this Manvantara. In the exoteric works he is referred to by some very uncomplimentary names; such as "Kali-Karaka," *strife*-maker, "Kapi-vaktra," *monkey-faced,* and even "Pisuna," the spy, though elsewhere he is called Deva-Brahma.

Even Sir W. Jones was strongly impressed with this mysterious character from what he gathered in his Sanskrit Studies. He compares him to Hermes and Mercury, and calls him "the eloquent messenger of the gods." All this led the late Dr. Kenealy ("Book of God") on the ground that the Hindus believe him to be a great Rishi, "who is forever wandering about the earth, giving good counsel," to see in him one of his twelve *Messiahs*. He was perhaps, not so far off the real track as some imagine.

What Narada *really is*, cannot be explained in print; nor would the modern generation of the profane gather much from the information. But it may be remarked, that if there is in the Hindu Pantheon a deity which resembles Jehovah, in tempting by "suggestion" of thoughts and "hardening" of the hearts of those whom he would make his tools and victims, it is Narada. Only with the latter it is no desire to obtain a pretext for "plaguing" and thus showing that "*I am* the Lord God."

It is he who brings on wars and puts an end to them. In the old Stanzas Pesh-Hun is credited with having calculated and recorded all the astronomical and cosmic cycles to come, and with having taught the Science to the first gazers at the starry vault. And it is Asuramaya, who is said to have based all his astronomical works upon those records, to have determined the duration of all the past geological and cosmical periods, and the length of all the cycles to come, till the end of this life-cycle, or the end of the seventh (Root) Race.

There is a work among the Secret Books, called the "Mirror of Futurity," wherein all the Kalpas within Kalpas and cycles within the bosom of Sesha, or infinite Time, are recorded. This work is ascribed to *Pesh-Hun* Narada. There is another old work which is attributed to various Atlanteans. It is these two Records which furnish us with the figures of our cycles, and the possibility of calculating the date of cycles to come. The chronological calculations (given in Vol. 2 - Ed.) are, however, those of the Brahmins ...; but most of them are also those of the Secret Doctrine.

The chronology and computations of the Brahmin Initiates are based upon the Zodiacal records of India, and the works of the above-mentioned astronomer and magician - Asuramaya. The Atlantean zodiacal records cannot err, as they were compiled under the guidance of those who first taught astronomy, among other things, to mankind.

Now whether Asuramaya is to be considered a modern myth, a personage who flourished in the day of the Macedonian Greeks, or as that which he is claimed to be by the Occultist, in any case his calculations agree entirely with those of the secret records.

From fragments of immensely old works attributed to the Atlantean astronomer, and found in Southern India, the calendar elsewhere mentioned was compiled by two very learned Brahmins in 1884 and 1885. The work is proclaimed by the best Pundits as faultless - from the Brahmanical standpoint - and thus far relates to the chronology of the orthodox teachings. If we compare its statements with those made several years earlier in "Isis Unveiled," with the fragmentary teachings published by some Theosophists, and with the present data derived from the Secret Books of Occultism, the whole will be found to agree perfectly, save in some details which may not be explained; for secrets of higher

Initiation - as unknown to the writer as they are to the reader - would have to be revealed, and that *cannot be done. SD 2, pp. 47 - 51*

2. Suffice it to say, that Narada is the Deva-Rishi of Occultism *par excellence*; and that the Occultist who does not ponder, analyse, and study Narada from his seven esoteric facets, will never be able to fathom certain anthropological, chronological, and even Cosmic Mysteries. He ... plays a part in the evolution of this Kalpa from its incipient, down to its final stage. He is an actor who appears in each of the successive acts (Root Races) of the present manvantaric drama, in the world allegories which strike the key-note of esotericism, and are now becoming more familiar to the reader. *SD 2, pp. 82 - 83*

THE UPANISHADS

1. The Books of the Vedanta (the last word of human knowledge) give out but the metaphysical aspect of this world-Cosmogony; and their priceless thesaurus, the *Upanishads - Upa-ni-shad* being a compound word meaning "the conquest of ignorance by the revelation of *secret, spiritual* knowledge" - require now the additional possession of a Master-key to enable the student to get at their full meaning. The reason for this I venture to state here as I learned it from a Master.

The name, "*Upanishads*," is usually translated 'esoteric doctrine.' These treatises form part of the *sruti* or "revealed knowledge," *Revelation*, in short, and are generally attached to the *Brahmana* portion of the Vedas (commentaries intended for the guidance of the "twice-born"), as their third division. There are over 150 *Upanishads* enumerated by, and known to Orientalists, who credit the oldest with being written *probably* about 600 years B.C. but of *genuine* texts there does not exist a fifth of the number. The Upanishads are to the Vedas what the Kabala is to the Jewish Bible. They treat of and expound the secret and mystic meaning of the Vedic texts. They speak of the origin of the Universe, the nature of Deity, and of Spirit and Soul, as also of the metaphysical connection of mind and matter. In a few words: They CONTAIN *beginning and the end of all human knowledge, but they have now ceased to* REVEAL *it,* since the day of Buddha. If it were otherwise, the Upanishads could not be called *esoteric*, since they are now openly attached to the Sacred Brahmanical books, which have, in our present age, become accessible even to the *Mlechchhas* (out-castes) and the Euopean Orientalists.

One thing in them - and this in all the *Upanishads* - invariably and constantly points to their ancient origin, and proves (a) that they were written, in some of their portions, *before* the caste system became the tyrannical institution which it still is; and (b) that half of their content have been eliminated, while some of them were re-written and abridged. "The great teachers of the higher Knowledge and the Brahmins are continually represented as going to Kshatriya (military caste) kings to become their pupils." As Cowell pertinently remarks, the *Upanishads* "breathe an entirely different spirit" (from other Brahmanical writings), "a freedom of thought unknown in any earlier work except in the Rig Veda hymns themselves." The second fact is explained by a tradition recorded in one of the MSS. on Buddha's life. It says that the Upanishads were originally attached to their Brahmanas after the beginning of a reform which led to the exclusiveness of the caste system among the Brahmins, a few centuries after the invasion of India by the "twice-born." They were complete in those days and were used for the instruction of the chelas who were preparing for their initiation.

This lasted so long as the Vedas and the Brahmanas remained in the sole and exclusive keeping of the temple Brahmins - while no-one else had the right to study or even read them outside of the *sacred* caste. Then came Gautama Buddha, the Prince of Kapilavastu. After *learning* the whole of the Brahmanical wisdom in the *Rahasya* or the *Upanishad*, and finding that the teachings differed little, if at all, from those of the "Teachers of Life" inhabiting the snowy ranges of the Himalayas, the Disciple of the Brahmins, determined to save the whole world by popularizing it.

Then it was that the Brahmins, seeing that their sacred knowledge and Occult wisdom was falling into the hands of the "*Mlechchhas,*" abridged the texts of the Unpanishad, originally containing thrice the matter of the Vedas and the Brahmanas together, without altering however, one word of the texts. They simply detached from the MSS. the most important portions containing the last word of the Mystery of Being. The key to the Brahmanical secret code remained henceforth with the initiates alone, and the Brahmins were thus in a position to publicly deny the correctness of Buddha's teaching by appealing to their *Upanishads*, silenced for ever on the chief questions. Such is the esoteric tradition beyond the Himalayas.

Sri Sankaracharya, the greatest Initiate living in the historical ages wrote many a Bashya (commentary - Ed.) on the *Upanishads*. But his original treatises, as there are reasons to suppose, have not yet fallen into the hands of the Philistines, for they are too jealously preserved in his *maths* (monasteries). And there are still weightier reasons to believe that the priceless Bashyas on the esoteric doctrine of the Brahmins, by their greatest expounder, will remain for ages yet a dead letter to most of the Hindus, except the *Smartava* Brahmins. This sect, founded by Sankaracharya (which is still very powerful in India) is now almost the only one to produce students who have preserved sufficient knowledge to comprehend the dead letter of the Bashyas. The reason of this is that they alone, I am informed, have occasionally real Initiates at their head in their mathams, as for instance, in the "Sringa-giri," in the Western Ghauts of Mysore. On the other hand, there is no sect in that desperately exclusive caste of the Brahmins, more exclusive than is the Smartava; and the reticence of its followers to say what they may know of the Occult sciences and the esoteric doctrine, is only equalled by their pride and learning (the Hindu theosophist, Subba Row was a representative of the Sringa-giri math, Mysore - Ed.). ***SD 1, pp. 269 - 271***

2.The followers of one of the greatest minds that ever appeared on Earth (Sankaracharya - Ed.), the *Advaita* Vedantins are called *Atheists*, because they regard all save Parabrahm (the Absolute), the *secondless*, or Absolute Reality - as an illusion. Yet, the wisest Initiates came from their ranks, as also the greatest Yogis. The *Upanishads* show that they most assuredly know not only what is the *causal* substance in the *effects* of friction, and that their forefathers were acquainted with the *conversion of heat into mechanical force*, but that they were acquainted with the *noumena* of every spiritual as well as of every cosmic phenomenon. ***SD 1, p. 522***

WONDERS OF THE ANCIENT WORLD

I. It is through ... "Sons of God" (divine Teachers and instructors of mankind, the guides of early humanity - Ed.) that infant humanity got its first notions of all the arts and sciences, as well as of spiritual knowledge; and it is they who laid the first foundation-stone of those ancient civilizations that puzzle so sorely our modern generation of students and scholars. *SD1, p. 208*

2. Let those who doubt this statement explain the mystery of the extraordinary knowledge possessed by the ancients - alleged to have developed from lower and animal-like savages, the *cave-men* of the Paleolithic age - on any other equally reasonable grounds. Let them turn to such works as those of Vitrivius Pollio of the Augustan age, on architecture, for instance, in which all the rules of proportion are those *taught anciently at initiations,* if he would acquaint himself with the truly divine art, and understand the *deep esoteric significance hidden in every rule and law of proportion.*

No man descended from a Paleolithic cave-dweller could ever evolve such a science unaided, even in millenniums of thought and intellectual evolution. It is the pupils of those incarnated Rishis and Devas of the third Root Race who handed their knowledge from one generation to another, to Egypt and Greece with its now lost *canon of proportion*; as it is the Disciples of the Initiates of the 4th (Root Race - Ed.), the Atlanteans, who handed it over to their *Cyclops*, the "Sons of Cyclops" or of the "Infinite," from whom the name passed to the still later generations of Gnostic priests. "It is owing to the divine perfection of those architectural proportions that the Ancients could build those wonders of all the subsequent ages, their Fanes, Pyramids, Cave-Temples, Cromlechs, Cairns, Altars, proving they had the powers of machinery and a knowledge of mechanics to which modern skill is like a child's play, and which that *skill* refers to itself as the 'works of hundred-handed giants.'" (*Kenealy,"Book of God"*)

Modern architects may not altogether have neglected those rules but they have superadded enough empirical innovations to destroy those just proportions. It is Vitruvius who gave to posterity the rules of construction of the Grecian temples erected to the immortal gods; and the ten books of Marcus Vitruvius Pollio on Architecture, of one, in short, *who was an initiate*, can only be studied esoterically.

The Druidical circles, the Dolmens, the Temples of India, Egypt and Greece, the Towers and the 127 towns in Europe which were found "Cyclopean in origin" by the French Institute, are all the work of Initiate Priest-Architects, the descendants of those primarily taught by the "Sons of God," justly called "The Builders." This is what appreciative posterity says of those descendants:

"They used neither mortar nor cement, nor steel nor iron to cut the stones with; and yet they were so artfully wrought that in many places the joints are not seen, though many of the stones, as in Peru, are 18ft. thick, and in the walls of the fortress of Cuzco there are stones of a still greater size." (*Acosta*, vi., 14) "Again, the wall of Syene, built 5,400 years ago, when that spot was exactly under the tropic, which it has now ceased to be, were so constructed that at noon, at the precious moment of the solar solstice, the entire disc of the Sun was seen reflected on this surface - a work which the united skill of all the astronomers of Europe would not now be able to effect." (*Kenealy,"Book of God"*) ***SD 1, pp. 208 - 209, foot-note***

THE WISDOM OF THE AGES

1. The outline of a few fundamental truths from the Secret Doctrine of the Archaic ages is now permitted to see the light, after long millenniums of the most profound silence and secrecy. I say "a *few* truths," advisedly, because that which must remain unsaid could not be contained in a hundred such volumes, nor could it be imparted to the present generation of Sadducees. But even the little that is now given is better than complete silence upon these vital truths.

The world of today, in its mad career towards the unknown - which it is too ready to confound with the unknowable, whenever the problem eludes the grasp of the physicist - is rapidly progressing on the reverse, material plane of spirituality. It has now become a vast arena - a true valley of discord and of eternal strife - a necropolis, wherein lie buried the highest and the most holy aspirations of our Spirit-Soul. That soul becomes with every new generation more paralyzed and atrophied. The "amiable infidels and accomplished profligates" of Society, spoken of by Greeley, care little for the revival of the *dead* sciences of the past; but there is a fair minority of earnest students who are entitled to learn the few truths that may be given to them now; and *now* much more than ten years ago (1877 - Ed.) when "Isis Unveiled," or even the later attempts to explain the mysteries of esoteric science, were published. *SD 1, p. xxii*

2. The main body of the Doctrines given (in *The Secret Doctrine* - Ed.) is found scattered throughout hundred and thousands of Sanskrit MSS., some already translated - disfigured in their interpretations, as usual, - others still awaiting their turn. Every scholar, therefore, has an opportunity of verifying the statements herein made, and of checking most of the quotations. A few new facts ... and passages quoted from the Commentaries will be found difficult to trace. Several of the teachings, also, have hitherto been transmitted orally; yet even those are in every instance hinted at in the almost countless volumes of Brahminical, Chinese and Tibetan temple literature.

However, it may be, and whatsoever is in store for the writer through malevolent criticism, one fact is quite certain. The members of several esoteric schools - the seat of which is beyond the Himalayas, and whose ramifications may be found in China, Japan, India, Tibet, and even in Syria, besides South America - claim to have in their possession the *sum total* of sacred and philosophical works in MSS. and type: all the works, in fact, that have ever been written, in whatever language or characters, since the art of writing began; from the ideographic hieroglyphs down to the alphabet of Cadmus and the Devanagari.

It has been claimed in all ages, that ever since the destruction of the Alexandrian Library, every work of a character that might have led the profane to the ultimate discovery and comprehension of some of the mysteries of the Secret Science, was, owing to the combined efforts of the members of the Brotherhoods, diligently searched for. It is added, moreover, by those who know, that once found, save three copies, left and stored safely away, such works were all destroyed. In India, the last of the precious manuscripts were secured and hidden during the reign of the Emperor Akbar. *SD 1, pp. xxiii*

3. The Secret Doctrine teaches no *Atheism*, except in the Hindu sense of the word *nastika,* or the rejection of *idols,* including every anthropomorphic god. In this sense every occultist is a *Nastika*. *SD 1, p. 279*

4. The esoteric truths presented in Mr. Sinnett's work (*Esoteric Buddhism*) ... contain ... a few tenets from a hitherto hidden teaching which are now supplemented by many more, enlarged and explained in the present volumes (*The Secret Doctrine Vols. 1 and 2*). But even the latter giving out many fundamental tenets *from the* Secret Doctrine *of the East,* raise but a small corner of the dark veil. For no-one, not even the greatest living adept, would be permitted to, or could - even if he would - give out promiscuously, to a mocking, unbelieving world, that which has been so effectually concealed from it for long aeons and ages. *SD 1, p. xvii.*

5. One more important point must be noticed, one that stands foremost in the series of proofs given of the existence of one primeval, universal Wisdom at any rate for the Christian Kabalists and students. The teachings were, at least, partially known to several of the Fathers of the Church. It is maintained, on purely historical grounds, that Origen, Synesius, and even

Clemens Alexandrinus, had been themselves initiated into the mysteries before adding to the Neo-Platonism of the Alexandrian school that of the Gnostics, under the Christian veil. More than this, some of the doctrines of the Secret schools - though by no means all - were preserved in the Vatican, and have since become part and parcel of the mysteries, in the shape of disfigured additions made to the original Christian programme by the Latin Church. Such is the now materialised dogma of the Immaculate Conception. This accounts for the great persecutions set on foot by the Roman Catholic Church against Occultism, Masonry, and *heteredox* mysticism generally. ***SD 1, p. xliv***

6. The days of Constantine were the last turning-point, the period of the Supreme struggle that ended in the Western world throttling the old religions in favour of the new one, built on their bodies. From thence the vista into the far distant Past, beyond the "Deluge" and the Garden of Eden, began to be forcibly and relentlessly closed by every fair and unfair means against the indiscreet gaze of posterity. Every issue was blocked up, every record that hands could be laid upon destroyed.

Yet there remains enough, even among such mutilated records to warrant us in saying that there is in them every possible evidence of the actual existence of a Parent Doctrine. Fragments have survived geological and political cataclysms to tell the story; and every survival shows evidence that the now *Secret* Wisdom was once the one fountain head, the ever-flowing perennial source, at which were fed all its streamlets - the later religions of all nations - from the first down to the last. This period, beginning with Buddha and Pythagoras at the one end and the Neo-Platonists and Gnostics at the other, is the only focus left in History wherein converge for the last time the bright rays of light streaming from the aeons of time gone by, unobscured by the hand of bigotry and fanaticism. *SD 1, p. xlv*

7. In other words - "THERE IS NO RELIGION (OR LAW) HIGHER THAN TRUTH" - SATYAT NASTI PARO DHARMAH" - the motto of the Maharajah of Benares, adopted by the Theosophical Society.

As already said in the *Preface,* the Secret Doctrine is not a version of "Isis Unveiled" - as originally intended. It is a volume explanatory of it rather, and though entirely independent of the earlier work, an indispensable corollary to it. Much of what is in ISIS could hardly be understood by theosophists in those days. The Secret Doctrine will now throw light on many a problem left unsolved in the first work, especially on the opening pages, which have never been understood.

Concerned simply with the philosophies within our historical times and the respective symbolism of the fallen nations, only a hurried glance could be thrown at the panorama of Occultism in the two volumes of ISIS. In the present work, detailed Cosmogony and the evolution of the four races that preceded our Fifth race Humanity are given, and now two large volumes explain that which was stated on the first page of Isis Unveiled alone and in a few allusions scattered hither and thither throughout that work. Nor could the vast catalogue of the Archaic Sciences be attempted in the present volumes before we had disposed of such tremendous problems as Cosmic and Planetary Evolution, and the gradual development of the mysterious Humanities and races that preceded our "Adamic" Humanity. Therefore, the present attempt to elucidate some mysteries of the esoteric philosophy has, in truth, nothing to do with the earlier work. *SD 1, pp. xli - xlii*

8. The Secret Doctrine is the common property of the countless millions of men born under various climates in times with which History refuses to deal, and to which esoteric teachings assign dates incompatible with theories of Geology and Anthropology. The birth and evolution of the Sacred Science of the Past are lost in the very night of Time; and that, even, which is historic - *i.e.*, that which is found scattered hither and thither throughout ancient classical literature - is, in almost every case, attributed by modern criticism to lack of observation in the ancient writers, or to superstition born out of the ignorance of antiquity.

It is only by bringing before the reader an abundance of proofs all tending to show that in every age, under every condition of civilization and knowledge, the educated classes of every nation made themselves the more or less faithful echoes of one identical system and its fundamental traditions - that he can be made to see that so many streams of the same water must have had a common source from which they started. What was this source? If coming events are said to cast their shadows before, past events cannot fail to leave their impress behind them. It is, then, by those shadows of the hoary Past and their fantastic silhouettes on the external screen of every religion and philosophy, that we can, by checking them as we go along, and comparing them, trace out finally the body that produced them.

There must be truth and fact in that which every people of antiquity accepted and made the foundation of its religions and its faith. Moreover, as Haliburton said, "Hear one side, and you will be in the dark; hear both sides, and all will be clear." The public has hitherto had access to, and heard but one side - or rather the two one-sided views of two diametrically opposed classes of men, whose *prima facie* propositions or respective premises differ widely, but whose final conclusions are the same - Science and Theology. And now our readers have an opportunity to hear the other - the defendants' justification and learn the nature of our arguments.

.... When it becomes undeniably proven that the claim of the modern Asiatic nations to a Secret Science and an esoteric history of the world, is based on fact; that, though hitherto unknown to the masses and a veiled mystery even to the learned (because they never had the key to a right understanding of the abundant hints thrown out by the ancient classics), it is still no fairy tale, but an actuality - then the present work will become but the pioneer of many more such books.

The statement that hitherto even the keys discovered by some great scholars have proved too rusty for use, and that they were but the silent witnesses that there do exist mysteries behind the veil which are unreachable without a new key - is borne out by too many proofs to be easily dismissed. *SD 2, pp. 794 - 796*

GLOSSARY

Adam Kadmon. (Hebrew) Archetypal Humanity; the "Heavenly Man." In the *Kabala* Adam Kadmon is the Logos, the manifested Deity emerging from the Ultimate Source.

Adi Buddha. (Sanskrit) The omniscient, infinite source of all things, having no beginning or end. A term used in Northern Buddhism.

Adityas. (Sanskrit) The planetary gods of the seven sacred planets.

Advaita or Adwaitism. (Sanskrit) A sect of Hindu Vedanta. The non-dual school of Vedantic philosophy founded by Sankaracharya, the greatest of the historical Brahmin sages.

Agnishwattas. (Sanskrit) A compound of two words: *agni*, "fire", *shwatta*, "tasted" or "sweetened"; a class of Angels who helped stimulate mind in man; also called Solar Angels, and Lords of the Flame in the Ageless Wisdom.

Aitareya Upanishad. (Sanskrit) The name of a Upanishad of the *Rig Veda*. Some of its portions are purely Vedantic.

Akasha. (Sanskrit) Literally, brilliant, shining. Supersensuous, subtle spiritual essence which pervades all space; the primordial spirit substance.

Amshaspends. (Persian) Hosts of angels in the Zoroastrian religion and tradition.

Arhats. (Sanskrit) A term used in the Western lands for Adepts or Yogis. Those who have passed the fourth initiation.

Arupa. (Sanskrit) Literally without form, formless; but usually applies to ethereal forms in the spiritual worlds.

Astral Light. (Sanskrit) An invisible region surrounding our globe. Also a cosmic "picture gallery" or indelible record of whatever takes place on the astral and physical levels

Asuras. (Sanskrit) Exoterically demons and not gods; but esoterically the reverse.

Atman. (Sanskrit) The highest part of man; the higher self or spirit.

Aum. (Sanskrit) The sacred sound and syllable of the Universe. Also represents the trinity in one.

Avalokiteswara. (Sanskrit) In the exoteric interpretation, the first divine ancestor and protector of the Tibetans, an avatar. Also known as Padmapani - the "lotus bearer" and the "lotus born." In esoteric philosophy he is the Supreme Soul, the Logos, both celestial and its correspondence in man, the Higher Self. The mantra "Om mani padme hum" is used to invoke his help.

Avatar. (Sanskrit) The descent or passing down of celestial energy of an inspiring divinity in order to illuminate a human being for the help of humanity. An Avatar is one who has a combination of three elements: an inspiring divinity; a highly evolved intermediate nature or soul, and a pure clean physical body. Examples of Avatars were: Rama, Krishna, Buddha, Christ.

Besant, Annie. (1847-1933) British socialist, theosophist, women's rights' activist, writer, orator and supporter of Indian home rule. In 1889 she read and reviewed in a positive light *The Secret Doctrine*, which dramatically changed her atheistic views on life. Subsequently, in 1890, she met H.P. Blavatsky in London and decided to dedicate her life to Theosophy. She first travelled to India in 1898 and in 1907 became the international president of the Theosophical Society with its headquarters in Adyar, Madras. She was also involved in politics, and in her connection with the National Congress party, campaigned for democracy in India. Besant continued to work for the Theosophical Society and for the independence of India until her passing in 1933.

Bhagavad Gita. (Sanskrit) Literally, The Lord's Song. A part of the *Mahabharata,* the great epic poem of India. It contains a dialogue between Krishna - the "Charioteer" - and Arjuna, his disciple, in which they have a discussion on the highest spiritual philosophy.

Brahma. (Sanskrit) One must distinguish between Brahma, neuter, and Brahma, the creator God of the Indian Pantheon, who exists periodically in his manifestation only and then again goes into *pralaya* (a period of rest).The former, Brahma, neuter, or Brahman, is the impersonal supreme and uncognizable Principle of the Universe.

Brahmanas. (Sanskrit) Hindu sacred books composed for Brahmins. These include commentaries on those portions of the Vedas which were intended for guidance of the Brahmins.

Brahmins. (Sanskrit) The highest of the four castes in India, also known as the priestly caste.

Bodhisattva. (Sanskrit) Literally, "he whose essence has become intelligence" (bodhi); those who need but one more incarnation to become perfect Buddhas and to be entitled to Nirvana. However the bodhisattva vow is to renounce Nirvana and remain on Earth to help humanity and all sentient beings.

Buddhi. (Sanskrit) The spiritual Soul and sixth principle in man. Also the vehicle of man's highest principle, Atman (Spirit). Compassion and intuition emanate from this principle.

Clemens, Alexandrinus. A Church Father and a voluminous writer who had been a Neo-Platonist and disciple of Ammonus Saccas in Alexandria. He lived between the second and third centuries of our current era.

Cosmocratores. (Greek) The Builders of the Universe; the world architects or creative Forces personified.

Crookes, Sir William. (1822-1919) English chemist and physicist noted for the discovery of the element thallium, for his studies foundational in the development of atomic physics, and for his theory on radiant matter. During the 1870s he became a member of the *London Theosophical Lodge.*

Daityas. (Sanskrit) Giants, titans, and exoterically, demons, but esoterically identical with certain Asuras, the intellectual gods, the opponents of the gods of ritualism.

Danavas. (Sanskrit) Almost the same as *Daityas*; giants and demons, the opponents of the ritualistic gods.

Demiurge or **Demiurgos.** (Greek) The Artificer; the Supernal Power which built the Universe. Freemasons derive from this word their phrase: "Supreme Architect of the Universe." Esoterically it is the third aspect of the Logos, and was the only Deity that Plato, as an Initiate of the Mysteries, dared mention.

Devachan. (Sanskrit) Literally, the "dwelling of the gods." A high illusory and heavenly state intermediate between earth lives into which the purified Self enters after its separation from the Kama Rupa (desire body).

Devas. (Sanskrit) Celestial beings, whether good, bad, or indifferent. Devas inhabit the three dimensions of consciousness above the physical.

Dhyani Bodhisattvas. (Sanskrit) Literally, the "Meditative Ones". There are also seven of these

Celestial Bodhisattvas, emanated from the Dhyani Buddhas. Each has governance over one of the seven globes of our planetary chain.

Dhyani Buddhas. (Sanskrit) Literally, "Buddhas of Meditation"; also called Celestial Buddhas and Buddhas of Contemplation. Also known as "They of the Merciful Heart." There are seven Dhyani Buddhas each one having governance of a Round of our planetary chain.

Dhyan Chohans or **Dhyani Chohans.** (Sanskrit-Tibetan) Literally, "Lords of Meditation." The highest gods answering to the Roman Catholic Archangels. They are the divine Intelligences charged with the supervision of the Cosmos. They are especially worshipped in Nepal.

Elementals. Nature spirits. Medieval mystics taught there were four general kinds: fire (salamanders), air (sylphs), water (undines), and earth (gnomes). The term also refers to thought forms that human beings create with their minds.

Elohim. (Hebrew) The Jewish equivalent for Dhyan Chohans, the "Messengers" and divine Intelligences charged with the supervision of the Cosmos.

Eye of Dangma. (Sanskrit) The inner sight of a purified Soul, Seer, and an Initiate, who has attained full wisdom.

Fifth Root Race. This is the present Root Race being developed (also known as the Aryan) and it has seven sub-divisions or sub-races. The development of mind is significant for this Root race.

Fludd, Robert. (1574-1637) Prominent English physician who used the methods of the Austrian physician and alchemist, Paracelsus. He had both scientific and occult interests. Remembered also as an astrologer, mathematician, Rosicrucian, and cosmologist.

Fohat. (Tibetan) Cosmic electricity; the universal propelling vital force. In the manifested universe it is the ever present electrical energy, a ceaseless formative and destructive power. In Esoteric Philosophy it is the active male potency of Sakti - the female reproductive power in nature.

Fourth Root Race. This is referred to as the Atlantean. It has seven major subdivisions or sub-races. The development of the emotions is significant for this developmental stage of humanity.

Gandharvas. (Sanskrit)The celestial choristers and musicians of India. In the *Vedas* these deities reveal the secrets of heaven and earth and esoteric science to mortals. They had charge of the sacred Soma plant and its juice, the ambrosia drink in the temples which was purported to give omniscience.

Gnosis. (Greek) Literally, "knowledge." This term was used by the schools of religious philosophy, both before and during the first centuries of Christianity, to denote the object of their inquiry. This Spiritual and Sacred knowledge, the *Gupta Vidya* of the Hindus, could only be obtained by Initiates into Spiritual Mysteries of which the ceremonial "Mysteries" were a type.

Gnostics. (Greek) The philosophers who formulated and taught the Gnosis of Knowledge. They flourished in the first three centuries of the Christian era; the following were eminent: Valentinus, Basilides, Marcion, Simon Magus, etc.

Hegel, Georg Wilhelm Friedrich. (1770-1831) German philosopher and greatest systematic thinker in the history of Western philosophy. His overall, encyclopedic system is divided into the science of logic, the philosophy of Nature, and the philosophy of Spirit. At the core of his social and political thoughts are concepts of freedom, reason, self-consciousness and recognition. His main treatise was titled: *The Philosophy of Right*.

Hermetic Literature. Any writing connected with the esoteric writings of Hermes, who, whether the Egyptian Thoth or the Greek Hermes, was the God of Wisdom with the Ancients. They were highly prized by some of the early Christians and Church fathers, such as St. Augustine, Cyril, and Origen.

Hermes Trismegistus. The "thrice-great Hermes"; the mythical Egyptian person after whom Hermetic philosophy was named. In Egypt he was the God Thoth or Thot. This was also a generic name for Greek writers on philosophy and alchemy.

Herodotus. (484-423 BC) Greek ancient historian born in the Persian Empire. A contemporary of Socrates. Referred to as the "Father of History."

Herschel, Sir William. (1738-1822) German born British astronomer. Founder of sidereal astronomy for the systematic observation of the heavens. He discovered Uranus.

Horus. One of the most significant ancient Egyptian deities. God of Sky and Kingship. Depicted as a falcon-headed man wearing the pachent - a red and white crown as a symbol of Kingship over the entire Kingdom.

Isis. In Egypt, Isis is both the goddess of Wisdom and the Virgin Mother. She is the female reflection of the god Osiris. H.P.B. named her first book after this goddess (*Isis Unveiled*).

Iswara. (Sanskrit) The divine spirit in man; the Lord or the personal god. A title given to Siva and other gods in India. Siva is also called Iswaradeva or sovereign deva.

Jivanmukti. (Sanskrit) An adept or yogi who has reached the ultimate state of holiness; a Mahatma or Nirvanee, a dweller in bliss and emancipation. Also one who has virtually experienced Nirvana in the midst of life.

Jivatma. (Sanskrit) The divine spirit of man; the seventh and highest principle. Also the ONE universal life.

Josephus, Flavius. First century Roman Jewish scholar, historian, and hagiographer. Born in Jerusalem, then part of Judea. He published a lengthy history of the Jews in which he describes the crucifixion of Jesus.

Judaeus, Philo. (25 BC- 50 AD) Hellenistic Jewish philosopher who lived in Alexandria, the Roman province of Egypt. Used philosophical allegory to attempt to fuse and harmonize Greek philosophy with Jewish philosophy. His writings were important to several Christian Church Fathers.

Judge, William Quan. (1851-1896) Anglo-Irish mystic and esotericist who was a co-founder with H.P. Blavatsky and H.S. Olcott of the Theosophical Society. Born in Dublin, he moved to America with his family at the age of 13. He became a lawyer, specializing in corporate law. When Blavatsky and Olcott moved to India, Judge stayed in the USA to manage the American Theosophical Society. He lectured extensively, wrote many books including *Ocean of Theosophy* and edited a successful theosophical magazine called *The Path*.

Kabala or **Kabbalah.** (Hebrew) The hidden wisdom of the Hebrew Rabbis of the middle ages derived from the older secret doctrines concerning divine matters and cosmogony. They were combined into a theology after the time of the captivity of the Jews in Babylon. All the works that fall under the esoteric category are termed Kabalistic.

Kalpa. (Sanskrit) The period of a revolution, generally a great cycle of time. Sometimes it represents the period known as a Maha-manvantara, or great manvantara, after which the globes of our Earth chain disintegrate. It is also called a "Day of Brama."

Kant, Immanuel. (1724-1804) The most significant thinker of the Enlightenment in Europe and one of the greatest philosophers of all time. His comprehensive and systematic work in the theory of knowledge, ethics, and aesthetics greatly influenced subsequent philosophers. Originally a theological student, he became attracted to Math and Physics, especially the work of Sir Isaac Newton. Among his many original works is *Critique of Pure Reason* - a treatise on Metaphysics.

Keely, John Ernst Worrell. (1837-1898) American inventor of Philadelphia who discovered a new motive power based on vibratory sympathy, which he originally described as *vaporic* or *etheric* force.

Kepler, Johannes. (1571-1630) German mathematician, astronomer, and astrologer. A key figure in the 17th century scientific revolution and best known for his discovery of the laws of planetary motion.

Kircher, Father. (1602-1680) Geman Jesuit scholar notable in the fields of comparatie religion, geology, and medicine. He has been compared to Leonardo Da Vinci for his enormous range of interests. He also displayed a keen interest in technology and mechanical inventions. Referred to as "the last Renaissance man."

Kriyashakti. (Greek) The power of thought; one of the seven forces of Nature. The creative potency of the *Siddhis* (powers) of fully developed yogis.

Kshatriya. (Sanskrit) The warrior caste and second of the four castes into which the Hindus were originally divided.

Kwan Yin. (Chinese) The female aspect of the Logos, the Universal Soul. Known as the "Mother of Mercy."

Kwan-Shai-Yin or **Kwan-Shi-Yin.** (Chinese) The male aspect of the Logos of the Northern (Mahayana) Buddhists.

Lao-Tze or **Lao-Tse.** Ancient Chinese philosopher and writer of the 5th or 4th century BC. Reputed author of the Tao-Te-Ching and founder of the philosophy of Taoism.

Laplace, Pierre, Simon. (1749-1827) French scholar, mathematician, physicist, and astronomer. He made crucial contributions to the arena of planetary motion by applying John Newton's theory of gravitation to the entire solar system.

Leibnitz, Gottfried Wilhelm. (1646-1716) German mathematician and philosopher. Wrote works on philosophical politics, law, ethics, theology, and history. One of the most prolific inventors in the field of mechanical calculators.

Lipikas. (Sanskrit) The celestial recorders, the angelic "Scribes"; those who record every word and deed, said or done by man on this earth. They are the agents of Karma - the Law of Cause and Effect.

Logos. (Greek) The outward expression and manifested aspect of the Ultimate Source which is ever concealed. It represents also the manifested Deity with every nation, and people. "The Word" of St. John's Gospel and the first born or manifested Deity emerging from the Absolute.

Lunar Pitris/Gods/Fathers. God-like beings who achieved a state higher than the human on the Moon chain. Nevertheless, they had not reached the grade or potency of being able to help stimulate the fire of mind in man. Instead, their function on this Earth chain was to provide the etheric (called astral in earlier theosophical writings) rupas and vehicles on which the physical form of man was moulded. They are distinguished from the Solar Pitiris, who were of a higher order of deities than the Lunar Pitiris and could assist man in developing his dormant mental faculties.

Mahamanvantara. (Sanskrit) A great period of manifestation known as a "Day of Brahma."

Mahat. (Sanskrit) Literally, "The Great Mind"; Universal Mind; the first principle of Universal Intelligence and Consciousness.

Mahapralaya. (Sanskrit) The great rest period that follows a Mahamanvantara or "Day of Brahma."

Marcus Aurelius Antonnius. (AD 121-180) Roman Emperor famous for his Meditations on Stoic Philosophy. Remembered as an exemplar of Epictetus' stoic philosophy.

Martyr, Justin. Born in Samaria in the second centruy AD. An early Christian who adopted Platonism and is regarded as a foremost interpreter of the theory of the Logos. He was martyred alongside some of his students and is considered a saint by the Roman Catholic Church.

Manvantara. (Sanskrit) A period of manifestation, as opposed to pralaya, dissolution or rest, and applied to various cycles.

Mulaprakriti. (Sanskrit) Undifferentiated primordial substance. Root matter.

Nagas. (Sanskrit) Literally nag means serpent and it a symbol of eternity. In China and Tibet, the terms "Dragons" and Nagas refer to wise men and yogis.

Neo-Platonism. Literally, the "new Platonism." An elect pantheistic school of philosophy founded in Alexandria by Ammonus Saccas, of which his disciple Plotinus was the head (189-270 C.E.). It sought to reconcile Platonic teachings and the Aristotlean system with Oriental Theosophy,

Nirguana. (Sanskrit) Unbound and without attributes; that which is devoid of all qualities, the opposite of Saguana, that which has attributes. Parabraman is Nirguana; Brahma (male and the creator god)

is Saguana. Nirguana is a term which shows the impersonality of Parabrahman, the Absolute.

Nirvana. A state of absolute existence, bliss, and consciousness, into which the Ego of a man who has reached a very high degree of perfection and holiness during life goes, after the body dies, and occasionally, as in the case of Gautama Buddha and others, during life.

Occultism or **Occult Science.**The science of things hidden. The penetrating deep into the causal mysteries of Being.

Olcott, Henry Steele. (1832-1907) American military officer, journalist, lawyer, co-founder and first president of the Theosophical Society. He was one of the first Americans to make a formal conversion to Buddhism. He helped recreate and renew study of Buddhism in Sri Lanka. Indeed he is still honoured in Sri Lanka as a pioneer of religious nationalism, and a hero in their struggle for independence.

Origen, Adamentius. (184-254 BC) Greek scholar, ascetic and early Christian theologian, born and spent half his career in Alexandria. Prolific writer on multiple branches of theology. He was anathematized at the Second Council of Constantinople due to his writings and teachings on metempsychosis (reincarnation) and the pre-existence of the soul. One of the most influential figures in early Christianity.

Ormazd. (Zend.) The god of the Zoroastrians, or the modern Parsis. He is symbolized by the sun, as being the Light of Lights. Esoterically, he is the synthesis of his six *Amshaspends* or Elohim, and the creative Logos

Osiris. Ancient Egyptian god of the After Life, and the dead; but more appropriately, he is called the god of transition.

Parabrahm or **Parabrahman.** (Sanskrit) Literally, "Beyond Brahma" (the male creator god). The Supreme Infinite Brahma (neutral); the Absolute; Attributeless and the Secondless Reality. The impersonal and nameless Universal Principle.

Paramartha. (Sanskrit) The Absolute existence.

Peripatetics. A school of philosophy in ancient Greece based on the teachings of Aristotle. The school dates from 335-322 BC.

Plato. (428-348 BC) The greatest of the Greek philosophers. He was an initiate in the Mysteries and laid the foundation of Western culture. In 387 BC Plato established the Academy in Athens, an institute of philosophy and scientific research. He was a student of Socrates and a teacher of Aristotle.

Plotinus. (AD 205-270) Philosopher and religious genius who lived in Alexandria, Egypt, and who transformed the revival of Platonism, which was subsequently called Neo-Platonism. His own quest was for mystical reunion with the Divine.

Plutarch of Athens. (d. AD 432) Greek philosopher who became head of the Platonic Society of Athens and was one of the teachers of the philosopher, Proclus. Plutarch wrote *Commentaries* on some of Plato's *Dialogues* and Aristotle's work.

Poseidon. (Greek) The last remnant and island of the great Continent of Atlantis, referred to by Plato.

Prajaparti. (Sanskrit) Progenitors; the givers of life to all on this Earth. They are seven and then ten - corresponding to the seven and ten Kabalistic Sephiroth; to the Mazdean Amshaspends; Brahma the Creator, is called Prajapati as the synthesis of these Lords of Being. In Christianity they are "the Seven Spirits before the Throne of God."

Prakriti. (Sanskrit) Nature, matter, as opposed to Spirit or Purusha - the two primeval aspects of the One Unknown Relaity.

Pralaya. (Sanskrit) A period of repose - planetary, cosmic, or universal. The opposite to a manvantara

Proclus. (412-485 AD) Greek Neo-Platonist philosopher and one of the last major classic philosophers. He set forth one of the most elaborate and developmental systems of Neo-Platonism.

Protogonos. (Greek) The "first born"; used of all the manifested gods and of the Sun in our system. It can be applied to the Logos, and Logoi.

Purusha. (Sanskrit) Spirit - a primeval aspect of the One Unknown Reality.

Pythagoras. (570-495 BC) Ionian Greek philosopher, great mathematician, geometrician and scientist. Born on the island of Samos, he travelled to Egypt and Greece, and maybe India. The first to call himself "a lover of wisdom," he established a movement known as Pythagoreanism and a school of wisdom at Krotona, Greece. He is best known for the Pythagorean theorem. Pythagorean ideals influenced Plato and through him the Western world.

Ra. Ancient Egyptian god of the Sun. A major god in the Egyptian religion.

Rig Veda. (Sanskrit) The first and most important of the four Vedas - the most ancient and sacred works of the Hindus.

Rishis. Adepts, sages, inspired ones of the Indian Continent.

Root Races. Seven Root Races or "developmental stages" form the evolutionary cycle of human life on this globe. Each is divided into 7 minor Races, which are further divided into sub-races and branchlets. The third Root Race was known as the Lemurian, the fourth, the Atlantean, and at the present we have just passed the middle of the fifth Root Race, known as the (Indian) Aryan.

Rosicrucianism. Secret Society of mystics allegedly formed in medieval Germany devoted to the study of ancient mystical philosophy and religious doctrines and their application to life.

Rounds. This concerns out planetary chain, which consists of 7 globes (A,B,C,D, E,F,G) existing simultaneously. Six are invisible, the only visible one of the earth chain being our globe (D). The doctrine of the Rounds refers to the Life Cycle Wave beginning its evolutionary course on Globe A and circulating around the 7 globes in turn, 7 times. The entire cycle is called a planetary manvantara.

Row, T. Subba. (1856-1890) A Brahmin, Subba Row was one of the most outstanding members of the early Theosophical movement in India. He was very learned in Vedanta philosophy and Occult Knowledge and also well versed in ancient Indian scriptures. He was a representative of the Sringa-giri Math (monastery) at Mysore and had considerable influence among orthodox Hindus.

Rupa. (Sanskrit) Literally it means form.

Sankaracharya, Sri. Some scholars place him in the 8th century AD. A great religious reformer of India and teacher of Vedanta philosophy. He established many maths (monasteries) and founded the most learned sect amongst the Brahmins, called the Smartava.

Seraphim. (Hebrew) Celestial beings described by Isaiah as of human form with the addition of three pairs of wings. The Seraphim of the Old Testament seem to be related to the Cherubim. In the *Kabala* the Seraphim are a group of angelic powers allotted to the Sephira, Geburah - Severity.

Sephira. (Hebrew) An emanation of Deity; the parent and synthesis of the ten Sephiroth when she stands at the head of the Sephirothal Tree; in the *Kabala*, Sephira, or the "Sacred Aged", is the divine Intelligence and the first emanation from the "Endless" or Ain Soph (the Absolute).

Sephiroth. (Hebrew) The ten emanations of Deity represented in the Kabalstic Tree of Life; the highest is formed by the Ain Soph, or the Limitless Light, and each Sephira produces by emanation another Sephira.

Shastras. (Sanskrit) Hindu treatises or books of divine or accepted authority, including books on law. A Shastri means to this day, in India, a man learned in divine and human law.

Shistas or **Sishtas.** (Sanskrit) Certain great Sages left after every minor *Pralaya* (that which is called "obscuration"), when the globe goes into its night or rest, to become, on its re-awakening, the seed of the next humanity.

Smaragdine Tablet of Hermes. As explained by Eliphas Levi, "this Tablet of Emerald is the whole of magic in a single page." This is a tablet, however, alleged to have been found by Saint Abraham's wife on the *dead body of Hermes*. But this is probably an allegory. It may mean that Saraswati, the wife of Brahma, or the goddess of secret wisdom and learning, finding still much of the ancient wisdom latent in the dead body of Humanity, revivified that wisdom.

Solar Pitris/Angels/Fathers. A high order of Angels (Dhyan Chohans) whose function it was to stimulate the fire of mind in man. Also known as Agnishwattas and Manasaputras.

Speusippus. (408-399 BC) Ancient Greek philosopher, Plato's nephew by his sister Potone. After Plato's death he inherited Plato's Academy and remained its head for 8 years. Following a stroke he passed the chair to Xenocrates. Although the successor to Plato, he diverged from some of his teachings.

Swabhavat. (Sanskrit) Literally, "that which is becoming." This is a state or condition of cosmic consciousness where spirit and matter which are fundamentally one, are no longer dual as in manifestation, but one.

Swedenborg, Emmanuel. (1688-1772) The great Swedish seer and mystic. Of all mystics, Swedenborg has influenced "Theosophy" the most, yet he left a profound impact on official science. During his time, as an astronomer, mathematician, physiologist, naturalist, and philosopher he had no rival.

Tetragrammaton. (Greek)The four-lettered name of God, its Greek title: the four letters are in Hebrew "yod, he, vau, he" or in English capitals IHVH. The true pronounciation is now unknown; the sincere Hebrew considered this name too sacred for speech, and in reading the sacred writings he substituted the word "Adonai" meaning Lord.

Theodosius. (347-395 AD) The last Roman Emperor. Also, the last emperor to rule over the eastern and western halves of the Roman Empire.

Theurgists. Practitioners of theurgy and sometimes referred to as wonder-working magicians.

Theurgy. The practice of rituals sometimes seen as magical in nature performed with the intention of invoking the presence of one or more gods with the goal of uniting with the divine.

Upadhi. (Sanskrit) The vehicle, carrier or bearer of something less material than itself. For example, the soul is the upahdi of spirit and the body is the upadhi of the soul.

Upanishads. (Sanskrit) Sacred writings of India that are interpretations of the *Vedas*. The term *Upanishad* is explained by the Hindu pundits as "that which destroys ignorance, and this produces liberation" of the spirit. It was from these very mystical and esoteric works that was later developed the highly philosophical and profound system called *Vedanta*.

Vaisvasvata Manu. (*Sanskrit*) The name of the forefather and progenitor of the present Root Race of humankind (the fifth).

Vedanta. (Sanskrit) A system of mystical philosophy derived from the efforts of Sages through many generations to interpret the sacred meaning of the Upanishads. Deemed the noblest of the six Indian Schools of philosophy.

Vedas. (Sanskrit) The most ancient and sacred literery and religious works of the Hindus. They are four in number: the *Rig-Veda*, the *Ajur Veda*, the *Sama Veda*, and the *Atharva Veda*, this last being commonly supposed to be of later date than the former three.

Vishnu. (Sanskrit) The second person of the Hindu trinity which is composed of the gods, Brahma, Vishnu, and Siva.

Wachtmeister, The Countess. (1838-1910) Prominent theosophist and close friend of H.P. Blavatsky. Born in Florence to a French father and English mother, she lost her parents when very young and was sent to an aunt in England. In 1863, she married her cousin, the Count Wachtmeister. They moved to Stockholm where in 1868, the Count was appointed Minister of Foreign Affairs. Her husband died in 1871 but she lived on in Sweden, then later moved to London. In 1881, she joined the London Theosophical Lodge and later met H.P.B. in 1884. She proved to be of great help to Blavatsky when she was in Wurzburg, Germany, writing *The Secret Doctrine*. Subsequently, the Countess wrote a book about her experiences entitled *Reminiscences of Helena Petrovna Blavatsky and the Secret Doctrine*. After H.P.B's death, she went to India, and later toured the USA and Australia lecturing on Theosophy.

Xenocrates. (396-314 BC) Greek philosopher, mathematician, and leader of Plato's Academy from

399-314 BC. His teachings followed those of Plato which he attempted to define more closely with mathematical elements.

Yoni. (Sanskrit) The female principle represented by the womb.

Yugas. Ages of the world, according to Hindu philosophy, of which there are four: The *Krita* (Gold), the *Treta* (Silver), the *Dwapara* (Bronze), and *Kali* (Iron). It is believed that we are currently experiencing the Kali Age and have been doing so since the death of Krishna approximately 5,000 years ago.

Zendavesta. Sacred book of Zoroastrianism, containing its cosmogony, law, liturgy, and the taechings of the prophet of Zoroaster, Zarathushtra.

Zohar. A compendium of Kabalistic Philosophy, which shared with the *Sepher Yetzirah* the reputation of being the oldest extant treatise on the Hebrew esoteric religious doctrines. Tradition assigns the authorship to Rabbi Simeon be Jochai, AD 80, but modern scholars are inclined to believe that a very large portion is no older than 1280, when it was certainly edited and published by Rabbi Moses de Leon, of Guadalaxara of Spain.

Sources for the Glossary: H.P, Blavatsky, *Theosophical Glossary*; The Theosophy Company, Los Angeles, California, 1952 - a photographic reproduction of the 1892 original edition; G. de Purucker, *Occult Glossary*; Theosophical University Press, Pasadena, California, 1953; and Wikipedia.

Printed in the United States
By Bookmasters